About Island Press

Since 1984, the nonprofit Island Press has been stimulating, shaping, and communicating the ideas that are essential for solving environmental problems worldwide. With more than 800 titles in print and some 40 new releases each year, we are the nation's leading publisher on environmental issues. We identify innovative thinkers and emerging trends in the environmental field. We work with world-renowned experts and authors to develop cross-disciplinary solutions to environmental challenges.

Island Press designs and implements coordinated book publication campaigns in order to communicate our critical messages in print, in person, and online using the latest technologies, programs, and the media. Our goal: to reach targeted audiences—scientists, policymakers, environmental advocates, the media, and concerned citizens—who can and will take action to protect the plants and animals that enrich our world, the ecosystems we need to survive, the water we drink, and the air we breathe.

Island Press gratefully acknowledges the support of its work by the Agua Fund, Inc., The Margaret A. Cargill Foundation, The Nathan Cummings Foundation, Betsy and Jesse Fink Foundation, The William and Flora Hewlett Foundation, The Kresge Foundation, The Forrest and Frances Lattner Foundation, The Andrew W. Mellon Foundation, The Curtis and Edith Munson Foundation, The Overbrook Foundation, The David and Lucile Packard Foundation, The Summit Foundation, The Summit Fund of Washington, Trust for Architectural Easements, The Winslow Foundation, and other generous donors.

The opinions expressed in this book are those of the author(s) and do not necessarily reflect the views of our donors.

Water Ethics

WATER ETHICS

Foundational Readings for Students and Professionals

Peter G. Brown and
Jeremy J. Schmidt

ISLANDPRESS

Washington | Covelo | London

Library of Congress Cataloging-in-Publication Data

Brown, Peter G.
 Water ethics : foundational readings for students and professionals / Peter G. Brown and Jeremy J. Schmidt.
  p. cm.
 Includes bibliographical references and index.
 ISBN-13: 978-1-59726-564-5 (cloth : alk. paper)
 ISBN-10: 1-59726-564-0 (cloth : alk. paper)
 ISBN-13: 978-1-59726-565-2 (pbk. : alk. paper)
 ISBN-10: 1-59726-565-9 (pbk. : alk. paper)
 1. Water-supply—Management—Moral and ethical aspects. 2. Water quality management—Moral and ethical aspects. 3. Water resources development—Moral and ethical aspects. 4. Water rights. I. Schmidt, Jeremy J. II. Title.
 TD345.B815 2010
  178—dc22

                                                                                    2009040579

Printed on recycled, acid-free paper

Manufactured in the United States of America
10 9 8 7 6 5 4 3 2 1

Keywords: water crisis, drought, integrated water resources management, adaptive management, common-pool resources, ecofeminism, utilitarianism, non-anthropocentrism, privatization, dominion

To the Emerald Planet.

Contents

ix

Part One

Introduction

Chapter 1

Water Ethics and Water Management

Jeremy J. Schmidt

WATER IS ESSENTIAL FOR LIFE, yet we have no systematic way to think about its value. For years water was considered as renewable as sunlight or wind, and the potential for its development seemed limitless. Now, having manipulated water for irrigation, energy, and burgeoning urban centers, we face the reality that although freshwater is renewable, it is as finite as many other resources.[1] It is now imperative to develop a cogent, grounded approach toward water management to curtail the growing, global water crisis.

The lack of such a strategy for managing water has meant that it is often used callously, carelessly, and without regard to ethical concerns. For instance, over the last fifty years 3,300 dams in India have inundated vast land areas and displaced an estimated 40 million people.[2] In Australia, the effects of severe drought have been exacerbated by reliance on infrastructure designed to increase water supply. Between 1975 and 1997, Perth received 14% less rainfall than the 20th century average but saw a 48% reduction in reservoir levels. From 1998 to 2006 rainfall managed just 48% of the 20th century average and reservoir levels dropped by 66%.[3] In both cases, entire watersheds have been manipulated based on beliefs regarding what ought to be done with water. Yet both instances failed to follow these manipulations through to their normative consequences for, respectively, displaced people or long-term sustainability.

Responding to contemporary water problems requires attending to questions of value. How should we capture, store, or distribute water? At

3

what cost? For whom? And for how long? Further, these questions are inherently ethical because, as with any essential resource, determining a fair and just distribution of water has direct effects on human and nonhuman lives and the systems that sustain them. Despite the layered, interwoven nature of water use decisions and ethical values, moral questions have received comparatively little attention in the decision-making frameworks that dominate water policy and management. As such, this book looks explicitly at ethical issues regarding water. It begins by clarifying the connection between water and ethics, and showing how ethical considerations are unavoidable in water management decisions. This introduction ends by outlining the book's structure, content, and rationale for a systematic evaluation of water's value. The principal purpose of the book is to provide an overview of the emerging field of water ethics by drawing on representative points of view regarding ethical issues with respect to water.

What Is a Water Ethic?

Ethics deals with problems that arise in disagreements regarding what ought to be done. These disagreements may arise in at least three areas:

1. Claims about facts or states of affairs, such as those about adequate water quantity or quality—because we need to know what we mean by "adequate"

2. Claims about correctly ordered social relationships, such as whether water should be allocated according to economics or on the basis of factors such as human rights or rights to property or healthy ecosystems

3. Claims about personal experiences, such as water's significance to people of a particular culture or belief.[4]

Given water's pervasiveness and its necessity for life, these three types of disagreements often overlap; one person may float a gift down a river, believing it to be part of healthy spiritual and biophysical renewal. Another may view this same act as pollution. Thus a water ethic is best defined broadly, as a normative framework guiding actions that affect water.

The last two decades have witnessed a global movement by water policy experts to connect ethics and water. In 1997, the United Nations Educational, Scientific, and Cultural Organization's (UNESCO's) World Commission on the Ethics of Scientific Knowledge and Technology (COMEST) initiated investigations into the use of freshwater. The subsequent COMEST report was organized around three themes: (1) a sense of shared purpose and harmony with nature, (2) a balance between traditional human values and technological innovation, and (3) harmony between "the sacred and utilitarian in water, between the rational and the emotional."[5] In 2004, UNESCO published a series of fourteen essays that were initially produced to provide input into the 3rd World Water Forum in Kyoto in 2003. The overview essay for this "Water and Ethics" series argues that two central problems confront a water ethic: (1) finding an appropriate scale for an ethic and (2) respecting value differences among individuals, groups, and society.[6] In 2007, the 3rd Marcelino Botin Foundation Water Workshop was held in Santander (Spain) where water experts focused on the manifold ways in which ethics and water are critically linked to issues of water management, economics, and poverty (among others).[7]

The rise of ethical discourse in global water policy networks has already led to a key debate regarding how a water ethic fits with other normative claims. From one perspective, a water ethic may be viewed as another aspect of existing concerns over the value of nature or regulating best management practices in natural resource policy. In this case, establishing a water ethic is similar to debates in environmental philosophy and applied ethics insofar as the aim is to provide an evaluative framework that prescribes correct behavior. An alternate view argues that the long history of religious myths, legal mores, and social institutions means that a water ethic does not fit well within the neatly defined categories used in other debates or disciplines.[8] To date, global policy discourse on water ethics takes the latter view. For instance, the COMEST report appeals to several principles that often compete with one another in environmental philosophy such as intrinsic value, equality, the common good, stewardship, and economic pricing.[9] It is difficult to predict how, or whether, this debate will be resolved but here it is worthwhile to note the divergent and influential sources of the water ethics discourse in order to understand some of the different perspectives of water policy experts, academics, and philosophers.

Regardless of whether we think of a water ethic as its own distinctive area of concern or as an instance of more general debates, our water use decisions have real consequences for both human and nonhuman lives. And if we are to support our decisions we must offer reasons. One logical question may arise: If we have good reasons for our water use decisions, is it possible to avoid talking about ethics altogether? The next section shows why ethical judgments are unavoidable, even when we have well-developed, rational frameworks for water use decisions.

Ethics and Water Management

The field of water and environmental management is concerned with the actual decisions made regarding resource allocation and use.[10] Hence resource managers seek to understand the characteristics of particular problems in order to clearly define what may count as a solution. By looking within this process, it is evident that water management frameworks unavoidably make a number of ethical judgments. So, while this section focuses on the concepts of integrated water resources management and adaptive management, it is important to bear in mind that *any* decision-making framework requires value judgments regarding how to define and resolve problems. It should be noted that the management approaches discussed here are not the only ones that exist, nor are they necessarily the best ones. Rather, they were chosen because they are extremely influential conceptual frameworks and because their underlying concepts offer interesting examples of how rational decision making, in itself, does not obviate the need for ethical judgment.

Integrated Water Resources Management

The concept of integrated water resources management (IWRM) dominates the global discourse in water management. Though its precursors extend back centuries, the modern history of IWRM has been traced to Spain, where in the 1920s water managers began using river basins as the natural unit for decisions.[11] Similarly, North American water managers increasingly promoted the coordinated development of water projects for multiple uses through institutions such as the Tennessee Valley Authority, which was created in the 1930s. From the 1960s onward, increasing attention was given to the social and environmental consequences of water development, with a push to manage both within a single system of decision making.[12] As IWRM ascended to a global policy phenomenon in the 20th century, it developed three core agendas: (1) the integration of "cross-sectoral" concerns from agriculture, industry, and urban uses; (2) the evaluation of water's full ecological, economic, and social value; and (3) the promotion of decision making at scales appropriate to coordination and resolution of water-related concerns.[13] Given IWRM's wide ambit, defining it in succinct terms has proven problematic. Nonetheless, an oft-cited definition was offered by the Global Water Partnership's Technical Advisory Committee, which defines IWRM as,

> a process which promotes the co-ordinated development and management of water, land and related resources, in order to maximize the resultant economic and social welfare in an equitable manner without compromising the sustainability of vital ecosystems.[14]

Ethical Judgments in IWRM

Defining the normative position of IWRM began in 1977 at the United Nations Conference on Water in Mar del Plata. There, policy experts argued that explicitly normative attitudes were responsible for the undervalued, fragmented approach to water management. They held that these attitudes were regarded as antiquated, subjective, and (thereby) incapable of meeting the demands of industrial society.[15] Accordingly, IWRM practitioners made the first order of business the establishment of objective facts and a rational planning framework the two pillars for correcting the inequitable distribution of water.[16]

However, IWRM's attempt to provide an impartial description of the type of management needed to meet water demands harbors implicit ethical content. For instance, the evaluation of the world's water as "inequitably distributed" is itself an evaluative standard. Inequitable based on what? Is it the human settlement pattern that is the problem? or the distribution of water on Earth? Without asking these questions a new agenda was established for integrating different water uses such that the greatest benefits could be achieved for industrial society. Thus, despite the pretense of objectivity, IWRM makes normative judgments about facts and the current state of affairs in global water distribution.

IWRM also makes judgments about correctly ordered social relationships. At a second conference in Dublin in 1992, water experts met to prepare a statement in preparation for the UN Conference on Environment and Development in Rio de Janeiro. The principles of the Dublin Statement read as follows:

1. Freshwater is a finite and vulnerable resource, essential to sustain life, development, and the environment.

2. Water development and management should be based on a participatory approach, involving users, planners, and policy makers at all levels.

3. Women play a central role in the provision, management, and safeguarding of water.

4. Water has an economic value in all its competing uses and should be recognized as an economic good.

In these four principles it is evident that correctly ordered relationships involve numerous factors such as economics, gender, development, and participation. Yet it is not clear how value neutral (if at all) any of these categories are. We may ask, Development for whom? Which women play a central role in safeguarding water? Why does water have an economic value in all of its competing uses? Could it not also have spiritual or social value? Here we see that the attempt to establish value neutral principles does not escape making certain moral judgments regarding water. Importantly, and as works in this volume show, these principles themselves rely on their fit with scientific, legal, and ethical norms for their plausibility.

Problems with the Ethic of IWRM

It is clear that IWRM makes certain ethical judgments about the world's water and how social relationships should be ordered. These judgments

may be critically assessed from several vantage points. First, we may disagree with how the world's water resources are connected with ethical
obligations. The claimed "inequitable distributions" may in fact not be
the central problem; perhaps it is the location or relative water demand of
certain types of human societies. Second, we may contest definitions of
correctly ordered social relationships, such as those of economics, for
failing to give place and weight to other forms of social order such as
community-based management. Third, we may question how well modern ideas of human equality and market transactions fit with the long-
established customs of religions such as Islam, Hinduism, or Christianity.

Consequently, though *integration* may appear a neutral term, there are
in fact numerous ethical judgments within IWRM. Defenses of these
judgments, however, are in short supply within IWRM theory, which has
yet to offer substantive justification for its ethical assumptions.[17]

Adaptive Management

While IWRM dominates global water discourse, the concept of adaptive
management is gaining prominence in North America and on the world
stage. Born out of insights from ecology in the 1970s, adaptive management theorists were very concerned with the top-down, command-and-
control style of environmental governance at the time.[18] A cause for
concern was the underlying assumption of stability in early water management and environmental regulation. For instance, the large projects
that reengineered entire watersheds for flood control or irrigation were
criticized because they assumed that the natural variations of rivers,
such as 50- or 100-year floods, were predictable and stable. In fact,
claimed adaptive managers, ecological systems are in constant flux, and
polices that encourage human control over nature are more susceptible
to changing environmental conditions.

In adaptive management, assumptions of stability are replaced with an
attitude that management practices are experimental attempts to learn
about evolving social and ecological systems.[19] Working from the idea of
change, the key to success in adaptive management is the preservation of
relationships, and the processes, functions, and feedbacks in social and
ecological systems that support complexity and which increase the system's ability to absorb and recover from disturbances. This is what is

referred to as resilience.[20] By increasing resilience, managers attempt to adapt to change and to strengthen relationships that are of particular value, such as those enabled by freshwater.[21]

Understanding and increasing resilience also reduces the chance that surprise events and disturbances, such as flash floods or forest fires, will overwhelm the adaptive capacity of ecological systems. In less resilient systems these disturbances could flip entire systems and radically reorient the relationships therein. For example, increasing amounts of phosphorous in a lake could flip it into a process of eutrophication. Likewise, deforestation could change a rain forest to a savanna. Once systems move from one state to another, there is no guarantee that the original conditions, or even other forms of complex living systems, can be regained.

Ethical Judgments in Adaptive Management

Building from the assumption of change, management actions are judged acceptable when they accord with the "Golden Rule," which states that the goal of adaptive management is to "strive to retain critical types and ranges of natural variation in ecosystems."[22] Accordingly, adaptive managers promote the design of social systems and institutions that preserve natural variation; yet this requires a number of secondary judgments regarding such things as the appropriate scale for decision making, the role of stakeholder involvement, and assessments of the social, ecological, and economic values. In dealing with these concerns, adaptive management expects the successful integration of different perspectives to be temporary and objective oriented.[23] As a result, the key to long-term success is pragmatic, turning on what is referred to as social learning.[24]

In the process of social learning, adaptive management makes numerous judgments regarding correctly ordered social relationships, such as arguing that water's value ought not to be reduced to single metrics, such as dollars, that are too simple to capture its full importance.[25] Likewise, adaptive management must judge between different personal claims, such as when scientific experts disagree over the "facts" and the underlying assumptions used to explain a system's behavior.[26] From a philosophical perspective, Bryan Norton has defended adaptive management by recovering the much maligned term *sustainability*. To be sustainable by Norton's account is to understand truth as what prevails "in the long-run" and to engage in the process of social learning through experimentation, place-based values, and democratic decision making.[27]

Problems with the Ethic of Adaptive Management

The judgments made by adaptive management face certain difficulties. First, it isn't entirely clear that all of the communities that persist today have equal claims to truth simply because their existence implies that they are successful experimenters. Rather, the choice to define success in terms of long-term experimentation is itself an ethical standard. For instance, conditions may exist today as the result of long-term "experiments" that are unethical, such as discriminatory practices based on race or gender. In this sense,

> A society given over to "experiments in living," in [John Stuart] Mill's phrase, is not one that simply increases the chances of living in the best way. It is one sort of society rather than another, and there are various forms of living that it rules out; indeed, those ruled out could include those most worth living.[28]

Second, there is a broader question regarding the centrality of social learning: What should we learn? If we focus on the making of *ex post* judgments after a management experiment this implicitly values one institutional starting point or social order as more desirable than another. For instance, adaptive management in Australia has perpetuated colonial inequities by explaining adaptive success in rangeland management in terms of the property rights institutions of European immigrants, rather than the aboriginal practices that created rangeland relationships to begin with.[29]

Book Structure: A Framework for Moving Forward

Ethical concerns are an inherent feature of water use decisions. The looming question remains: What ought we to do?

To begin, it is important to clarify what it means to be in a water crisis. In this book it means that we are at a turning point, where our decisions now, at this stage of water use decisions, will influence the trend of future events, such as the role of water in sustaining other species and future

generations of humans. At present, the literature on water ethics is fragmented; with numerous, relatively isolated efforts all attempting to encourage improved water use decisions without well-defined terms of reference. Hence the purpose of this book is to map out how different
moral points of view turn us toward different notions of the good and,
consequently, legitimate different water use decisions. To do so we situate different streams of thought within their historical and intellectual
heritage.

The book is assembled, in rough-and-ready terms, as a chronology re-
flective of how the academic literature has matured. This does not mean
that the ideas themselves progress from oldest to newest—in fact, many
"new" ideas are restated versions of old, even ancient insights. Rather, organizing the book in this way helps demonstrate how ethical attitudes toward water have evolved over time, both within certain traditions and in
the responses of those who dissent from them. Hence this book is not ordered according to different topics or regions, such as by country or in
terms of economics, privatization, or human rights. As the outline below
shows, we attempt to follow certain ethical perspectives through to their
normative conclusions at different scales and in consideration of their
implications for water use decisions. As such, each section begins with a
brief introduction to the key ideas and debates discussed.

The rationale for structuring the book as we have is that, in many
cases, ethical disagreements arise not only from technical issues, such as
how to best structure a water market, but because of broader worldviews
regarding the earth, its water, and our place within it. At the same time,
we have sought to represent a wide variety of different regions and topics. From a geographic perspective, the essays in this volume cover a large
area and include case examples from Arab regions as well as individual
countries such as Canada, China, Kenya, Nepal, Peru, Spain, and the
United States. Likewise, the different principles considered are used to
support decisions on a broad array of topics, including economics, gender, property, religion, resource management, and law.

Part 2: Dominion and the Human Claim to Water

The book begins by considering religious ideas of human dominion and
the plurality of norms that support human claims to water. The deep-

rooted and historically persistent beliefs of different religious and legal systems legitimate many of our current property systems and the types of social and environmental relationships that we have with water. Importantly, these systems are tacitly relied on to support different resource policies that vary from neoliberal agendas to calls for personal stewardship of environmental resources.

Part 3: Utilitarianism

Without doubt, the dominant ethical principle in modern resource policy is that of utilitarianism—the idea that resources should be used to maximize happiness for the greatest number of people. Yet it is also based on certain conceptions of water as a resource and on organizing the political economy to achieve the utilitarian ideal through specific social instruments, such as bureaucracies, markets, and private property. This section considers ethical issues that arise in utilitarianism and the ways in which success is calculated at individual, community, and global scales.

Part 4: Water as a Community Resource

A different attitude was developed in common-pool resource theory— the idea that tenure systems are a mix of public and private institutions replete with norms deeply embedded in community history. From this perspective, water policies reflect principles that balance individual propensities toward purely selfish behavior with those that ensure communal success through distributions of water and other resources. Efforts in community-based management are also considered from the perspective of adaptive management.

Part 5: Water: Life's Common Wealth

A different way to think about ethics and water resource management has come in a family of ideas that we refer to as life's commonwealth. Within this group, the community is defined to include all living things, and in some versions all things living or nonliving. The authors do not necessarily characterize the nature of these moral obligations in the same way. However, these essays offer a different perspective on the history of legal norms, their influence on contemporary resource management practices and on the types of ethical considerations required in a view where humans do not have an exclusive claim to natural resources.

Part 6: Ethics in Complex Systems

The final section considers water as part of a complex hydrological system. From the perspective of a complex system, two decision-making options are available. One is to seek to manage water as rationally and fully as possible so as to design a sustainable balance between human and environmental systems. A second considers natural systems too complex to manage well and suggests we should adopt an attitude of humility and forbearance toward these systems. In addition, we should attempt to recover aspects of our moral heritage in a redeemed relationship with water as essential for a responsible relationship with life and the world.

Notes

1. As historian Donald Worster remarked, "[F]or the first time in history there is a broad critical spirit rising against imperialism in general, and against water imperialism in particular. It is spreading from country to country and wherever it goes, it seems to be making the same demand: Stop massive interventions in the waterscape. Look for ways that people can live less obtrusively, more harmoniously with their riverine systems. Develop more democratic forms of decision-making about rivers and watersheds." D. Worster, "Water in the age of imperialism," in *A history of water*, Vol. III, ed. T. Tvedt and T. Oestigaard (London: I.B. Tauris and Co. Ltd., 2006), 5–17. Quote at 16.
2. A. Roy, *The cost of living*. (New York: The Modern Library, 1999).
3. M. Young, "C21 water opportunities for Canada," (lecture, Policy Research Initiative, Ottawa, Ontario. March 19, 2007).
4. J. Habermas, *Between facts and norms: contributions to a discourse theory of law and democracy*. Translated by William Rehg. (Cambridge: MIT Press, 1998). See generally, J. Habermas, *The theory of communicative action*. Translated by Thomas McCarthy. 2 vols. (Boston: Beacon Press, 1981).
5. [Lord] Selborne, "The ethics of freshwater: a survey," (Paris: UNESCO, 2000).
6. J. Priscoli, L. Dooge, and R. Llamas, "Water and ethics: overview," (Paris: UNESCO, 2004).
7. R. Llamas, L. Martinez-Cortina, and A. Mukherji, eds., *Water ethics*. (New York: CRC Press, 2009).
8. C. West, "For body, soul or wealth: the distinction, evolution, and polity implications of a water ethic," *Stanford Environmental Law Journal* 26 (2007): 201–232.
9. Selborne, 2000.
10. B. Mitchell, *Geography and resource analysis*, 2nd ed. (New York: Longman, 1989).

11. M. Rahaman and O.Varis, "Integrated water resources management: evolution, prospects and future challenges," *Sustainability: Science, Practice and Policy* 1 (2005): 15–21.

12. G.White, *Strategies of American water management.* (Ann Arbor: University of Michigan Press, 1969).

13. K. Conca, *Governing water: contentious transnational politics and global institution building.* (Boston: MIT Press, 2006).

14. Global Water Partnership, "Integrated Water Resources Management," (Stockholm:Technical Advisory Committee Background Papers, 2000) 4: 22.

15. A. Biswas, ed. *United Nations water conference.* (Oxford: Pergamon Press, 1978).

16. Ibid.

17. A. Biswas, "Integrated water resources management: a reassessment," *Water International* 29 (2004): 248–256.

18. C. S. Holling, ed., *Adaptive environmental assessment and management.* (New York: John Wiley & Sons, 1978); C. S. Holling and G. Meffe, "Command and control and the pathology of natural resource management," *Conservation Biology* 20 (1996): 328–337.

19. C. S. Holling and Lance H. Gunderson, eds., *Panarchy: understanding transformations in human and natural systems.* (Washington, DC: Island Press, 2002).

20. B.Walker and D. Salt, *Resilience thinking.* (Washington, DC: Island Press, 2006).

21. C. Folke, "Freshwater for resilience: a shift in thinking," *Philosophical Transactions of the Royal Society of London B* 358 (2003): 2027–2036.

22. Holling and Meffe, 1996, 334.

23. L. Gunderson, "Adaptive dancing: interactions between social resilience and ecological crises," in *Navigating social-ecological systems*, ed. F. Berkes, J. Colding, and C. Folke (Cambridge: Cambridge University Press, 2003), 33–52.

24. Holling and Gunderson, 2002.

25. C.Walters, "Challenges in adaptive management of riparian and coastal ecosystems," *Conservation Ecology* 1 (1997): 1.

26. R. McLain and R. Lee, "Adaptive management: promises and pitfalls," *Environmental Management* 20 (1996): 437–448.

27. B. Norton, *Sustainability: a philosophy of adaptive ecosystem management.* (Chicago: University of Chicago Press, 2005).

28. B.Williams, *Ethics and the limits of philosophy.* (Cambridge, MA: Harvard University Press, 1985), 172.

29. P. Nadasdy, "Adaptive co-management and the gospel of resilience," in *Adaptive co-management*, ed. D.Armitage, F. Berkes, and N. Doubleday (Vancouver: University of British Columbia Press, 2007), 208–227.

Part Two

Dominion and the Human Claim to Water

Chapter 2

Editors' Introduction

The last transfiguration in the process of evolution appears as the ethics of mankind. . . . By his arts, institutions, languages, and philosophies he has organized a new kingdom of matter over which he rules. The beasts of the field, the birds of the air, the denizens of the waters, the winds, the waves, the rivers, the seas, the mountains, the valleys, are his subjects. The powers of nature are his servants, and the granite earth his throne.

— Major John Wesley Powell, 1888

IN THE LITERATURE ON ETHICS, and in environmental ethics in particular, the term *dominion* has come to represent the position that water, and indeed all of the earth's natural resources, is to be used at humanity's discretion. Regardless of any other uses these resources may be put to now or in the future, human uses take priority. Human claims to water vary from property rights to the rightful place of water within social or religious belief systems. Many authors criticize a dominion view of water as anthropocentric, instrumental, and patriarchal. Here we offer a brief explanation of the idea of dominion, introduce criticisms of it, and provide some subsequent responses to these criticisms.

In 1969, Lynn White Jr. wrote that Christianity was the most anthropocentric religion the world had ever seen.[1] This claim can be taken in two ways. On one hand, strong definitions of anthropocentrism state that all and only humans count morally. On the other hand, weaker versions of anthropocentrism suggest that although humans have greater value, other species, or processes, may also merit moral consideration, though not in the same manner as humans.[2] White's thesis relied upon Biblical passages such as Genesis 1:28 where it says, "And God blessed them [the first humans], and God said unto them, 'Be fruitful, and multiply, and replenish the earth, and subdue it; and have dominion over the fish of the sea, and over the fowl of the air, and over every living thing that moveth upon the earth.'"

As a major influence in Western ethics, the anthropocentric dimension in the Judeo-Christian tradition has been further criticized for justifying an *instrumental* view toward things of lesser or no moral value and for treating such things as a means to meet obligations or desires. Hence, the natural world and other species were not seen as ends in themselves. This chapter's epigraph from Major John Wesley Powell takes this view. An important influence on early North American water policy, Powell conceived of the world and its water as tools in the progress of (Western) civilization.

In many cases, the biblical narrative is criticized further in its appeal to a patriarchal logic where women, non-Western peoples in general, and other species lack the properties associated with full membership in the moral community.[3] Historically, these qualities have included Western forms of logic and rationality; even physical attributes such as skin color and brain size have been equated with moral superiority. Together, anthropocentrism, instrumentalism, and patriarchy form an overarching narrative—a story which positions men in the role of masters over themselves, women, the natural world writ large, and water.

As ecofeminists argue, with men as masters, the dominion framework operates by creating normative dualisms—rules for pairing things that are (claimed to be) intrinsically distinct—that are applied to establish and maintain power relationships favoring the dominant group. For instance, the pairings of God–man, man–woman, and human society–nature have historically formed the basis for making claims about the nature of authority. God has authority over man, man over woman, and so on, or so the claim goes. The power differential in these dualisms is maintained in two ways: First, the two groups are ascribed unequal value. For instance,

men are granted a higher value than women or nature based on something distinctive to men and claimed to be absent in others. Second, the
two groups are radically exclusive. Here the dominion model asserts that
there is something intrinsic to the dominant group that the lower group
lacks the capacity to attain. For instance, men are described in terms of
their transcendent rationality or physical strength, while women are cast
as immanently emotional and dependent on men for identity and protection; unable to achieve rational or physical autonomy.

Further exacerbating these problematic assumptions is the homoge-
neous treatment of so-called lesser groups in the association of women,
nature, and citizens of indigenous cultures with undesirable characteristics as amorphous "others" of little or no inherent moral worth. Save, that
is, any value they derive in relationship to the dominant group. Critics of
this view point out that the narrative is empirically indefensible. Moreover, the versions of science, religion, and rationality it legitimates contribute to ethical and environmental problems by oppressing other humans, other species, or nature.[4] Of particular interest here is the role of
water in the dominion narrative and the ethical implications of seeing
water through its lens.

In the biblical creation account, which is often appealed to as the genesis, or at least an influential description, of the dominion thesis, divinely
ordered land comes forth out of the formless sea. In this story, the normative pairing of order and chaos, land and water, finds a strong counterpart
in many of the Western world's oldest myths such as those of ancient
Mesopotamia and Greece.[5] As a result, the metaphors that underlie Western notions of the good life carry peculiar normative assumptions regarding the values associated with water. However, even though the association of water with physical and moral chaos can be found at the roots
of several religions, religion alone is not responsible for our understanding of our relationship with water. Indeed, there is no single architect of
the modern dominion narrative; instead there are overlapping narratives.
For instance, Carolyn Merchant argues that the sources of Western culture from ancient Greece also legitimate the domination of nature.[6]

Mastery over nature was important in the transition from natural theology to the modern conception of the hydrological cycle.[7] And, in the subsequent harnessing of water's immense potential through technological

advances that followed, entire landscapes were redesigned for the express purposes of humans. A good example is the massively overhauled hydrology of the modern German landscape that, according to some, has been nothing less than a military coup against an oppressive natural regime.[8] These technoscientific developments and the moral advancement of society were, especially post-Darwin, adamant in their desire to jettison theological baggage and to coalesce human accomplishments in the name of progress. Progress would be both managerial and moral; it would reflect new institutions for states and nations while also reflecting new moral achievements in the betterment of the human condition. In this sense, progress was also reflected in the social and physical landscapes and the role of water within them.[9]

It is important to note that those who attack the idea of dominion often simplify complex religious, legal, and scientific traditions in terms that are not acceptable to adherents of those belief systems. Not surprisingly, there has been considerable response in defense of the Judeo-Christian position regarding the environment, much of which falls under the broad category of ecotheology.[10] While we cannot cover all of the debates here, one rejoinder has been to point out that, contrary to the claim that Judeo-Christian beliefs legitimate literal interpretations regarding human dominion over creation, the interpretation of the Genesis story has traditionally been metaphorical. As a result, even though the early chapters of Genesis can be understood in the dominion framework, they needn't be interpreted as promoting a literal call for humans to subdue and control nature. Rather, the term *dominion* is more accurately interpreted from the original biblical texts as implying that humans are here to steward and care for the earth and are not endowed with absolute privilege.[11] Such a view looks often to passages such as Genesis 2:15, "And the Lord God took the man, and put him into the garden of Eden to dress it and to keep it."

While the theological foundations of the dominion model gradually gave way to scientific explanations of water's behavior, there has been a resurgence of religious concern about water and other natural resources. Despite the attempted severance of religious worldviews from scientific progress, new forums for religion, ecology, and environmental stewardship are increasingly looking at the state of the world's water from a faith perspective.[12] This is where Part 2 begins.

Contents

This section begins with a consideration of how different religions conceive of ethical responsibility in modern decisions regarding water. The first essay, by His All Holiness Ecumenical Patriarch Bartholomew, argues that Christians have a moral duty to protect water as part of their broader obligations to fellow humans. In this short excerpt, the Patriarch explains the role of water in the broader economy of God's divine plan and the consequent stewardship of water required by humans. The second essay, by Faraj Al-Awar, Mohammad J. Abdulrazzak, and Radwan Al-Weshah, considers water and ethics in Islam. They pay specific attention to the premises of modern water management, such as integrated water resources management (IWRM), and its reliance on prevailing social attitudes for success. The third essay, by Rajendra Pradhan and Ruth Meinzen-Dick, looks thoughtfully at how human and cultural rights fit within broader social values, such as those offered by Christianity, Islam, and Hinduism. In particular, they consider how different gender beliefs operate in the plurality of different social, religious, and cultural rights to water. The fourth essay, by Greta Gaard, takes a critical view of dominion and its underlying assumptions regarding gender, race, and the environment. Gaard argues that the type of reasoning legitimated in the dominion model is inherently biased toward men in particular and humans in general. In response, she offers an ecofeminist perspective on issues of ethics, equity, and water.

Notes

1. L. White, "The historical roots of our ecological crisis," *Science* 155 (1969): 1203–1207.

2. B. G. Norton, "Environmental ethics and weak anthropocentrism," *Environmental Ethics* 6 (1984): 131–148.

3. V. Plumwood, *Feminism and the mastery of nature.* (New York: Routledge, 1993).

4. C. Merchant, *Reinventing Eden: the fate of nature in Western culture.* (New York: Routledge, 2004); V. Plumwood, *Environmental culture: the ecological crisis of reason.* (New York: Routledge, 2002).

5. S. Shaw and A. Francis (eds), *Deep blue: critical reflections on nature, religion and water*. (London: Equinox, 2008); K. Armstrong, *The great transformation: the world in the time of Buddha, Socrates, Confucius and Jeremiah*. (London: Atlantic Books, 2006).

6. Merchant.

7. Yi-Fu Tuan, *The hydrological cycle and the wisdom of God: a theme in geoteleology*. (Toronto: University of Toronto Press, 1968).

8. D. Blackbrown, *The conquest of nature: water, landscape and the making of modern Germany*. (New York: W. W. Norton & Company, 2006).

9. S. Schama, *Landscape and memory*. (New York: Vintage Books, 1995).

10. See, L. Sideris, *Environmental ethics, ecological theology, and natural selection*. (New York: Columbia University Press, 2003).

11. R. Berry (ed), *Environmental stewardship: critical perspectives past and present*. (New York: T & T Clark, 2006), especially at 17–31.

12. Works such as *Deep Blue* by Shaw and Francis (2009), which is principally concerned with religious issues affecting water, present a perspective that is complimentary to this volume.

Chapter 3

Byzantine Heritage[1]

His All Holiness Ecumenical Patriarch Bartholomew

Liturgy and Life

The spiritual heritage of Orthodoxy has had a profound effect over the centuries on the public and spiritual life of the Orthodox peoples, defining in an impressive way their particular ethos. This is the case not only with respect to the liturgical experience of the faith, but also with respect to the extension of this experience to the secular realm. In the Orthodox tradition and understanding, the world was initially very good but subsequently became rebellious; within this fallen creation humanity is called to achieve, through divine grace and personal willingness and endeavor, assimilation to God and deification by grace. Through the Orthodox Church, the sanctifying and restoring divine grace of God is extended to the entire cosmos. This is the grace that springs from the Holy Altar, on which the mystery of the divine economy in Christ is constantly celebrated and the sacredness of the divine creation is praised through unceasing thanksgiving and doxology to the all-wise Creator. This doxology has in sight God's manifold gifts to humanity, but especially the saving sacrifice on the cross of the God-Man, God's Son and Word, which reveals the incomprehensible efficaciousness of the cross as the way of transforming and improving the world.

In this way, *the natural world acquires deep significance, because it participates in the plan of divine economy. It is not a place of exile and imprisonment of the spirit, but an instrument and garment that is being sanctified and is participating*

in the divine economy. The natural world is destined to partake of the renewal and glorification that encompass the body of the Lord that ascended into heaven. Consequently, preoccupation with nature does not
contradict Christian interests or militate against Christian duties. This
presupposes, of course, that such preoccupation is given its rightful place
within the context of the rest of the Christian duties, such as the ministry
of the word, the ministry of the table, the active engagement in good
works, and so on. Having all these things in mind, the Mother Church
does not refrain from concern with the problems of the natural environment, knowing that this environment should be of good service to humanity and fulfill the purpose for which it was destined. It is, then, in the
context of this interest that we have initiated and now participate in this
third international symposium on religion, science, and the environment,
whose specific theme this year is "The Danube: A River of Life."

The Gift of a River

The Danube is a superb gift of God to the peoples of Central and Eastern
Europe because it has been indeed a source of life for all the peoples of
Europe. In Roman times, the Danube marked the limit of the civilized
world; and in Byzantine times, it was the natural bridge of communication between the peoples of that region and the civilized world. At all
times the Danube has *been* the means by which material goods and spiritual and cultural ideas have constantly been transported among the peoples of North and South, East and West.

Indeed, when the capital of the Roman Empire was transferred from
Rome to Constantinople, the great commercial artery of the Danube
connected the highest civilization of Byzantium with the greatest commercial market of the then known world, that of Constantinople. Thus,
through the richness and natural flow of its waters, the Danube served for
centuries—and still serves to this day—both the physical and the spiritual
dimensions of the life of the peoples of Europe and of the East. This was
particularly the case during the Christian period, but the river still remains a source of hope and life for the people living beside it and for the
people of Europe as a whole.

As a consequence, indifference toward the vitality of "the river of life"
on the part of those near to it or farther away could be described as a

blasphemy against God the Creator and a crime against humanity. This is because a threat to its life is a threat to the life of all. The dumping of industrial, chemical, or nuclear waste into the flow of the river of life constitutes an arbitrary, abusive, and certainly destructive interference in the natural environment on the part of humanity. For *pollution or contamination of the waters of the river damages the entire ecosystem of the broader region,* which receives its life from the unceasing flow of water through the river's surface and subterranean arteries.

Laws for Nature

It is obvious, then, that the constantly increasing interest of the European peoples, not only in developing greater use of the river, but also in more direct intervention to preserve its purity, constitutes their supreme duty. This is based on the fact that the life of the Danube is a divine gift that contributes to the life of several European nations. If the pollution and contamination of the waters of the river of life continue, the peoples of Europe will destroy a source of their own life for the sake of insignificant and short-lived economic or other interests.

In light of this, it is clear that the international and interreligious symposium on religion, science, and the environment has rightly included in its mission the study of the problem of the Danube and has rightly conducted this study while sailing down the river of life. *The sensitivity of the Orthodox peoples in general concerning this problem is self-evident; but it has to become a matter of consciousness and personal responsibility for each of us, if it is to be resolved more quickly.* In His perfect wisdom, God has laid down the aims and laws that pertain to the operation of the entire divine creation and has provided for the self-sufficient protection of its life. Therefore, He designated the human person as a steward, not a destroyer of the divine creation. He did this because humanity is the finest member, the king, of the entire divine creation. Consequently, if humanity's stewardship is unfaithful to the divine commandment to work and maintain the creation within which it was placed, then humanity is unfaithful to itself, destroying God's house that sustains its own life.

The Ecumenical Patriarchate and the local Orthodox Churches— among whom the Most Holy Church of Romania is included, under the inspiring leadership of Your beloved Beatitude, our most honorable brother Patriarch Teoctist of Romania—and the entire pious people of Romania, from His Excellency the President of the Republic to the last citizen, are conscious of their mission for the protection of the natural environment. They also know that indifference toward the divine creation would be considered today an unacceptable moral stance. This is because the Orthodox Church cannot afford to show lack of concern for the natural world, which was included by God in the plan of the divine economy in Christ. The Orthodox Church knows full well that the renewal of the entire creation was envisaged in Christ. Thus, the social realism of the Orthodox faith and the Orthodox dogmatic stance in regard to the creation easily lead to the conclusion that every Christian is both able and obliged to contribute actively, not only to the salvation of the river of life, the Danube, but also to the protection of the entire ecosystem of humanity and of other related ecosystems.

Note

1. Originally published in: Chryssavgis, J. (ed). *Cosmic grace, humble prayer*. © 2003 Wm. B. Eerdmans Publishing Company, Grand Rapids, MI. Reprinted by permission of the publisher; all rights reserved. Pp. 267–269.

Chapter 4

Water Ethics Perspectives in the Arab Region[1]

Faraj Al-Awar, Mohammad J. Abdulrazzak,
and Radwan Al-Weshah

Introduction

Water ethics, as a specific and distinct philosophical field, is emerging in academic arenas, professional discussions, and dialogues on water governance. Concerns of water conservation, as well as adequate access to basic needs of water and sanitation and the deprivation of poor and marginalized communities throughout the world of such a fundamental human right, mostly due to the lack of empowerment and the inability to pay for the service, pose a difficult ethical dilemma that needs to be solved based on societal and ethical frameworks. These frameworks are also necessary to address issues such as the allocation of limited water resources and its relationship to efficiency, productivity, valuation, as well as principles of equity and social justice. Such ethical perspectives are especially significant for consideration of environmental conservation and sustainability for future generations within the contexts of integrated water resources management. . . .

Rational Water Governance

Water governance refers to the range of political, administrative, economic, and social systems that are put in place to develop and manage water resources and the delivery of water services.[2] The general principles of rational and effective water governance are basically equity and efficiency in allocation of water resources and access to clean water and sanitation; balance between social, economic, and environmental water utilization and maintenance of ecosystem integrity; holistic and integrated management approaches; as well as full community participation in the management of local water resources. These principles, which obviously coincide with the water ethics principles discussed in the previous section, are addressed through integrated water resources management (IWRM) approaches that are characterized by transparency of decision-making, as well as accountability and responsiveness to society's value system(s). Therefore, rational water governance and its IWRM tools are the main mechanisms through which a society's water ethics framework is implemented.

Integrated Water Resources Management

The concept of IWRM has been coined and advocated by the international community since the early 1990s, and it gained wide acceptance as an appropriate management tool for rational water governance. IWRM is an ecosystem-based approach that takes into consideration the inter-relationships between natural resources systems and socio-economic objectives, and attempts to integrate them with national development and poverty alleviation objectives. It should be noted that the IWRM approach can be implemented only within a society-adopted ethical framework. All management tools of IWRM should be based on established ethical principles for water resources management in order to be adopted by society. Otherwise some of these tools, especially economic instruments, might reduce access to clean water and sanitation among poor and marginalized groups of population.

The integrated nature of the IWRM approach ensures equitable access to water for all population sectors while taking full consideration of economic efficiency and environmental integrity. In other words, the individual human right of access to basic needs of water is ensured while the interests of the society as a whole in economic development and preserved environment are fully considered. Therefore, the concept of solidarity among various water users, with varied geographical and inter/intra-sectoral interests, is inherently embedded in the approach. Moreover, examples where IWRM has been a useful tool in solving international and trans-boundary water conflicts suffice to show the importance of solidarity between different parties in solving such conflicts.[3]

Water Ethics Perspectives in the Arab Region

The Arab Region is experiencing one of the fastest growing water deficits in the world. The majority of the Region's countries have been consuming more water than their renewable supply for quite some time. However, this is no longer an option due to its high costs and negative environmental consequences that have been leading to a vicious cycle linking deteriorating status of water resources, in terms of quantity and quality, to deteriorating livelihoods. General lack of familiarity with participatory and integrated management approaches; fragmented institutional structures and conflicting mandates; outdated water pricing policies; imbalanced sectoral water allocation; persistence on solving increasing demand problems through expensive supply augmentation; and delegation of responsibility without the necessary devolution of power and financial resources in decentralization plans are among the major problems facing water management throughout the Region. . . .

Ethical Framework for IWRM Implementation in the Arab Region

With the issues of water scarcity and mismanagement coming up, countries in the Arab Region are faced with the pressing need to initiate cooperation among each other through regional programs and develop their own national plans for the adoption of IWRM approaches. As a matter of fact, some countries in the Region have already started to establish the necessary institutions and develop national plans for IWRM implementation. It should be noted, however, that most of the national efforts in the Region for IWRM implementation have been dominated by neo–liberal economic policies that are globally gaining ground since the early 1990s as the main vehicles for growth and poverty reduction. . . .

However, many negative impacts of market-led economies have surfaced throughout developing countries in the past decade and a half. The most significant of these impacts, faced in certain cases, have been increasing poverty levels among the most severely disadvantaged sectors of society, as well as environmental pollution and degradation when rules of free market economy are left alone in control.[4] Promoting the change to across-the-board free-market water pricing systems, for example, has always proved to be politically difficult due to the insensitivity of such systems to the weak ability of poor populations to pay for their access to basic water needs. This is specifically true in places where water has been historically heavily subsidized, as the case has been for a long time in the Arab Region. Therefore, the introduction of IWRM approaches should be done in such a way that earlier-acknowledged governmental responsibility to provide adequate water services for poorer sectors of Arab societies is not abandoned. On the contrary, adoption of the IWRM approach should be used as a means to achieve water-related international goals of poverty reduction. . . .

Water Ethics in Islam

Water is given great importance in Islam, and it is considered as a blessing from God that sustains life. In addition, ensuring social justice for Muslims is among the cornerstones of the Religion. Most of the Prophet's "hadith" is about the preservation of justice and equality, including equality in water use and access to water resources for all sectors of society. Consequently, true Muslim believers cannot grab water in excess to their needs since they are obliged to allow free access to any amounts of water beyond these needs.[5]

Islamic thought is the chief cultural and ethical source of predominantly Muslim Arab societies. Consequently, any ethical framework for water management in the Arab Region has to be in agreement with Islamic beliefs and condoned by relevant Islamic rules. Therefore, looking into Islamic ethical bases for integrated water resources management is a necessary prerequisite step for developing such a framework. Actually, extensive Islamic rulings cover a wide range of issues in environmental and water management from environmental stewardship and water conservation to sectoral allocation, water pricing, and privatization in the water sector. Below is an analytical description of these rulings, which are all based on Islamic values that call for social justice and participation of all sectors of society in the management of its common natural resources.

Environmental Stewardship and Water Conservation

According to Islam, humans are the most favoured of God's creatures. However, they are responsible for ensuring that nature, God's gift to humanity, is well conserved and taken care of so that it would be equitably available for all on planet Earth. Therefore, the environment must be protected by humans, with clear command against upsetting the natural order through pollution or overexploitation. Accordingly, in the Quran, God commands the believers to "make not mischief on earth," i.e., they should not degrade or pollute natural resources. Water conservation in quantity and quality is specifically encouraged within Islamic laws. The Quran tells the believers that they may use God's gifts, such as water, for their basic needs for survival, provided that they do use it in moderation not in excess.[6]

Among the most used water conservation tools is the reuse of treated wastewater for irrigation. Treating and reusing wastewater, especially domestic sewage, has many advantages in water management, since they allow the conservation of freshwater for the highest-value uses. Moreover, the reuse of nutrient rich wastewater helps control the environmental impacts of dumping raw sewage in streams and water bodies and enhances agricultural productivity. However, with the utmost importance given to personal cleanliness and public hygiene in Islamic tradition, most Arab societies have been skeptical in their initial response to the idea of wastewater reuse for irrigation. But several "fatwas" have been issued after consulting with scientists and engineers, such as the "fatwa" of the Council of Leading Islamic Scholars in Saudi Arabia for example, stating that treated wastewater can theoretically be used for all purposes as long as it does not pose any health risk to society.[7] As a result, treated wastewater reuse for irrigation in GCC countries, including Saudi Arabia, has been practiced since 1978.

Water Pricing

In Muslim nations, water pricing is complicated and disputable since, as mentioned above, the Islamic perception is that water is a common public good which should neither be bought nor sold.[8] However, according to Kadouri et al., most contemporary Islamic scholars have concluded that, in spite of its original nature as a common good, individuals have the right to use, sell, and recover value-added costs of developed infrastructure for water supply services.[9] Accordingly, water resources in Islam are categorized as follows:

- *Public property*, which is water in its original state as a natural resource with free access for all

- *Restricted private property*, such as lakes and rivers, where owners may have certain rights, but also have obligations (e.g., should not hold back surplus water)

- *Private property*, which is developed through investment in infrastructure works

Based on the discussion above, in principle it is not against Islamic ethical beliefs to charge a price for water supply. However, it is important to note that within Islam, such prices should be a "fair price" that would lead to greater equity in water use which should be the first consideration in any economic instrument used for water management. Thus water tariffs based on price elasticity of demand are allowed in Islam as they are equitable in principle. On the other hand, cost recovery is also allowed in Islam due to its positive effect on enhancing water conservation and water services for poor communities.[10] Moreover, since Islam encourages environmental protection, the price can include the cost of wastewater collection and treatment.

Privatization

The goal of full cost recovery of water service delivery is best reached through the participation of private partner(s) with the public sector. Islam supports privatization of water supply and sanitation provision in principle as long as it leads to a fair and free market, which results in equitable cost sharing. After all, Prophet Muhammad was a businessman prior to his Prophecy, and he set an example for ethical business dealings. Muslim scholars agree that privatization is allowed within Islam as long as users are served equitably and charged a fair water price.

Sectoral Allocation

According to Islam, and during the days of the Islamic state, water use was prioritized in order to make the most of available water quantities for the whole population. As such, irrigation was given third priority, behind domestic use and "quenching of thirst," which was assigned the first priority. Consequently, contemporary Islamic scholars consider reallocation of water among sectors and giving priority to basic water needs for life as a necessity that is not in conflict with Islamic belief. Moreover, reallocating water from the agricultural to the domestic sector enhances social justice and equality in water use, which are very important in the Muslim faith. These are very important considerations in some countries of the Arab Region in which sectoral reallocation of water has become a dire need.

Participation

Contrary to the centralized governance and decision-making systems that exist in most Arab countries, community participation in all public matters such as the management of water resources is mandatory in Islam. In the Quran, believers are defined as those who would, among other things, manage "their affairs by mutual consultation." As such, according to Islam, this consultation is required of all those who are entitled to a voice, including women. Therefore, all members of society should be proactive in developing and implementing proper participatory water management schemes. Furthermore, the role of each and every individual in society is important when it comes to spreading awareness for water use and conservation. It should be mentioned here that Muslim clerics have an important role to play with respect to preaching and educating people according to the aforementioned principles of ethical water use.[11]

Conclusion

As mentioned in earlier sections, efforts for IWRM implementation in the Arab Region have been heavily dominated by neo-liberal policies that are gaining ground around the globe. Neo-liberal management tools such as decentralization of water resources management, privatization of water services, water pricing reforms aiming at full cost recovery, and sectoral water re-allocation leading to higher efficiency are all being planned and/or implemented for the water sector in the Arab Region with the presumption that treating water as an economic good and using all these tools for managing water resources improves the overall efficiency in the sector and eventually leads to water conservation and expansion of access to water and sanitation in the Region. However, typical negative impacts of free market–based neo-liberal policies for water resources management, like initial reduction in access to water for poor populations due to their inability to pay for the services, and the consequent increase in poverty level, as well as environmental pollution and degradation, have been well known wherever these policies have been put to work. Therefore, developing an ethical framework, based on universal human right to water and other global principles of water ethics, to guide the whole implementation process of the above mentioned management tools has become a necessary step for successful transformation toward IWRM adoption in the Arab Region. It is obvious from the previous section that this can be done within predominantly Muslim Arab societies since there is no contradiction between Islamic belief and worldwide accepted ethical standards of integrated water resources management principles which balance equity, efficiency, and sustainability across society. As a matter of fact, one can summarize the Islamic perspective of proper and ethical water management by a single principle, i.e., enhancing equity among water users and justice for all. Therefore, IWRM measures can be implemented in the Arab Region while fully recognizing and adhering to ethical principles of equity, solidarity, and stewardship and respecting the societies' heritage and cultural background.

Notes

1. Originally published in the *Arab Gulf Journal of Scientific Research (AGJSR)*, 24(4): 167–182. Reprinted with permission.

2. UNDP, "Water governance and poverty reduction: draft practice note for the bureau for development policy, energy and environment group." (New York: UNDP, 2003).

3. Ibid.

4. P. Woodhouse, "Development policies and environmental agendas," in *Development theory and practice: critical perspectives*, ed. U. Kothari and M. Minogue (Basingstoke: Palgrave, 2001), 136–156.

5. N. Faruqui, "Islam and water management: overview and principles," in *Water Management in Islam*, ed. N. Faruqui, A. Biswas, and M. Bino (Canada: United Nations University Press, 2001), 1–32; T. Naff and J. Dellapenna, "Can there be confluence? A comparative consideration of Western and Islamic fresh water law," *Water Policy* (2002) 4: 465–489.

6. Faruqui, 2001.

7. W. Abderrahman, "Water demand management and Islamic water management principles: a case study," *Water Resource Development* 16 (2000): 465–473.

8. Faruqui, 2001.

9. M. Kadouri, Y. Djebbar, and M. Nehdi, "Water rights and water trade: an Islamic perspective," in *Water Management in Islam*, ed. N. Faruqui, A. Biswas, and M. Bino (Canada: United Nations University Press, 2001), 85–93.

10. Faruqui, 2001.

11. Faruqui, 2001.

Chapter 5

Which Rights Are Right? Water Rights, Culture, and Underlying Values[1]

Rajendra Pradhan and Ruth Meinzen-Dick

Introduction

Throughout history, humans have been aware of the value of water. People, plants, and animals live or die depending on their water consumption. Cities and states rise or fall depending on their control over water. Religions link water to the sacred and divine. As human populations and water consumption have grown dramatically over the last fifty years, water scarcity has been increasing worldwide, even in places that once seemed water abundant. With scarcity has come greater attention to clarifying water rights as a way of mitigating conflict over water. The result has been competition not only over water itself, but also among different ways of defining rights, and the underlying values and meanings placed on water.

   Much of the current international debate over how to handle water scarcity has posed the underlying question of values of water as a simple dichotomy between economic efficiency and basic welfare or human rights. This was exemplified in March 2000, at the Second World Water Forum in the Hague, where the Water Vision Commission submitted a report recommending full-cost pricing of water services and measures to ensure that water was used efficiently. The forum of non-governmental organizations (NGOs), trade unions, and a number of protesters countered by insisting that "a clean healthy environment and access to basic water and sanitation services are universal rights, and cannot therefore be negotiated as commodities."[2] Related to this is a debate over whether water services and water resources themselves should be privatized, nationalized, or transferred to communities. Advocates of economic efficiency are generally associated with support for privatization, whereas supporters of the welfare or human rights value of water often support state or community management of water services. A third group places the highest value on environmental uses of water, arguing that anthropogenic uses of water should be minimized in order to protect natural habitats.

Posed in terms of such polar positions, the debate over water values generates more heat than light. A closer look at the multiple forms of water rights derived from state, customary, local, or religious laws, however, reveals more complexity in the principles and values regarding water, including religious, community, and livelihood values, that is missing from most international discussions. These values, which are embedded in cultures, underlie how rights are defined, both in the abstract and in specific situations. They also affect how water rights are actualized by different parties.

In this paper, we examine the link between water rights and the broader meanings, values, and notions of equity attached to water, as reflected in state, local, and selected religious laws. We examine different conglomerations of rights to water (understood broadly to include both rights to use and rights to control or make decisions) for different uses. More specifically, we will discuss the state laws of selected Western and non-Western countries; Hindu, Muslim, and Christian laws (especially those relating to drinking water); and several local or customary laws dealing with water. The concluding section argues that, rather than seeking a single, hegemonic type of water law or valuation of water, recognizing the pluralistic legal frameworks, types of rights, and meanings of water is not only a more realistic viewpoint, but also one which can lead to more productive negotiations over water rights and water use.

Law and Legal Pluralism

Rights to resources derive from law, which in turn has a dialectical relationship with underlying cultural values, such as those of justice, equity, solidarity, and hierarchy, on one hand, and cultural meanings and values of resources on the other. The very term "rights" in English conveys a sense of what is fair, just, and equitable. There is, however no such thing as a single, unitary right, nor is there a single, consistent law or a single consistent legal system. In most domains of social life and in most social settings more than one legal system (defined broadly) is relevant. For many social scientists, especially anthropologists, law is not limited to acts, rules, administrative orders, and court decisions, enacted or made by various state organs. Law is understood very broadly, at least by many legal anthropologists, as cognitive and normative orders that are generated and maintained in a social field.[3] Any social field, such as a village, an ethnic community, an association, or a state, is able to generate and enforce rules or normative and cognitive repertoires and may influence or be influenced by other social fields. It is thus possible to have various kinds of law, including state law, religious law, customary law, donor or project law, and local law.

The coexistence and interaction of multiple legal orders within a single social setting or domain of social life is called legal pluralism.[4] It enables individuals to make use of more than one law in order to rationalize and legitimize their decisions and behavior. The different overlapping legal orders that can apply to a particular situation regarding water are illustrated in Figure 5-1. Which specific law or combination of laws individuals or groups will use or orient themselves to in specific cases "will mostly be a matter of expediency, of local knowledge, perceived contexts

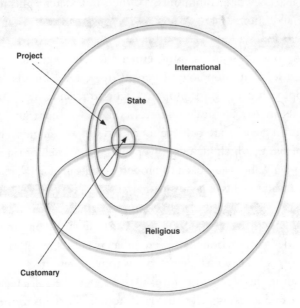

Figure 5-1 Illustration of overlapping legal orders related to water.

of interaction, and power relations."[5] During disputes and negotiations, claims are justified with reference to legal rules. In a process known as forum shopping, disputants use different normative repertoires in different contexts or forums depending on which law or which interpretation of law they believe is most likely to support their claims.[6]

The different normative and cognitive orders may be sharply differentiated in some contexts, as for example, in the courts, but they are less sharply differentiated in the everyday life of local communities. At the local level we find a mixture of several normative orders: long historical tradition, e.g., customary law,[7] new forms of self-regulation, elements of old and new state laws, and donor or project law (regulations). This whole mixture of norms and rules that are expressed and used at the local level is called local law.[8]

Water Rights

The term "water rights" is understood in different ways.[9] It is often interpreted narrowly, for example, by many lawyers and irrigation management experts, to mean the right to use a share of water allocated to an individual, a water users' association, a company, or a district by a statal or para-statal agency or a community.[10] Others link water rights to a system of water allocation.[11] This understanding of the term has the virtue of suggesting not just water shares but also the mechanism of allocating shares. In contrast, scholars using either the common property framework or a legal–anthropological perspective offer a broader and more useful approach that regards property rights as relationships among people with regard to a physical resource. In this view, water rights, like property rights in general, are better understood not as a single right but as a bundle of rights, which includes several types and levels of rights.

Following Wiber's approach to property rights in general, in this paper we define water rights as claims to use or control water by an individual or group that are recognized as legitimate by a collectivity larger than the claimants and that are protected by law. Individuals or groups (users, communities, corporations, states, etc.) may make claims of various kinds over resources.[12] They include the rights to use a resource and derive income from it, the rights to control use and to make rules regarding resource use and users, as well as the right to transfer rights to the resource to another through sale, lease, gift, or inheritance.[13] These various kinds of rights may be grouped into two broad categories of rights: use rights of access and withdrawal, and decision-making rights of regulation, control and decision making.[14] Decision-making rights may also be considered as rights of governance.[15] To fully understand water rights it is necessary to address both use and control rights, and not just use rights as is often done in some literature.

It is not sufficient to assert claims to a resource: unless claims are accepted by a collectivity larger than the claimants, they are not considered legitimate. The relevant legitimizing institution often varies. Depending on the context, it may be a users' group, a village or ethnic community, a village council, or a state agency. These legitimizing institutions or collectivities often compete, offer alternative legitimacies based on different laws (state, customary, local, religious, etc.), and, hence, define water rights and rights holders differently. Claims accepted and validated as legitimate by one collectivity or law and thus recognized as rights are not necessarily recognized and accepted as valid by another collectivity or law.

The importance of underlying values in legitimating water rights thus becomes clear. Claims to and recognition of claims over resources are based not only on specific laws, principles, and rules, but also on wider cultural norms and values. Wider cultural norms or values can themselves be one law among other laws that may be called upon to define rights and spell out who has rights, the types of rights they have, and the procedures and conditions by which persons (individual or corporate) establish, maintain, transfer, and lose rights. In most cases, individuals shop for and select specific law from among the plural legal orders most suitable to their claims. But they may also take recourse to more diffuse normative orders in order to legitimize their claims or decisions. Which norms or laws are considered valid and acceptable for a particular claim, by a specific person, is open to negotiation and contestation and depends mostly on social and especially power relations between claimants. In some cases, wider cultural values, such as those of community solidarity, "common property" notions of natural resources, and rules applicable in times of distress, may be used to acquire "tolerated access" but not necessarily rights to resources.[16]

Over time and in some contexts, these wider values may be accepted as norms or laws relevant for specific claims, and the claimants may be able to acquire rights instead of tolerated access. The concept of water rights thus does not refer to a single and unitary right but to bundles of rights that vary across property regimes, legal orders, and cultures (meanings and values of water). Moreover, the bundles of rights are not static but complex, dynamic, flexible, and subject to change because of ecological, livelihood, knowledge, and social and political uncertainties.[17]

It is important to differentiate between general rights in principle and specific rights that an individual can avail. F. and K. von Benda-Beckmann refer to these rights as categorical and concretized rights, respectively, or "the legal construction of rights from the actual social relationships that connect concrete right holding individuals, groups and associations with concrete and demarcated resources."[18] Beyond categorical and concretized rights, it is also important to look at the actualization of rights, the ability of an individual to make use of a resource or to make decisions about it.

The configurations of bundles of rights to water differ not only across different laws and cultures but even with the same law or culture across different property regimes, sources of water, and uses of water. The bundles of rights to water in a water source such as a river, for example, often differ from rights to water once it is appropriated and conveyed by infrastructure. Similarly, there often are different bundles of rights to water for different uses, such as religious or domestic uses and more economic uses of water. Some of the confusion in the debate over water rights is related to the fact that distinctions among different uses or sources of water are not made. For example, advocates of the human rights value of water refer mainly to drinking and domestic uses of water (and perhaps to some extent, to irrigation and environmental uses) but rarely to commercial or industrial uses of water.

Examples of Different Laws, Cultural Values, and Meanings of Water

The international discourse regarding water and water rights, whatever its differences, in general assumes the primacy of state and even international laws over religious and local laws. Before the many meanings, uses, and rights relating to water are erroneously collapsed into a single meaning, use, and right; however, it is useful to step back and analyze the different meanings and bundles of rights relating to water in different kinds of laws and in different cultures. In this section, we briefly describe broad patterns of values underlying different types of law, moving from global law to the most context-specific law: international declarations, state law . . . religious law . . . and local law pertaining to water.

International Law and Declarations

The past decade has witnessed an increasing number of international forums and declarations regarding water. The 1992 International Conference on Water and the Environment generated the Dublin Principles that were endorsed in drinking water–related discussions at the Rio Summit. These principles reflected relatively uncontroversial underlying values or concerns with the environment (water as a unitary resource), local participation, and gender equity (women as major water users should be involved in water management). However, they also introduced a relatively more controversial principle: water is an economic good, with an economic valuation. This economic valuation and emphasis on efficiency was expanded in the World Bank's Water Policy paper and was reflected in that organization's push for water markets and water charges in its lending programmes.[19]

The economic valuation of water has received increasing attention since the Second World Water Forum in 2000. A report by the Vision Commission for the forum began with a statement reflecting the many values of water:

> Water is life. Every human being, now and in the future, should have access to safe water for drinking, appropriate sanitation, and enough food and energy at reasonable cost. Providing adequate water to meet these basic needs must be done in an equitable manner that works in harmony with nature, for water is the basis for all living ecosystems and habitats and part of an immutable hydrological cycle that must be respected if the development of human activity and well being is to be sustainable.[20]

However, it was the subsequent recommendations focusing on efficiency and pricing that drew the most attention and protest. The commission's recommendation on pricing was only that users should pay the full cost of delivering water, not an economic "rent" or charge for the value of the resource itself, but this point was generally ignored by both proponents and opponents in the subsequent debate. As noted above, the NGO forum and trade unions argued that water should not be commodified and pressed instead for water to be recognized as a basic human right.

International declarations concerning water are important in shaping discourse and, to some extent, norms regarding water, but they do not generally have a direct effect on water rights. One notable exception is the Ramsar Convention on Wetlands, stressing the value of water for environmental protection rather than human use. This document has been ratified as an international treaty. In other cases, international declarations only have an effect if they are adopted by states and translated into national law or are pushed by donor organizations to be incorporated into project regulations. For example, the Asian Development Bank and the World Bank have supported the government of Sri Lanka in devising a new Water Resources Policy (adopted March 2000) and revising its Water Resources Act to include tradable water entitlements that allow individuals to claim "rent" on water resources. National and international environmental NGOs (e.g., Environmental Foundation and Friends of the Earth) oppose this regulation on the grounds that "water is a basic need of any living form," and that the proposed changes would threaten the environment, food security, and the ability of the poor to get waters.[21]

Statutory Law

In many countries the state, by means of state law, claims for itself rights to regulate, control, manage, and even own natural resources such as water. There are several reasons for a state's claims to such rights, related to state authority, national welfare and development, and revenue mobilization. First, vital natural resources are considered public goods to be regulated, managed, and perhaps even utilized by the state for public welfare. Many countries adhere to some form of Public Trust Doctrine, a principle dating back at least to Roman law, which maintains that the state holds navigable waters and certain other water resources as a common heritage for the benefit of the people. Under this doctrine, control over water is an aspect of sovereignty which the state cannot give up.[22] In fact, this is more than a legal principle; it is a political reality: a state that cannot meet the basic water needs of its population is not likely to survive. The welfare aspect of the state's involvement in water resources is especially strong and relevant, at least as far as rhetoric goes, in terms of domestic water uses (drinking water). The construction and management of flood control mechanisms, irrigation systems, and even hydroelectricity plants are also seen as part of the welfare functions of the state. Closely related to its welfare functions are the development functions of a state: the state (often with international aid) is the major actor in the development of water resources and other infrastructures which lead to economic growth.

Water resources, besides being public goods, are also sources of revenue for the state. The revenue generated directly through taxes and fees for the utilization of water resources may be modest, but at least in the past, the governments of South Asian countries have raised a large part of the revenues through high taxes on irrigated land. The construction of irrigation structures thus served the dual purpose of providing welfare service to the population and raising more revenue for the state (and more income for agrarian elites). More recently, revenue from hydroelectricity has become significant for countries such as Bhutan.

State laws reflect the values accorded to water as a public good and as a source of revenue and the state's own roles in providing welfare and development and earning revenue. But despite these common elements, states differ in the relative emphasis they give to different values and even in how they define values such as "equity."[23] These differences are seen not only among countries, but even within a single country over time. For example, as the post-apartheid government of South Africa took on functions and responsibilities such as ensuring the equitable distribution of water to all, providing for health and sanitation, and ensuring a sustainable environment, its water law was reformed to award the highest priority to meeting the basic water needs of the whole population as well as to preserving base stream flows for ecological services. . . .

Religious Values

Water has multifaceted meanings and values in different religions and cultures. A complete treatment of the meanings attached to water in any one religion is beyond the scope of this paper, let alone a comparative analysis of different religions. In this section we examine some of the cross–cutting themes related to water in Hindu, Judeo–Christian, and Is-lamic religious traditions. These are important because religious law and norms often have quite a bit to say about water, and these rules and the underlying values have a profound effect on human behavior which can-not be understood with reference to secular values or bodies of law alone.

Water is often associated with the creation of the universe. Manu for example, describing the origin of the universe, wrote, "He [The Self-Existent Lord] thought deeply, for he wished to emit various sorts of creatures from his own body; first he emitted the waters and then he emitted his semen in them. That (semen) became a golden egg . . . (and) Brahma himself, the grandfather of all people, was born in that egg."[24] In the Biblical creation story, "In the beginning . . . the Spirit of God moved on the face of the waters" (Genesis 1), and water is mentioned three times in the first few verses. This concept instills reverence for water as an element and as the source of life itself.

Associated with the "creative" aspect of water is a linking of water and nature. The Bible mentions water more than any other element.[25] God's care for people is illustrated repeatedly by providing water: "He watereth the hills from his chambers: the earth is satisfied with the fruit of thy works" (Psalm 104). Contemporary Christianity identifies caring for wa-ter resources as part of the duty of the stewardship of nature.

In many religions the symbolism of water as a life-giving element is associated with its ability to remove sins and purity. In ancient times, re-ligious rights and basic hygienic provisions were interlinked.[26] Thus, wa-ter is required for both everyday cleansing and for rituals. For Hindus, water is a medium for purification, through sprinkling, drinking, or bathing. Water has important ritual uses, for example, as offerings to deities and ancestors, for purification of things and persons, and to mark changes in the status of individuals (e.g., life-cycle rituals). Bathing in sa-cred rivers (with the Kumbh Mela as an ultimate example) has special purifying properties for the soul as well as for the body. Judaic, Christian, and Islamic tradition also stress the importance of cleaning the body with water[27] as well as the use of water in many rituals. The Christian sacra-ment of baptism is a clear example of the link between water and spiri-tual purification, as well as rebirth. In these cases, the purity (symbolic, if not actual) of water is valued, and the emphasis is on water quality, rather than on quantity alone. Indeed, water from certain sources becomes holy water, and is considered so no matter what its bacteriological or chemical content.

Religions may also associate water with social relations of cooperation and conflict. Among Hindus, water symbolizes social relations of hierarchy, inequality, and separation between different castes. Water marks the boundary between the pure and impure castes, and within the impure castes between the touchable and untouchable castes. In the Judeo-Christian tradition, Rachel drawing water at the well for Abraham's servant (as well as his camels) establishes that she is the proper wife for Isaac (Genesis 24). The New Testament (John 4) uses a parallel story to indicate inclusiveness: at Jacob's well, Jesus breaks local taboos by asking a Samaritan adulteress to draw water for him, although most Jews would not have had dealings with such a person; again, water is linked back to spiritual, rather than only to material, life.

Despite the symbolic meaning of water in many religions, there is also a recognition that water is a basic human need. Hence many religions recognize the right to quench one's thirst as a basic human right. This is done not so much by creating a "liberty" for individuals to take water, as by creating a "duty" for others to supply water freely,[28] or by making the provision of water an act of merit. Islamic law and hadiths stress the importance of providing water to guests and extend the "right of thirst" to animals and plants as well.[29] In Christianity, Jesus says that on Judgment Day, giving water to those whose thirst will be one of the defining criteria for separating those who are to go to the kingdom of heaven from those who are to be cast out, because when they gave water to "the least of these my bretheren, ye have done it unto me" (Matthew 25: King James Version). In Islam, the Prophet Muhammad also warns that those who refuse superfluous water to a thirsty traveler will be ignored by God on the day of judgment. In Hindu religious texts, one of the duties of the householder is to offer hospitality to guests, which includes the offer of water: "He should offer a guest, as soon as he arrives, a seat, some water, and food" (Manu, III). Offering water to quench thirst is an important religious imperative, a duty. Furthermore, offering water benefits the donor: "A man who gives water obtains satiation" (Manu, IV). At least one reported case in the hills of Nepal suggests some Nepalese believe that a person who prevents others from gaining access to drinking water, even if the source is on private land, goes to hell.[30]

Hindu religious laws on one hand restrict free access to water for the lower castes but at the same time emphasize the virtues of offering drinking water. It is more accurate to say that Hinduism has dual values relating to drinking water; on one hand, water is a common good, to which all should have use rights for drinking purposes but not necessarily to control rights. On the other hand, the ideology of purity and pollution, hierarchy and separation, limits the use rights of the impure castes. Water is a common good for drinking purposes but the common nature of water is limited to people of similar caste status. This has serious implications for access and use rights to water, especially from taps and wells for untouchable castes. The Untouchable castes do not have access and use rights to taps and wells used by touchable castes. State law, which at least in its rhetoric proclaims equality of all citizens and the equal access to water, provides an alternative norm for the lower castes to claim equal use rights to water for drinking purposes. Research in Bhaktapur in the Kathmandu valley shows that caste considerations in terms of access and use rights to public taps and wells have declined significantly ("after democracy we cannot exclude the impure castes") but they are still important for the more orthodox and for ritual uses of water. All castes, whatever their ritual status, have access and use rights to rivers. Rivers, because they flow, are always ritually pure, even if they are physically filthy. . . .

The case of drinking water in the Hindu tradition illustrates the important distinction between use rights and decision-making rights. Low castes have the right to use water for drinking and basic needs, but high castes and elite groups have decision-making rights that allow them to develop water sources and exclusion rights that enable them to keep low castes from drawing water for themselves or engaging in other acts related to water management. . . .

Implications for Actualizing Water Rights

It is extremely important to look at the interplay among different types of law and their underlying values if we are to better understand the rights to water enjoyed by specific individuals and groups. In this section we illustrate this point with examples from a case study of domestic wa-

ter supply in Bangladesh and a general analysis of women's rights to water for various purposes.

Sadeque's study of domestic water supply in Bangladesh shows the influences of all the types of law and values indicated above.[31] International
concerns with providing drinking water to improve public health are apparent in UNICEF programs which are increasing the number of hand
tubewells. In contrast, national policies for water accord priority to irrigation to ensure food security. The regulations of a program to finance
hand tubewells require the formation of a beneficiary group that will
collect co-financing payments and share the costs of as well as the water
from the pumps. In practice, however, one household usually provides
the payment. While other group members will still have use rights, local
norms specify that the household that finances a well can locate it near
their homestead, and is designated as the caretaker. This gives them pref-
erential use rights, and the role of caretaker provides decision making and
exclusion rights. Here, project regulations specifying a group of users,
Muslim norms of not denying drinking water, and Hindu notions of
caste purity and water use coexist with additional local notions that children should not draw water because they do not take proper care of the
pump. Which law or regulation is used in a specific situation and for particular persons determines who will have rights, and which law is to be
used is subject to negotiation and contestation. Social, economic, power,
and other relationships among the claimants often determine which law
is considered relevant and thus who are rights holders and the type of
rights they have.

Despite implicit values of gender equity (or even preference for
women) in most international declarations on water, conflicting values
and norms regarding gender roles in other social fields limit women's
ability to obtain or actualize rights to use and especially to control water.[32] In recent years, some national laws and project regulations have included provisions for women to participate in a variety of user organizations, though water rights are still often assumed to be held by household
heads, who are usually male.

In irrigation, rights to water are acquired by acquiring rights to land
(by purchase, inheritance, gift, etc.) in the command area and, in the case
of farmer-managed systems, by contributing to the construction of the

system. As a categorical right anyone, irrespective of gender, may acquire water rights. But impediments to women's acquisition of land or to their ability to contribute labor mean that many women are not able to concretize their rights. Farmer-managed systems may put women at a greater disadvantage than government projects do because labor contributions are required to maintain water rights, and gender ideology prohibits women from contributing their labor for the repair and maintenance of irrigation systems where men are present. Not only local norms but also religious values of purity and pollution may create barriers. For example, Nepali women of child-bearing years cannot provide labor because their participation is considered polluting to the system hence they cannot acquire or maintain their water rights unless special provisions are made for them to hire male laborers.[33] Government project regulations may give women a better chance of actualizing their use rights because water fees, rather than labor contributions, are required. However, in both management systems, women often find it difficult to actually acquire water for their fields because they are less powerful than men irrigators. Nevertheless, in some cases women have been able to irrigate their fields without contributing labor, either through force,[34] personal relations,[35] or through "tolerated use" of water for recognized livelihood needs.

Even when they are able to use the water (by virtue of being a member of a household with a land right or having an independent title to land), women often cannot concretize decision-making rights because of the gender ideology that women should not participate in the public domain. Here donor pressures, national policies, and project regulations are often making special provisions for women to be members of water users' associations and even to sit on the management committees of these associations. Women's participation in these forums is not just a matter of rhetoric—it has major implications for their decision-making rights. However, even when formal membership rules do not create a barrier for women, practical considerations (such as the time to attend meetings) and the relative values placed on men versus women speaking in public mean that they are not able to actualize their decision-making rights. At the same time, it needs to be pointed out that though women may lack decision-making power, they may be able to influence decisions through personal relations.[36]

Women's rights to water vary across uses and property and management regimes. Women usually have weak rights to use irrigation water and almost non-existent rights to make decisions in farmer-managed systems because irrigation is considered a male domain. In irrigation systems managed by state agency or constructed or rehabilitated by state or donor aid, women may have better use rights and even decision-making rights, at least in categorical terms. Women usually have stronger use rights to drinking water. This is partly because fetching water is considered a woman's task, and thus it does not violate local norms. Many drinking water programmes have made specific provisions for including women in organizations and as caretakers of pumps or local infrastructure, in part because of donor pressures to include women, and in part because women are felt to have the greatest stake in the facilities and thus be the most diligent managers.

Though state and project laws regarding women's rights to use and make decisions regarding water may not be accepted and considered legitimate by men (and often by women too), these laws provide a forum and a source of alternate legitimacy that women can call upon to press their claims, especially during disputes.[37] Furthermore, such regulations may, over a period of time, be accepted by specific local communities and become part of their local law as, for example, in community forestry in Nepal, where women have managed to establish relatively strong use and decision-making rights.

Conclusion

Human uses of water increased almost exponentially in the latter half of the twentieth century. The results have included a growing scarcity of water for many human needs and the destruction of many aquatic-based ecosystems. The ensuing debate about priorities for water use and management has been polarized, to some extent, between those who stress the value of water as a source of human welfare and those who argue that it should be treated as an economic good, with a third group pushing for awarding priority to water for nature. Yet this debate misses the multifaceted values and meanings of water, which vary across cultures, different types of law, different water uses, and over time. Ingram and Brown argue:

> As the relative scarcity of water increases throughout the world and the commodity perspective it engenders rises in policy popularity, it becomes important to revisit the community value dimension of water lest it be crushed in a policy rush to resolve scarcity problems by treating water not only as an economic good but as strictly a commodity devoid of other values.[38]

In recent years considerable attention has been placed on ecological economics as a means of quantifying environmental values in order to include them in economic analysis, and even some allowance for distributional issues in economic approaches to water, e.g., through targeted subsidies for the poor, to meet what are considered basic human needs. But other values of water have been largely overlooked, and it may not be possible to include them in conventional economic approaches. For example, how should the destruction of a community and heritage be valued, or how can the sacred value of water be quantified? There are, as yet, no methodologies for spiritual economics. Indeed, it is somewhat ironic that when water becomes most scarce and valuable for life itself, it becomes too precious to price.

Nor are the values and meanings of water simply an academic issue, because values are reflected in various legal frameworks. Variants of state, project, religious, and customary law demonstrate many different values, and those values vary between different uses, especially drinking water versus productive uses. The rights to water for different uses and users derive from these different types of law, and hence the values they embody determine how water will be used and with what consequences for human welfare and natural ecosystems.

Rather than seeking to reconcile all these values or to establish the dominance of a single type of law for defining water rights, we argue that the many types of rights, laws, and values that shape human behavior must receive attention. A wider focus can lead to the more effective implementation of water-related projects, through more realistic expectations of what can and cannot be accomplished through statutory legal reforms or project regulations. Recognizing other values of water can also lead to better stewardship of water resources. Economic incentives alone will not be enough to get people to conserve water, share it equitably, and protect its quantity and quality for other species and future generations, but religious and community norms can contribute to such behavior.[39]

Finally, the interaction of many types of rights, laws, and values can provide leverage to empower marginalized groups, such as women, or poor households, and enable them to acquire water rights. It is important to consider not only water uses but also bundles of rights, including control and decision-making rights. The discussion of human rights to water is usually limited to use rights, primarily for domestic purposes, whereas it is decision-making rights that are at the core of governance issues. Questions about who controls and manages water and makes and implements decisions related to water about the level at which rights are exercised, and about the extent to which women and marginal groups are included, affect the equity and sustainability of water use.

Notes

1. Originally published as: R. Pradhan and R. Meinzen-Dick, "Which rights are right? Water rights, culture and underlying values," *Water Nepal* 9/10 (1/2) (2003): 37–61. Figure 1 from R. Meinzen-Dick and R. Pradhan, "Legal pluralism and dynamic property rights," CAPRi working paper 22 (Washington, DC: International Food Policy Research Institute, IFPRI, 2002) 36 pp. Reprinted with permission. Available at: http://www.capri.cgiar.org/pdf/capriwp22.pdf.

2. NGO and Trade Union Major Groups, "Second World Water Forum: NGO Major Group Statement to the Ministerial Conference," (The Hague, 2000). Accessed February 14, 2001, at http://www.worldwaterforum.org/index2.html.

3. For a discussion of social field, see S. Moore, "Law and social change: the semiautonomous field as an appropriate field of study," *Law and Society Review* 70 (1973): 719–746.

4. For a discussion of legal pluralism see J. Giffiths, "What is legal pluralism?" *Journal of Legal Pluralism* 24 (1986): 1–50; A. Griffiths, "Legal pluralism," in *An Introduction to law and social theory*, ed. R. Banakar and M. Travers (Oxford and Portland, Oregon: Hart Publishing, 2002), 289–311; S. Merry, "Legal pluralism," *Law and Society Review* 22 (1988): 869–896; H. Spiertz and S. Joep, "Water rights and legal pluralism: some basics of a legal anthropological approach," in *Negotiating Water Rights*, ed. B. Bruns and R. Meinzen-Dick (London: Intermediate Technology Publications, 2000) 162–199; K. von Benda-Beckmann, "Legal pluralism," *Tai Culture* 6 (2001) 18–40; F. von Benda-Beckmann, "Who is afraid of legal pluralism?" *Journal of Legal Pluralism* 47 (2002): 37–82.

5. Spiertz and Joep, 2000.

6. The freedom to choose from among different forums or laws is limited by various factors. See K. von Benda-Beckmann, *The broken stairways to consensus: village justice and state courts in Minangkabau.*Verhandelingen van het Koninklijk Instituut voor Taal-, Land- en Volkenkunde,Vol. 106. (Dordrecht, Leiden, Cinnaminson: Foris Publications, KITLV Press, 1981).

7. There are many kinds of customary laws, only some of which are based on long historical tradition (see F. and K. von Benda-Beckmann and Spiertz, 1997).

8. R. Pradhan, F. von Benda-Beckmann, K. von Benda-Beckmann, H. Spiertz, S. Khadka, and H. K. Azharul (eds.), *Proceedings of a workshop held in Kathmandu, Nepal, January 22–24, 1996.* (Sri Lanka: International Irrigation Management Institute, 1997).

9. Bruns and Meinzen-Dick (2000) identify three approaches to water rights studies: legal (state law), institutional (as in irrigation studies and many ethnographic studies), and common property. See also R. Pradhan and J. Brewer, "Water rights in Nepal" (Manuscript report prepared for IIMI, 1998); R. Meinzen-Dick and L. Jackson, "Multiple use, multiple users of water resources" (Paper presented at the International Association for the Study of Common Property, 6th Annual Conference, June 7, 1997) in *Multiple functions of common property regimes*, ed. B. Swallow, R. Meinzen-Dick, L. Jackson, T. Williams, and T. A. White, EPTD Workshop Summary Paper No. 5. (Washington, DC: IFPRI, 1997).

10. J. Teerink and M. Nakashima, *Water allocation, rights and pricing: examples from Japan and the United States.* (Washington: The World Bank, 1993).

11. N. Uphoff, *Improving international irrigation management with farmer participation: getting the process right.* (Boulder, CO: Westview Press, 1986); J. Brewer, R. Sakthivadivel, and K. Raju, "Water distribution rules and water distribution performance: a case study in the Tambraparani Irrigation System." Research Report No. 12, IIMI, 1997.

12. M. Wiber, "Levels of property rights and levels of law: a case study from the northern Philippines," *Man* (N.S.) 26 (1992): 469–492.

13. Each of these rights is constituted by a complex or bundle of rights. For example, there are different kinds of use rights: full and independent use rights, dependent use rights, rights for a particular season or crop, and so on.

14. E. Schlager and E. Ostrom, "Property-rights regimes and natural resources: a conceptual analysis," *Land Economics* 68 (1992): 249–262; R. Pradhan, F. von Benda-Beckmann, K. von Benda-Beckmann, H. Spiertz, S. Khadka, and H. K. Azharul, 1997; U. Pradhan, "Farmers' water rights and their relation to data collection and management," in *From farmers' fields to data fields and back*, ed. J Sowerine, G. Shivakoti, U. Pradhan, A. Shukla, and E. Ostrom (Kathmandu: International Irrigation Management Institute and IAAS, 1994), 187–198; Pradhan and Brewer, 1998; Meinzen-Dick and Pradhan, 2002.

15. R. Pradhan, "Water rights and legal pluralism in Nepal" (paper presented at the Eighth SAARC Law Conference, Kathmandu, Sept 22–24, 2000).

16. See for examples, R. Pradhan and U. Pradhan, "Negotiating access and rights: disputes over rights to an irrigation water source in Nepal," in *Negotiating water rights*, ed. B Bruns and R. Meinzen-Dick (London: Intermediate Technology Publications,

2000), 200–221; I. Sodemba and R. Pradhan, "Land and water rights in Thulo San-grumba, Ilam," in *Water, land and law: changing rights to land and water in Nepal*, ed. R. Pradhan, F. von Benda-Beckmann, and K. von Benda-Beckmann (Kathmandu: FREEDEAL. Wageningen: WAU. Rotterdam: EUR, 2000), 101–128; Meinzen-Dick and Pradhan, 2000.

17. Menizen-Dick and R. Pradhan, 2002; F. von Benda-Beckmann and K. von Benda-Beckmann, "Gender and the multiple contingencies of water rights in Nepal," in *Water, land and law: changing rights to land and water in Nepal*, ed. Rajendra Pradhan, Franz von Benda-Beckmann, and Keebet von Benda-Beckmann (Kath-mandu: FREEDEAL, WAU and EUR, Kathmandu, Wageningen and Rotterdam, 2000), 17–38.

18. F. von Benda-Beckmann and K. von Benda-Beckmann, 2000.

19. World Bank, "Water resources management." World Bank Policy Paper. (Washington, DC: World Bank, 1993).

20. World Water Commission, *A water secure world: vision for water, life, and the en-vironment*. (The Hague, 2000).

21. H. Winthange, "Right to water," Email Petition Circulated 21 January.

22. H. Ingram and C. Oggins, "The public trust doctrine and community values in water," *Natural Resources Journal* 32 (Summer, 1992): 515–537.

23. R. Boelens and G. Davila (eds.), *Searching for equity: conceptions of justice and eq-uity in peasant irrigation*. (Essen, the Netherlands: Van Gorcum, 1998).

24. Manu, *The Laws of Manu*, trans. W. Doniger and B. Smith (Delhi: Penguin Books, 1991). At 8-10.

25. M. Miller and J. Miller, *Harper's Bible Dictionary*. (New York: Harper and Row, 1952).

26. Ibid.

27. Examples include Islamic rules about washing before prayers, see, N. Fa-rouqui, "Water, human rights, and economic instruments: the Islamic perspective," *Water Nepal* 9/10 (2003) 197–214; Biblical references to the washing of lepers in Je-sus' time, and Jesus washing his disciples' feet.

28. Building on the work of John R. Commons, Ostrom and Ostrom (1972) point out that the inverse of one person's right, or liberty, is the duty of others to up-hold that right. See, V. Ostrom and E. Ostrom, "Legal and political conditions of wa-ter resource development," *Land Economics* 48 (1972): 1–14.

29. Faruqui, 2003; J. Wescoat, "The 'right to thirst' for animals in Islamic law: a comparative approach," *Environment and Planning D: Society and Space* 13 (1995): 637–654.

30. B. Upreti, "Community level water use negotiation: implications for water resource management," in *Water, land and law: changing rights to land and water in Nepal*, ed. R. Pradhan, F. von Benda-Beckmann, and K. von Benda-Beckmann (Kath-mandu: FREEDEAL. Wageningen: WAU. Rotterdam: EUR, 2000), 249–270.

31. S. Sadeque, "Nature's bounty or scarce commodity: competition and consen-sus over groundwater use in rural Bangladesh," in *Negotiating water rights*, ed. B. Bruns and R. Meinzen-Dick (London: Intermediate Technology Publications, 2000).

32. F. and K. von Benda-Beckmann, 2000.

33. U. Pradhan, "Property rights and state intervention in hill irrigation systems in Nepal" (PhD. diss., Cornell University, 1990).

34. M. Zwarteveen and N. Neupane, "Free riders or victims: women's nonparticipation in irrigation management in Nepal's Chhatis Mauja Irrigation System." Research Report No. 7. (Colombo: IIMI, 1996).

35. P. Bajracharya, "Gendered Water Rights in the Hile Khola Kulo Irrigation System, Shakejung VDC, Ilam," in *Water, land and law: changing rights to land and water in Nepal*, ed. R. Pradhan, F. von Benda-Beckmann, and K. von Benda-Beckmann (Kathmandu: FREEDEAL, WAU and EUR, Kathmandu, Wageningen and Rotterdam, 2000), 129–146; R. Meinzen-Dick and M. Zwarteveen, "Gender participation in water management: issues and illustrations from water user associations in South Asia," in *Gender analysis and reform of irrigation management: concepts, cases and gaps in knowledge*, ed. D. Merry and S. Baviskar (Colombo: IWMI, 1998), 173–192.

36. Meinzen-Dick and Zwarteveen, 1998.

37. Meinzen-Dick and Jackson, 1997.

38. H. Ingram, and F. Brown, "Commodity and community water value: experiences from the U.S. Southwest," in *Searching for equity: conceptions of justice and equity in peasant irrigation*, ed. Rutgerd Boelens and Gloria Davila (Essen, the Netherlands: Van Gorcum, 1998), 114–120.

39. N. Farouqui, A. Biswas, and M. Bino (eds.), *Water management in Islam*. (Tokyo: United Nations University Press and International Development Research Centre, 2001).

Chapter 6

Women, Water, Energy: An Ecofeminist Approach[1]

Greta Gaard

THROUGHOUT THE INDUSTRIALIZED WORLD TODAY, one of our most intimate contacts with water occurs over the toilet. Where did we get the idea that water was a place for waste? And how does that idea cohere with the fact that we need clean drinking water to survive?

Although the water-borne toilet has been found in civilizations as diverse as the Roman empire (27 B.C.E.–284 C.E.) and in western India's Harappa civilization (circa 2500 B.C.E.), it was not until 1596 that the flush toilet was invented by Sir John Harrington.[2] Almost 200 years later, improvements were made that solved the odors of Harrington's toilet, and the water closet caught on in the early 19th century at about the same time the Industrial Revolution hastened the shift of population from sparsely populated rural areas to more densely concentrated urban areas. Most towns were not prepared for the influx of population, and excrement collected in courtyards, alleyways, and streets; diseases such as diarrhea, gastroenteritis, dysentery, typhoid fever, and even cholera were easily spread. Sanitary campaigners across Europe argued for a shift away from cesspools and privy vaults (which were not designed to deal with such large volumes of waste and thus were in constant danger of overflowing) to a system of sanitary sewage.

By "sanitary sewage" they meant sewers built to carry the raw sewage away from the streets and into rivers and lakes, because engineers believed that "running water purified itself."[3] Not surprisingly, this theory proved false, causing major outbreaks of typhoid fever in downstream cities, and highly polluted waterways. Finally, at the beginning of the 20th century, modern sewage treatment methods were developed.

And this is where we are today: On one hand, we know we need pure water for drinking, for human and for environmental health; on the other hand, we still use waterways as sewers. This dichotomous view of water—pure water/wastewater—parallels other normative dualisms of thought: wilderness/civilization, nature/culture, virgin/whore, White/of color, reason/emotion. And these normative dualisms are at the root of Western culture's troubled relationship with nature. Examining the problems of water pollution and water power from an ecofeminist perspective, we can recognize the interconnections among women, water, and energy as well as among many other ecosocial problems we face today.

Ecofeminism and the Master Model

More than a theory about feminism and environmentalism, or women and nature, as the name might imply, ecofeminism approaches the problems of environmental degradation and social injustice from the premise that how we treat nature and how we treat each other are inseparably linked. To date, one of the most comprehensive ecofeminist philosophical critiques of the ecosocial problem has been developed by Val Plumwood in *Feminism and the Mastery of Nature*.[4] There, Plumwood described the oppression of humans and nature as stemming not from a single system such as patriarchy, capitalism, or anthropocentrism—as suggested by the analyses of radical feminism, Marxism, and deep ecology, respectively—but from a system of interlocking, oppressive structures based on a series of hierarchical dualisms that lie at the heart of Western culture and can be traced back to their origins in Platonic philosophy. As Plumwood explained, "The western model of human/nature relations has the properties of a dualism and requires anti-dualist remedies. She defined dualism as resulting from "a certain kind of denied dependency on a subordinated other."[5] Examining the various forms of oppression, particularly the intersections of race, gender, and colonialism, Plumwood showed how "by means of dualism, the colonized are appropriated, incorporated, into the selfhood and culture of the master, which forms their identity. The dominant conception of the human/nature relation in the West has features corresponding to this logical structure."[6] Exemplifying these dualisms are the following sets of contrasting pairs, whereby the privileged self of Western culture is constructed in opposition to the devalued other of nature:[7]

> self / other
> culture / nature
> reason / nature
> male / female
> mind / body (nature)
> master / slave
>
> . . .
>
> White / non-White
> financially empowered / financially impoverished
> heterosexual / queer
> reason / the erotic

As Plumwood has ably demonstrated, Western culture's oppression of nature can be traced back to the construction of the dominant human male as a self fundamentally defined by its property of reason and the construction of reason as definitionally opposed to nature and all that is associated with nature, including women, the body, emotions, and reproduction.[8] Feminists have also argued that women's oppression in Western culture is characterized by their association with emotion, the body, and nature.[9]

Conceptually dividing the interconnected whole of life into atomistic, dualised pairs, this form of thinking then creates conceptual linkages between the properties of the self as well as within the devalued category, and the association of qualities from one oppressed group with another serves to reinforce their subordination: the conceptual linkages between women and animals, women and the body, women and people of color, women and nature, or women and water, for example, all serve to emphasize the inferiority of these categories. These linkages reveal broader connections between the treatment not just of women and water but of indigenous people and water, impoverished people and water, water and emotions, and, of course, our human animal bodies as nature and water.

Hierarchical dualisms are manifested both politically through socioeconomic structures and psychologically through the identity of what

Plumwood calls "the Master Model," a gendered reason/nature dualism
that concentrates the intersection of privilege in terms of race/class/
gender/species/sexuality.[10] Both psychologically and politically, the logical structure of dualism separating self and other is kept in place through
a series of linking postulates that includes (a) backgrounding, or denied
dependency on the other, that is, "I built this house," usually meaning the
speaker hired an architect and paid laborers to build it for him or her, an
example of classism; (b) radical exclusion, or hyperseparation between
self and other, sometimes based only on a single characteristic such as
race or sexuality, that is, "I'm not 'swishy' like those fags" (heterosexism);
(c) incorporation, whereby the other is defined primarily in relation to
the self, that is, "that's the wife" (sexism); (d) instrumentalism, or objectification, whereby the other has no intrinsic value, that is, "lodgepole
pine" (anthropocentrism); and (e) homogenization, or stereotyping, that
is "all Blacks have rhythm" (racism).[11]

Building on the ecofeminist hypothesis that the position and treatment of women in Western culture is connected symbolically, psychologically, economically, and politically to the treatment of nature, this chapter explores ways that the treatment of women and water is integrally
connected to the treatment of indigenous people and the land itself.
These connections are most clearly seen by examining the institutionalized structures controlling the distribution of energy and power in North
America, for the production and distribution of energy is one of the ways
that women, indigenous people, economically disadvantaged people, and
water are used as resources in Western culture.

Environmental Sexism

In the beginning–creation myths from many civilizations speak of a split-
ting or opening in the dark, formless Oneness, a parting of the waters.[12]
The Hindu goddess Bindumati divided the Ganges; the goddess Isis divided the river Phaedrus. The Hindu triple goddess, Kali, is represented as
the primal Deep, or menstrual Ocean of Blood at the beginning and end
of the world. In ancient Sumer, the name for Mother of the Universe,
Nammu, was represented by an ideogram meaning *sea*. The Sumero-
Babylonian goddess Tiamat, from whose formless body the universe was
born at creation, is mother of the four "female" elements: water, darkness,
night, and eternity. In Assyrian and Babylonian myths, Tiamat alone pro-

duced the fluid of creation whose great reservoir was the Red Sea, comparable to Kali's Ocean of Blood. These myths associated women, water, and nature and held all three as sacred sources of creation.

Thousands of years later, the river Styx, principal river of the underworld in Greek myth, was compared to the menstrual blood of Mother Earth. Styx was also personified as a goddess, a daughter of Ocean. The mermaid, or literally "virgin of the sea," was a fish-tailed Aphrodite, the goddess of love, who in her death-goddess aspect received the souls of those who died at sea. Throughout northern Europe, in pre-Christian or pagan cultures, wells were seen as sacred outpourings and passageways into the Mother Earth, and many were famous for their healing properties. In all these associations of women and water, there is the corresponding association of birth and death, creation and destruction. There is the concept of life as renewable and circular, following a seasonal round of creation–preservation–destruction. But gradually, cultures that valued the circle of life were displaced by cultures that conceived of life as a linear trajectory, from birth to death to eternal heaven or hell, or annihilation.

Riane Eisler's *The Chalice and the Blade* describes the shift from earth-based, matrifocal cultures that viewed nature as alive and sacred and valued women and men equally;[13] she calls these "partnership" cultures, in contrast to the "dominator" cultures that slowly superseded them and in the process changed their views of nature from animistic to mechanistic, their deities from earth-based goddesses to sky gods, and their social system from networks to hierarchies. Although the associations between women and water survived the transition from partnership to dominator cultures, their meaning was reversed; no longer revered as the source of life, neither women nor water were seen as sacred in patriarchal religions. In A.D. 413, the Catholic Church decided that every child was born tainted with the original sin of conception. It was no longer the mother's birthwaters that would bring a child to life—though once considered sacred, they were now "unclean." Only the water blessed by a sexually abstinent male priest would bring the child eternal life through baptism.[14] Thus the associations between women and water continued, but in Western cultures their association signaled their shared subordination.

Today, as people have for centuries, we continue to treat water as an important resource. Pure water for drinking and food preparation has been a crucial advancement in the treatment of disease. Many cultures use water for irrigation and for cleansing. Water is recognized as an environment for both recreation and transportation, a habitat for fish and other animal life. But in all of these uses, water is not usually seen as a sacred, animate source of life but rather as an essential, though inanimate, resource. Exemplifying the instrumentalism inherent in Plumwood's master model, Western culture views water primarily as a means to its own ends, a servant to the dominant (not subordinate) population;[15] it is difficult, in this cultural context, to imagine that water would have purposes of its own.

Clean water is also treated as a resource that, like women and women's work, does not appear in our national accounting systems. On the international market, the United Nations System of National Accounts has no method of accounting for nature's own production or destruction until the products of nature enter the cash economy, nor does it account for the majority of the work women do. For example, Marilyn Waring has observed that in the colonial accounting systems of many developing countries, the water that rural women carry from the wells to their homes has no cash value, but the water carried through pipes has value.[16] Moreover, a clean lake that offers women fresh-water supplies has no value in these accounting systems; once the lake is polluted, however, and companies must pay to clean it up, then the clean-up activity itself is performed by men and recorded as generating income. Only when the water is dammed, its force used to create energy that is sent over high-voltage power lines and sold to cities, does the water enter the accounting. In these ways, both water and women do not count in the international market economy. . . .

Environmental Racism

Structurally analogous to environmental sexism, environmental racism involves a conceptual association between people of color and nature that marks their dual subordination. Environmental racism is seen in,

> the deliberate targeting of communities of color for toxic waste disposal and the siting of polluting industries. It is racial discrimination in the official sanctioning of the life-threatening presence of poisons and pollutants in communities of color. And, it is racial dis-

crimination in the history of excluding people of color from the mainstream environmental groups, decision making boards, commissions, and regulatory bodies.[17]

Environmental racism is also exemplified in cases where the dominant culture perceives subordinated others as a "resource" with no goals and purposes of their own, in cases where the subordinated other is defined solely in terms of the dominant culture. As the following examples suggest, the association of people of color and water/nature has been seen as an opportunity to use both as resources, to take away their power, and to provide that power to the masters.

The Columbia River

In the Pacific Northwest, 54% of energy production comes from hydroelectric dams. The Northwest Power Planning Council (NPPC) claims it provides the cheapest power in the country.[18] To make this claim, of course, the NPPC doesn't count the cost of choked rivers; flooded landscapes; salmon without access to spawning grounds; indigenous people cut off from traditional burial grounds, hunting grounds, and homelands; or the health hazards of high-voltage power lines.[19] Controlling the Columbia River through 11 dams on its U.S. course (17 dams in all), the Bonneville Power Authority (BPA) owns 15,012 circuit miles of high-voltage power lines, extracting the energy from the water and extending that energy in a 300,000-square-mile network that includes Oregon, Washington, Idaho, Montana, Wyoming, Nevada, Utah, and California.[20] Meanwhile, the same river that supplies this energy and irrigates the farmlands of eastern Washington is also used as an industrial sewer. By the year 2000, the health of the Columbia River had become severely threatened by the load of dioxins and furans, heavy metals (including aluminum, iron, copper, lead, arsenic, mercury, barium, and cadmium), bacteria from fecal contamination, pesticides (including atrazine, aldrin, dieldrin, and dichlorodiphenyl trichloroethane [DDT]), polychlorinated biphenyls (PCBs), and, of course, radioactive waste from the Hanford nuclear site.[21]

Very little is said about the impact of these dams on the Native Americans who, prior to the dams, were living a nomadic life in the areas surrounding the Columbia River: the Okanogan, Nespelem, San Poil, Wenatchee, Entiat, Chelan, Methow, Palouse, and Nez Perce. In 1872, these disparate bands were lumped together and the Colville Reservation was formed, named after Andrew Wedderburn Colville, a London entrepreneur in the rum and molasses business, who never set foot in America. Now called the Colville Confederated Tribes, these 12 diverse bands live around Nespelem, in the area north of the Grand Coulee Dam. Curiously, although the Native people are now known by names the White people conferred on them, the dams have taken the names of those they displace. Lake Entiat is the reservoir created by the Rocky Reach Dam; Chief Joseph, the dam built in 1955, is named after the Nez Perce leader who led his people in an unsuccessful flight from U.S. Army forces, attempting to find refuge in Canada.

Clues still remain. At the Rocky Reach Dam in Wenatchee, a series of Nez Perce portraits is contained in the dam's Museum of the Columbia. Before 1877, the Nez Perce nation was the richest and most powerful of the Columbia Plateau tribes.[22] They netted salmon from the Columbia, Clearwater, Snake, Imnaha, and Salmon rivers; they gathered camas bulbs and kaus roots; they hunted buffalo. And they called themselves the Numipoo, "We People." Early French fur traders named them the Nez Perce even though nose piercing was not practiced among the tribe; the guide book speculates "the name may have come from their tribal sign of passing the forefinger of the right hand beneath the nose from right to left," because all tribes had special hand identification signals at the time. Today, the Nez Perce are a conquered people. . . .

The dams' impact on salmon was brought to national attention through the 1999 debates between Al Gore and Bill Bradley for the Democratic presidential nominations,[23] but Native people have known about this impact for more than a century. In the 1855 treaties with the United States, many Columbia Basin tribes[24] reserved fishing rights to the seven species of salmon in the Pacific Northwest: the pink, sockeye, chum, chinook, and coho as well as the steelhead and cutthroat trout. Then and now, their reasons for defending the salmon are both spiritual and material:

- Salmon are part of the tribes' spiritual and cultural identity.

- Over a dozen longhouses and churches on the reservations and in ceded areas rely on salmon for their religious services.

- The annual salmon return and its celebration by Native peoples assure the renewal and continuation of human and all other life.

- Historically, these tribes were wealthy peoples because of a flourishing trade economy based on salmon.

- For many tribal members, fishing is still the preferred livelihood.

- Salmon and the rivers they use are part of a sense of place. Native people believe the Creator put their tribes where the salmon return. They feel obliged to remain and to protect this place.

- Salmon are indicator species: As water becomes degraded and fish populations decline, so too will the elk, deer, roots, berries, and medicines that sustain Native people.

- As the primary food source of Native people for thousands of years, salmon continue to be an essential aspect of their nutritional health.

- Because tribal populations are growing (returning to pre–1855 levels), the needs for salmon are more important than ever.

- The annual return of the salmon allows the transfer of traditional values from generation to generation.

- Without salmon returning to the rivers and streams, Native people feel they will cease to be Indian people.[25]

But when the dams disrupted the water flow in the Columbia River, they also disrupted the interconnected ways of life for both Native people and salmon. Historically, between 10 million and 16 million salmon and steelhead returned to spawning grounds each year in the Pacific Northwest.[26] By the 1960s, that number had dropped to about 5 million, and today, less than 1 million fish make the return journey, most of them hatchery fish. The combination of heavy commercial fishing, hatcheries (which introduced inbreeding and may have contributed to disease in wild fish populations), damage to traditional habitat through development, contaminated oceans, and dams have all taken their toll on the salmon. In turn, the Native people have suffered a loss of food source and a loss of identity.

Perhaps nowhere are the differences in the Indian and non-Indian ways of relating to nature more evident than in the treatment of water. The Columbia River tribes have always regarded water as a medicine because it nourishes all of life. Water flushes poisons out of humans, other living creatures, and the land. Traditional culture teaches that to be productive, water must be kept pure. When water is kept pure and cold, it takes care of the salmon and humans alike. Water that cannot take care of salmon cannot take care of humans. According to the Columbia River tribes, non-Indians have used the water without fully understanding that it must be treated with respect to remain powerful. By causing the water to warm, by restricting its flow, and by putting pollutants in it, non-Indians have made the water so sick that it can no longer be used as a cleansing agent, so inhospitable that at times it can no longer take care of the salmon.[27]

Hydro-Quebec and the First Nations People

In Canada, the conquest of Native people, water, and the land is exemplified in the story of dams. The homeland of the indigenous Innu, Nitassinan is a land of mountains, thundering rivers, vast boreal forests, sweeping tundra, and Atlantic seashore, but today this Innu homeland is divided between the Canadian provinces of Quebec and Labrador, and the majority of Innu people live in eleven villages along the north shore of the St. Lawrence River.[28] The Innu and the land have been repeatedly used as resources for the dominant culture, as Winona LaDuke explained in *All Our Relations: Native Struggles for Land and Life.*[29]

Before the dams were built, there was a great waterfall in Nitassinan, larger than Niagara Falls, called Patshetshunau, or "steam rising." In 1895, a geologist wrote that the noise of the falls "can be heard for more than ten miles away as a deep booming sound," and the cloud of mist was visible for a distance of 20 miles.[30] But in the 1960s, the Newfoundland premier convinced a group of investors to build a hydroelectric power plant at the renamed Churchill Falls and then signed over the right to sell most of the power to Hydro-Quebec at a price of less than three tenths of 1 cent per kilowatt hour for 40 years. Hydro-Quebec now has the right to renew the contract until 2044. The company has been able to sell the power at 9 times its purchasing price, making approximately $750 million from the dams in 1976 but paying Newfoundland a mere $70 to $80 million.[31] The Native Innu receive none of the profits but pay the costs nonetheless. Damming the 300-foot falls at Patshetshunau created the Smallwood Reservoir and flooded 5,698 square miles of Nitassinan, drowning the black spruce forest, pulling heavy metals such as mercury out of the soil, and flooding the Innu hunting, harvesting, and burial grounds. By 1977, a decade after the dam was built, 37% of Innu surveyed had elevated mercury levels in their bodies from eating contaminated fish.[32] Hydro-Quebec then turned to James Bay, in the Cree homeland.

The LaGrande Complex, or James Bay I, put 11,500 square kilometers of land underwater to produce 12,000 megawatts of electricity.[33] Damming the Eastmain and Rupert Rivers caused massive flooding, which once again leached methyl mercury from the soil, causing mercury contamination in the reservoirs with levels 6 or more times greater than what was considered safe. With the dam increasing or decreasing the rivers' flow based on the electrical demand at the end of the power line, many fish and beaver drowned. In 1984, a deadly release of dam water occurring during the annual migration of the George's River caribou herd drowned more than 10,000 caribou. Hydro-Quebec refused to accept responsibility, calling the deaths "mainly an act of God."[34]

The Cree and Innu were not informed of Hydro-Quebec's plans in enough time to stop the first two dams, but they were ready when James Bay II was proposed in the late 1980s. This new project would destroy four major river systems—the Great Whale, Lower Broadback, Nottaway, and Rupert—and would involve the total deforestation of about 922,040 square kilometers of land.[35] The project was intended to generate energy for sale to Vermont, New Hampshire, Maine, and New York, but environmentalists, students, and many Native and human rights groups organized and put a stop to this project in November 1994. . . .

Environmental Classism

In the preceding examples, there is a pattern of power companies locating their plants in rural communities, using up the water, polluting the land and the health of the people, and transferring the energy to the wealthier urban residents. In situations involving Euro-Americans, Western culture's domination of water and economically disadvantaged communities can be described as environmental classism. In the summer and fall of 2000, one battle against environmental classism took place on the international border of Whatcom County, the most northwestern county in Washington State, in the town of Sumas.

With a population of 700, Sumas is a rural community teetering on the edge of economic sufficiency. It relies largely on dairy farming and the patronage of tourists crossing the Canadian–American border between Sumas and Abbotsford. Already the Sumas–Abbotsford aquifer is contaminated with nitrates and pesticides, traceable to a high volume of dairy wastes and the over application of synthetic fertilizers.[36] The Environmental Protection Agency has repeatedly tested the groundwater and found ethylene-dibromide (EDB), a known carcinogen left over from berry farming; some estimate it will take 20 more years for the pesticides still locked in the soil to reach the aquifer.[37] Along with EDB, 50% of the wells in the city are contaminated with nitrates, a consequence of runoff from the many dairy farms, and 20% of these are above safe drinking levels.[38] The situation is so dire that water is trucked in to area residents; meanwhile, migrant farm workers (largely Hispanics) drink untreated water. It is in this context of water scarcity that a new power plant is being proposed.

In March 1999, National Energy Systems Company (NESCO) began the process of applying for a permit to build a new 660-megawatt power-generating facility within Sumas city limits and 500 yards from the town's elementary school. The proposed project would be the largest natural gas–fired generating facility in the state of Washington. If approved, on each day of operation, Sumas Energy 2 (SE2) will emit more than 3 tons of hazardous pollutants, including ammonia, lead, mercury, benzene, and toluene; it will consume up to 1.2 million gallons of water (a third of which is drinking water), 3 times the amount of water that is reserved for the next 20 years of growth and industry; it will create noise pollution in residential areas 3 times as loud as the level known to interfere with sleep; and it will require an additional 48 miles of high-voltage power lines to be extended through the county.[39] These costs to human and environmental health will not be offset with substantial benefits. Whatcom County does not need the extra power; in fact, the 660-megawatt capacity of SE2 is equal to the total electrical consumption of the entire county, including the county's industries.[40] Sumas residents and other local activists believe that the power generated by SE2 is intended for sale in Southern California.[41] For compensation, the town of Sumas will receive $900,000 per year in property taxes, offset by the inevitable decrease in property values caused by the plant's environmental pollution.[42] The plant will create only 24 full-time jobs, yet its owners are applying for a $24 million tax break.[43] Meanwhile, the health of the local residents, the animals, the water, air, and land will suffer.

Water, Power, and Human Relations

These examples of environmental sexism, environmental racism, and environmental classism reveal something about Western culture's attitude toward nature. They reveal how as inhabitants of Western culture we are conditioned to think about water and how we are conditioned to think about power. And our conception of power and energy, as well as our relationship to water, is based on a linear model that is now showing itself to be not only inaccurate, but life threatening. This linear model is based on the assumption that energy can be continuously extracted from nature—from water, from poor people, from people of color, from women—without giving back anything of sustenance. In the linear model of power production, energy is extracted, distributed, consumed, and in the process, wastes are produced: noise, electromagnetic radiation, flooding, pollution. In nature's energy model, production and consumption form a continuous flow; there is no waste.[44]

A fundamental insight of feminism has been its understanding of power and power relationships. From a feminist perspective, power in itself is a neutral entity that can be used in different ways. Domination of others—whether in the form of rape, slavery, animal experimentation, colonialism, clear-cutting, or damming—has been called "power over" and is part of the violent and oppressive framework that feminists reject. In contrast, teaching or supporting others in using their own inner strength, deriving strength from their relationships, or working in coalition with other groups for the good of life on this earth has been called empowerment, or "power with." It is this peaceful use of power that feminists advocate; its implications for social justice, for environmental justice, and for sustainable energy production can be denied only at the risk of human and ecological health. . . .

We need to change the socioeconomic infrastructure that mediates

Western culture's relationship with water, and to do this we need three types of change to occur simultaneously—changes in the practice of democracy, and in the areas of economic accounting and cultural beliefs. As the experiences of citizens from James Bay, Quebec, to Sumas, Washington, make clear, government is being heavily influenced by corporations and is not responding to citizen input. Voting more regularly or lobbying our elected officials does not seem to be influencing the political system when this system is too closely tied to corporate economics. To restore the genuine practice of democracy, corporations need to be brought under the control of the government, and the government must be brought back to serving the people for whom it stands. Shifting our cultural views from anthropocentrism to an interconnected worldview that includes "all our relations,"[45] we need a political system that recognizes the citizenship of mountains and lakes as well as the citizenship of humans of all races; we need an ecological democracy.[46]

Second, the life-sustaining value of pure water needs to be reflected through a form of economic accounting, that is, accounting that counts both the environmental costs of over-consumption and pollution as well as the value of free flowing rivers and pure, widely available drinking water. As the indigenous people of North America have advised, we need to account for both the material as well as the spiritual and psychological value of environmental health for all residents of the land. To safeguard against situations that allow corporations to place undue pressure on poor communities, urging them to accept polluting industries and toxic wastes, we need an economic system that pays a living wage to every worker, one that does not require workers to risk their health for their jobs, one that values the work that women do, and one that respects the value of indigenous peoples and indigenous homelands. We need an ecological economics.[47]

At the same time that we reclaim our democracy and adjust our economic accounting, we need to transform our inherited cultural beliefs, for a democracy is capable only of representing the beliefs of the people who participate in it. Democracies are not inherently ecological, feminist, or antiracist unless the people within them make them so. Currently, the democracies of North America do not give full citizenship to people of nondominant races and genders, and this exclusion is antidemocratic;

moreover, they rely on a separation between the public citizen and the private individual, thereby separating the functions of production, reproduction, and consumption. To remedy these errors, we need to "close the loop," in effect, to restore the connections between public and private, between culture and nature, between reason and the erotic, between energy and emotion, between the mind and the body; we need to recognize and nourish the interdependence of White and non-White citizens and people of all genders. We need a partnership culture, one that acknowledges our human identities as fundamentally interdependent with human and nonhuman others.

Ecological spirituality is part of this cultural shift and is needed as well. One spiritual path known for its ecological commitments, Buddhism suggests that the impediments to our spiritual unfolding are the same as our problems with social and environmental injustice and can be traced to three root forces—greed, hatred, and delusion.[48] These forces are also at the root of Western culture's troubled relationship with water. Greed is at the root of this culture's failure to account for the environmental costs of water pollution; rather, we profit by polluting. Hatred contaminates our relationship with nature, with racialized others, with our bodies as nature. Delusion, or wrong view, comes into play when we think we can treat water any way we want and get away with it, that this earth is not a closed system, and that the consequences of our polluting behaviors will not come back to us. Today, we can no longer flush and forget. An ecological spirituality recognizes the immanence of the sacred here and now, in the interdependence of all life, and in each glass of water. Power can be shared in ways that honor our various relations with each other and with the land. The choice is up to us.

Notes

1. Originally published as: G. Gaard, "Women, water, energy: an ecofeminist approach," *Organization and Environment* 14 (2001): 157–172. Reprinted by Permission of SAGE Publications.

2. J. Stauffer, *The water crisis.* (Montreal, Canada: Black Rose Books, 1999); L. Wright, *Clean and decent: the unruffled history of the bathroom and the water closet.* (New York: Viking, 1960).

3. Stauffer, 1999, 7.

4. V. Plumwood, *Feminism and the mastery of nature.* (New York: Routledge, 1993).

5. Ibid., 41.

6. Ibid., 41–42.

7. The list of hierarchical dualisms has been described by many feminists and ecofeminists alike. The specific form used here was initially developed by Plumwood (1993) and augmented with the final four dualisms (racism, classism, heterosexism, erotophobia) by G. Gaard, "Toward a queer ecofeminism," *Hypatia* 12 (1997) 114–137; the dualisms describing the separations involved in racism and classism are particularly important to the argument here.

8. Ibid.

9. E. Gray, *Green paradise lost.* (Wellesley, MA: Roundtable Press, 1979); S. Griffin, *Woman and nature: the roaring inside her.* (New York: Harper & Row, 1978); C. Spretnak (ed.), *The politics of women's spirituality.* (New York: Doubleday/Anchor, 1982); G. Steinem, *Revolution from within.* (Boston: Little, Brown, 1992).

10. Gaard, 1997; Plumwood, 1993.

11. The "linking postulates" are from Plumwood, 1993, pp. 48–55, but the examples are my own interpretation.

12. The mythical associations between women and water in this paragraph are taken from Barbara G. Walker, *The woman's encyclopedia of myths and secrets.* (San Franciso: Harper & Row, 1983). See entries for Creation, Kali, Mermaid, Nammu, Styx, Tiamat, Water, and Wells.

13. R. Eisler, *The chalice and the blade.* (San Francisco: Harper-Collins, 1987).

14. Walker, 1983, 90–91.

15. Plumwood, 1993.

16. M. Waring, *If women counted: a new feminist economics.* (San Francisco: Harper-Collins, 1988).

17. Ben Chavez, quoted in R. Bullard (ed.), *Confronting environmental racism: voices from the grassroots.* (Boston: South End, 1993), 3.

18. Northwest Power Planning Council. Available: http://www.nwppc.org (accessed, 2000).

19. On the health hazards of high-voltage power lines, see Becker, 1990; Becker and Selden, 1985; Lawrence, 1996. This controversial topic has been hotly contested by the scientific establishment (see Campion, 1997; Leary, 1996) because the connection between electromagnetic fields and cancer has not been proven in controlled laboratory tests. Meanwhile, environmental and public health activists continue to note the real-world correlations and have called for an exercise in judgment using the precautionary principle. . . .

20. Bonneville Power Authority. Available: http://www.transmission.bpa.gov (accessed, 2000).

21. Columbia Riverkeeper. Available: http://www.columbiariverkeeper.org (accessed, 2000).

22. Chelan County Public Utility District, *Nez Perce Indian portraits, Rocky Reach Dam.* (Wenatchee, WA: Author, 2000).

23. S. Power, "Salmon vs. dam issue colors presidential campaign," *Bellingham Herald*, A1–A2, November 29, 1999.

24. The Nez Perce Tribe, Confederated Tribes of the Umatilla Indian Reserva-

tion, Confederated Tribes of the Warm Springs Reservation of Oregon, and the Confederated Tribes and Bands of the Yakama Indian Nation are the only tribes in the Columbia Basin to have reserved rights to anadromous fish.

25. Columbia River Anadromous Fish Plan of the Nez Perce, Umatilla, Warm Springs, and Yakima Tribes. Available: http://www.critfc.org/textffRP_text.htm (accessed, 2000).

26. Power, 1999, A2.

27. Columbia River Anadromous Fish Plan, 2000.

28. W. LaDuke, *All our relations: Native struggles for land and life.* (Boston: South End, 1999), 49.

29. Ibid.

30. Ibid., 60.

31. Ibid.

32. Ibid., 61.

33. Ibid.

34. Ibid., 62.

35. Ibid.

36. S. Ayers, "Pollution cleanup list comes with teeth," *Bellingham Herald*, AI–A2, June 30, 1998.

37. Ibid.

38. E. Pizzillo, "Dairy inspection program produces 45 warnings so far," *Bellingham Herald*, AI–A2, January 18, 1999.

39. B. Bumford, "Generations Affected by Senseless Power (GASP) oppose Sumas Energy 2." Available: http://www.se2-gasp.org (accessed, 2000); A. Hanners, "Governor's veto of proposed Sumas power plant and political economics," *Whatcom Watch*, April 11, 2000.

40. Bumford, 2000.

41. G. Gaard, "Democracy takes beating in Sumas plant talks," *Bellingham Herald*, B4, August 20, 2000; A. Hanners, "The Sumas power plant: tax breaks in return for pollution," *Whatcom Watch*, 1,6, May 1999.

42. Bumford, 2000.

43. Hanners, 2000.

44. M. Mies and V. Shiva, *Ecofeminism.* (London: Zed Books, 1993).

45. LaDuke, 1999.

46. G. Gaard, *Ecological politics: ecofeminists and the Greens.* (Philadelphia: Temple University Press, 1998); V. Plumwood, "Has democracy failed ecology?" *Environmental Politics* 4 (1995): 134–168; C. Sandilands, "From natural identity to radical democracy," *Environmental Ethics* 17 (1995): 75–91.

47. Gaard, 1998; M. Mellor, "Women, nature, and the social construction of 'economic man,'" *Ecological Economics* 20 (1997): 129–140; Plumwood, 1995; Waring, 1988.

48. P. Payutto, "Buddhist solutions for the twenty-first century," in *Dharma rain: sources of Buddhist environmentalism*, ed. S. Kaza and K. Kraft (Boston: Shambhala Publications, 2000), 170–177.

Part Three

Utilitarianism

Chapter 7

Editors' Introduction

There are just two things on this material earth—people and natural resources.

—Gifford Pinchot[1]

The Utilitarian Ethic

Like other ethical perspectives, utilitarianism has a strong historical basis. It has antecedents in Epicureanism (300 BCE), which argued pleasure was the preeminent good, pain the sole evil. Its modern formulation relies on Jeremy Bentham (1748–1832) and John Stuart Mill (1806–73), who, though they disagreed on important matters, are typically referred to as the classical utilitarians. In its classical form, the principle of utility asserts that actions are right insofar as they promote the greatest happiness for the greatest number. Major elements in the appeal of utilitarianism, especially its flourishing in the 19th century, were that it provided a straightforward answer to two fundamental questions: (1) What is right? (2) Why should I do it?[2]

In answer to the question, What is right? utilitarianism suggests the use of a common metric of pleasure over pain, or happiness over unhappiness, the positive balance of which is defined as utility. In the 19th century, this idea was especially influential in providing some empirical measure of ethical correctness and aided utilitarianism in overcoming a form of ethics known as intuitionism, which supposed that ethical principles were to be derived from our intuitive sense about the good. As regards the second question, Why should I do it? utilitarianism offers at least two different responses. One of these emphasizes explicit duties to others, and grounds these duties in our sympathetic concerns for all affected persons. On this view, the well-to-do have obligations to help the less fortunate since this will result in an overall increase in utility. Those with lots of water should help the thirsty. The second answer suggests that, while there are duties to help all affected persons, these obligations can best be discharged *indirectly* by each person pursuing his or her own utility through market transactions. In this view we should individually seek to increase utility, and this will have the net effect of increasing the utility of society as a whole. In the period following World War II this school found common cause with like arguments of Adam Smith and his notion of the "invisible hand" that guides individual actions designed to increase one's own utility toward the benefit of all.

In its anthropocentric form, utilitarianism sees the natural world in terms of things that can be used to increase human happiness. Namely, those things we call natural resources. There are two general ways to secure natural resources to meet the utilitarian dictum and which roughly correspond to how duties are conceived: bureaucratic and individualist. Bureaucratic approaches to utility are characterized by their reliance on a centralized authority and experts who, for instance, engineer large dams or diversion projects in order to provide increased benefits to society. Alternately, individualist approaches are characterized by reliance on markets and the idea that there is, by definition, a gain in utility from all voluntary transactions. Hence, the effects of decisions increasing an individual's utility work to benefit society as a whole. We introduce this section by providing the context for understanding both forms of utilitarianism, their impacts on modern water policy, and the particular difficulties facing utilitarianism.

Bureaucratic Utilitarianism

One of the most interesting aspects of water policy in North America and elsewhere is that early management approaches often had very little to do with water directly. In fact, water policies were often derived from ideas regarding how to best manage forests and land, not lakes, wetlands, rivers, or glaciers. Especially during the late 19th and early 20th centuries, the belief that all natural resources could be managed effectively by scientific expertise propelled the notion that long-term improvements must be undertaken by a stable organization concerned with the public interest: that is, the government. The key to success was a conservationist ethic, a "wise use" philosophy that would ensure forests, and eventually water, could provide benefits for humans indefinitely. In the conservationist movement there was a strong suspicion of private ownership since this often led to rampant and very harmful exploitation of the resources.

Gifford Pinchot, the first head of the U.S. Forest Service, was one of the most influential proponents of conservation management. Pinchot believed that the classical formulation of the utilitarian ethic lacked foresight and that resources should be managed to promote the greatest amount of happiness for the greatest number *for the longest amount of time*.[3] When this framework was applied to water it had important repercussions. For instance, in North America it ushered in the era of municipal sewage systems and the large dams, irrigation, and diversion projects by the Bureau of Reclamation and the U.S. Army Corp of Engineers. However, many argue that long-term economic benefits to society did not always surpass costs to the local environment and, in many instances, had the ironic effect of undermining the livelihoods of the people they were designed to benefit.[4]

Individualistic Utilitarianism

In response to shortcomings of bureaucratic forms of utilitarianism, there has been a turn toward individualist strategies in which markets replace government agencies as the means of achieving increased utility. Rather than attempting to engineer the greatest happiness for the greatest number, the microeconomic approach allows individuals to make their own choices, and it uses price to provide an indication of what individuals can expect to exchange for increased utility. Buyers may be single people, households, or firms, but, at any scale, the aggregate effects of their actions are believed to translate into net benefits for society. Since those who have to buy water are likely to use less of it this means that there is less waste and more for others.

The microeconomic approach to water can also provide a market structure that allocates water in support of other social values. Some economists argue that virtually any desired distribution of water is attainable by carefully designing property rights to encourage certain types of transactions while discouraging others.[5] For example, when the Central Valley of California was dominated by agriculture, it was more efficient to allocate water to support that sector. However, since California has now become a heavily urbanized state, allocation of water rights to cities will bring about a different, and arguably more just, efficiency. However, despite the promises of water markets, several attempts to establish them have met with limited success. For instance, despite being lauded as an exemplar for free water markets, empirical results from Chile indicate that few, if any, transactions have taken place and that critical issues of social inequity remain.[6]

Difficulties with Utilitarianism

The principle of utility has provided the default ethic for water resources management and development throughout the 20th century.[7] However, as the scale of hydropower development, watershed engineering projects, privatization, and economic instruments for water valuation have expanded, criticisms of the utilitarian view have begun to polarize discussions on water and resource management. Here we highlight some of the ethical difficulties at the heart of these debates.[8]

The problem of individual and collective goods. As we discussed earlier, classical utilitarianism aimed to achieve the greatest happiness for the greatest number, and, in Pinchot's reformulation, for the longest time. However, it has been very difficult to transition from the idea that everybody seeks to maximize their own happiness to the notion that we are morally obliged to maximize the utility of others. In this sense utilitarianism needs to clearly define the scale at which the *greatest* good is calculated— is it the aggregate of individual happiness? or is it the measure of society's collective well-being? With regard to water, Ricardo Petrella considers utilitarianism's individualist strategy deficient because it assumes that the sum total of individual goods is the same as what is good for society.[9] However, there may be goods at larger, communal scales that do not reduce to individual calculations or obligations. For example, Bryan Nor-

EDITORS' INTRODUCTION   83

ton argues that considering the greatest good as an aggregate of individual utility forgoes opportunities to consider goods arising at larger scales critical for sustainability, such as those of communities and watersheds.[10]

The tyranny of the majority. A second criticism of utilitarianism is that it does not adequately protect rights. For instance, in its promotion of the greatest good utilitarianism authorizes overriding a minority if a net increase in utility is produced. Author and activist Vandana Shiva contends that using utility calculations can be inequitable when certain water uses are undervalued compared to others.[11] For instance, the construction of dams to serve a large city can override the rights of a fewer number of local people in calculating overall utility. This exclusion of certain types of rights, such as those of traditional water uses, may legitimate the dispossession of water from entire categories of water users in favor of increased benefits for private firms and their customers.[12]

Excessive burdens. A third criticism of utilitarianism is that it is too burdensome. That is, it is unreasonable to expect that, in deciding upon a course of action, I may accurately calculate my own utility against the utility of potentially countless others. From this perspective, there is little room in utilitarianism for me to live my life as defined by my own purposes and projects. For instance, those living upstream, if they adhere to utilitarianism, would need to have a large amount of knowledge regarding the utility of those living downstream to ensure that their actions increase happiness for themselves more than they decrease it for others. A similar problem arises in neoclassical economics and the assumption that consumers have "complete knowledge" in making transaction decisions.

Whose utility counts? Another criticism of utilitarianism is that it doesn't give us a good stopping rule for judging whose utility should be considered in decision making. This difficulty can also be thought of in terms of obligations to both humans and nonhumans. Peter Singer has argued that if we consider equal interests equally then at least some nonhumans (i.e., advanced primates) have the same level of interests as some humans (i.e., newborn babies).[13] Jeremy Bentham went further, as Singer does in some of his writings, saying that creatures that can suffer are worthy of moral consideration. In terms of water, a resource upon which all life invariably depends, some rule that circumscribes the number of interests to consider in a utility calculation is necessary to reach *any* decision. Yet utilitarianism offers no such rule.

Criteria for happiness. A final criticism of utilitarianism may be found in the terms used to calculate utility preferences, wherein some economic texts replace talk of utility with talk of preferences or interests. In these cases it is very difficult to understand why we have obligations to care about the preferences or tastes of others unless they are connected to happiness. And then if it is happiness we are concerned with we have not escaped from all the difficulties with the utilitarian project that we have just considered.

Contents

The essays begin with one that sees water as a resource for human well-being, through to the promise of water markets and considerations of the earth's entire hydrological cycle in terms of "ecosystem services." This ordering offers the opportunity to assess utilitarian claims at a number of scales, from bureaucratic and individual perspectives, to whether water's value is calculated as a communal or personal good and through to concerns about the extent to which we can quantify water's value in monetary terms.

The first essay, by William J. McGee, marks water's initial conception as a resource that may be harnessed for the greatest good of society. McGee's early-20th-century perspective highlights the important gains that technology and resource management offered for the bureaucratic coordination and development of water resources. The second essay, by Terry Anderson and Donald Leal, presents strong arguments for how bureaucratic water management is inefficient in terms of directing water to its highest value. The solution they offer is to move toward water markets, which offer the opportunity to increase efficiency through economic transactions and clearly defined property rights in Western water law. The third essay, by Steven Kraft, argues that, while water markets may allocate water to their highest value, they fail to ensure that the final distribution of water is just. Kraft considers distributive fairness key to acceptable water policies and offers principles for comparing utilitarian claims against the potential for markets to favor those who can afford, or who have access to, those markets that price water. The fourth essay, by Joseph L. Sax, responds to the focus on individual goods in policies designed to stimulate water market transfers. Sax argues that several legal traditions, including Western water law, have strong implications for protecting community rights rather than only those of individuals. The final essay, by Augustin Berque, considers the quantification and economic valuation of the world's water cycle as part of the earth's "ecosystem services." He argues that the inherent judgments in how we quantify water and determine its economic value are limited and should lead us to reorient water policies from their utilitarian focus and toward a clearer positioning of humans in relation to their environment.

Notes

1. Quoted in Bryan G. Norton, *Sustainability: a philosophy for adaptive ecosystem management.* (Chicago: University of Chicago Press, 2005), 181.
2. Henry Sidgwick, *Outlines of the history of ethics.* (Boston: Beacon Press, 1960).
3. G. Pinchot, *The training of a forester.* (Philadelphia: J. B. Lippincott Co, 1914).
4. See Marc Reisner, *Cadillac desert: the American West and its disappearing water,* revised edition (New York: Penguin Books, 1993); Sandra Postel, *Pillars of sand: how long can the irrigation miracle last?* (New York: W.W. Norton & Company, 1999).
5. T. Horbyluk and J. L. Lynda, "Welfare gains from potential water markets in Alberta, Canada," in *Markets for water: potential and performance,* ed. K. Easter, M. Rosengrant, and A. Dinar (Boston: Kluwer Academic Publishers, 1998), 241–258.
6. C. Bauer, "Results of Chilean water markets: empirical research since 1990," *Water Resources Research* 40 (2004): W09S06.
7. D. Feldman, *Water policy for sustainable development.* (Baltimore: John Hopkins University Press, 2007).
8. These criticisms are drawn from Peter G. Brown's, *Commonwealth of Life,* 2nd ed (Montreal: Black Rose Books, 2008). The reader who is interested in debates regarding the merits of utilitarianism may wish to consult James Rachels, *The elements of moral philosophy.* (New York: Random House, 1986); Peter Singer, *Practical ethics.* (New York: Cambridge University Press, 1979); William Frankena, *Ethics,* 2nd ed. (New Jersey: Prentice Hall, 1973); Smart, J., and B. Williams, *Utilitarianism: for and against.* (New York: Cambridge University Press, 1973).
9. R. Petrella, *The water manifesto: arguments for a world water contract.* (New York: Palgrave, 2001).
10. Norton, 2005.
11. V. Shiva, *Globalization's new wars: seed, water and life forms.* (New Delhi: Women Unlimited, 2005).
12. E. Swnygedouw, "Dispossing H_2O—the contested terrain of water privatisation," *Capitalism, Nature, Socialism* 16 (2005): 1–18.
13. Peter Singer, *Practical ethics.* (New York: Cambridge University Press, 1979).

Chapter 8

Water as a Resource[1]

William J. McGee

THIS IS AN AGE OF SCIENCE and ours a nation of science. Observation has matured in measurement and passed from the qualitative to the quantitative, generalization is a habit, and prevision has become a commonplace in current life. More than all else, the course of nature has come to be investigated in order that it may be re-directed along lines contributing to human welfare; invention has become a step toward creation, and is extending far beyond the merely mechanical and into the realms of the chemical and even the vital. Now is the time of conquest over nature in practical sense, of panurgy in philosophic sense—the day of prophecy made perfect in predetermined accomplishment.

Our country is growing rapidly. The rate varies along different lines. Our growth in agricultural production is unprecedented in the world's history; our growth in population is so much more rapid that exportation of food-stuffs is declining; our growth in mining outruns our increase in population; our growth in manufacturing far exceeds that in mining; and our growth in application of mechanical power is much more rapid than our advance in manufacturing. Along one line only is our growth more rapid than in the use of power—i.e., in that knowledge and mental capacity required to guide and develop the material progress.

Our rate of mental growth is not easily measured in that its manifestations are manifold. In 1905 it was pointed out that along the single line of university development the rate of advance is geometric—that during the first half of the 19th century our university strength measured in endowments, or faculties, or students, or alumni, or all combined doubled; that during the next quarter-century it doubled again; that from 1875 to 1890 it doubled again; that in the next decade it once more doubled, and that within the first seven years of the present century it would inevitably double again. Naturally such whelming growth can not continue indefinitely on any line; yet the advance can and does continue, largely by the development of new lines or by multiplication of the old, so patently that it is safe to characterize our progress in knowledge and mental power as geometric.

Our growth in knowledge of that definite character called science is notable—particularly in its ever-multiplying applications. Twenty-five years ago the writer compiled a geologic map of the United States, the first based wholly on observation and not at all on inference, and although a quarter of the area was left blank, it was complete enough for publication;[2] a year later he compiled the first map showing the distribution of coal in the United States, which was fairly complete for two-thirds of our area yet so incomplete for the remaining third as not to be deemed worthy of publication. The fact that today any geologic map may be made substantially complete, and that our coal deposits have been surveyed not only as to area but as to volume, strikingly illustrates the rapidity and sureness of our progress in practical knowledge. With the growth of science, its field has extended and its agencies have multiplied. When the Federal Geological Survey was started and the State surveys were reinvigorated only three decades ago, they stood almost alone for the development of the natural resources, aside from the land reckoned in area merely. Now the surveys have grown; an entire Federal Department and corresponding State instrumentalities have come up on the basis of resources comprising the land and its products and potentialities, a wide range of minerals, the forests which protect the streams, and of late the water itself. It is in harmony with the general development that the quantitative method is now applied not only to soil production in forests and crops, and to mine production and minerals in the ground, but finally to the rains and rivers which render the land habitable and the ground waters which render it fruitful.

No more significant advance has been made in our history than that of the last year or two in which our waters have come to be considered as a resource—one definitely limited in quantity, yet susceptible of conservation and of increased beneficence through wise utilization. The conquest of nature, which began with progressive control of the soil and its products and passed to the minerals, is now extending to the waters on, above, and beneath the surface. The conquest will not be complete until these waters are brought under complete control. . . .

Our stock of water is like other resources in that its quantity is fixed. It differs from such mineral resources as coal and iron, which once used are gone forever, in that the supply is perpetual; and it differs from such resources as soils and forests, which are capable of renewal or increase, provided the supply of water suffices, in that its quantity can not be augmented. It differs also in that its relative quantity is too small to permit full development of other resources and of the population and industries depending on them. Like all other resources, it may be better utilized. It must be better utilized in order to derive full benefit from lands and forests and mines. . . .

Hitherto water has seldom been regarded as a resource to be exploited and conserved; it has been viewed vaguely as a prime necessity, yet merely as a natural incident or providential blessing. In its assumed plentitude the idea of quantity has seldom arisen though the waste is least in those arid regions in which customs are better adjusted to the values and inter-relations of water. Under the English common-law prevailing in eastern United States, the water is held appurtenant to the land; under the Code Napoleon prevailing in Louisiana, it virtually appertains to the community; under the Spanish-Roman law prevailing in western United States, water is subject to prior appropriation and beneficial use, and hence appertains primarily to the individual or family, while the land is essentially appurtenant to the water traversing it. Some States recognize a residuary right of the people in the natural waters, or in the headwaters of streams used for water supply or navigation, and this recognition seems to be extending over the country; but the usage of the different sections is not uniform, the exercise of the right of the people generally varying with the aridity of the land or the density of the population.

It has been roughly estimated that the inland waterways of the country could be improved in ten years at a cost of $50,000,000 annually in such manner as to promote interstate commerce and at the same time greatly reduce the waste and extend the use of the waters. If done at the cost of the people, the burden would be $0.625 per capita per year, or $6.25 in all, for a population of 80,000,000.

It is rougly estimated that the direct benefits would comprise an annual saving in transportation of $250,000,000; an annual saving in flood damage of $150,000,000; an average annual saving in forest fires of at least $25,000,000; an annual benefit through cheapened power of fully $75,000,000; and an annual saving in soil erosion or corresponding benefit through increased farm production of $500,000,000—a total of $1,000,000,000 or $12.50 per capita annually, i.e., twenty times the cost. In addition, large benefits would result from extended irrigation, from the drainage and settlement of swamp and overflow land, and from purified and cheapened water supply with consequent diminution of disease and saving of human life.

It is estimated that the income derived from power developed by works for the improvement of navigation, if utilized at current market rates in cooperation with states and citizens, would alone compensate the entire cost of maintenance and continued development after the initial expenditure of $500,000,000 as a working capital.

Notes

1. Originally published as: W. J. McGee, "Water as a resource," *American Academy of Political and Social Science*, 33(3) (1909): 37–50. Reprinted by permission SAGE Publications

2. It appeared under the title "Map of the United States exhibiting the present status of knowledge of the geological groups." Fifth Annual Report of the U.S. Geological Survey, 1885 (pages 36–38, Plate II).

Chapter 9

Priming the Invisible Pump[1]

Terry L. Anderson and Donald R. Leal

MARK TWAIN SUPPOSEDLY QUIPPED: "Whiskey is for drinkin' and water is for fightin'." In the arid West, where water is the lifeblood of agriculture, this adage has become especially appropriate, as municipal, industrial, and environmental demands for water have grown and generated competing uses. Traditionally, growing demands have been met by increasing supplies made possible with dams and canals, such as the Central Arizona Project, which cost billions of dollars to deliver water primarily to municipal users in Phoenix and Tucson.

For most of the twentieth century, the federal government subsidized the construction and maintenance of water storage and delivery projects designed to make the desert "bloom like a rose." The Bureau of Reclamation and the Army Corps of Engineers administer the use of water from these projects, providing nearly 90 percent of it to agricultural users, who pay only a fraction of what it costs to store and deliver. The artificially low prices for federal water promote waste of water supplies that are coming under increasing stress from industrial, municipal, and environmental demands. And despite these demands, the political allocation of federal water has been unresponsive, with few transfers of water made to other uses. We have learned from this political allocation system that if water runs uphill to money, it gushes uphill to politics. . . .

This political, social, and economic climate is bringing pressure to change the way water is managed. In the face of efforts to curtail government spending and protect the environment, the formal and informal institutions that govern water allocation must foster conservation and more efficient allocation of existing supplies and take water's growing recreational and environmental value into account. Water markets provide a way of doing this.

Free market environmental principles have become a coalescing theme among environmentalists and fiscal conservatives who oppose political water projects that are both uneconomical and environmentally destructive. This theme first manifested its potency in the defeat of the 1982 Peripheral Canal initiative, a project to divert northern California water to southern California. Opponents successfully convinced voters that high construction costs combined with high environmental costs associated with draining fresh water from the Sacramento delta made the project an economic as well as an environmental disaster. Following the initiative's defeat, Thomas Graff, general counsel for the California Environmental Defense Fund, asked: "Has all future water-project development been choked off by a new conservationist–conservative alliance . . . ?"[2] The answer appears to be yes, as construction of new, large-scale federal water projects has come to a virtual halt.

Water marketing can provide a basis for extending the alliance into the twenty-first century by encouraging efficient use, discouraging detrimental environmental effects, and reducing the drain on government budgets. Equally important, water marketing can release the creative power of individuals in the marketplace, enabling water users to deal with allocation problems specific to their demands and their local environmental constraints. As economist Rodney Smith explained, with water marketing "a farmer can apply his first-hand knowledge of his land, local hydrology, irrigation technology, and relative profitability of alternative crops to decide how much water to apply and which crops to grow on his land."[3]

The Prior Appropriation Doctrine

As with all aspects of free market environmentalism, water marketing depends on well-specified water rights; that is, rights must be clearly defined, enforceable, and transferable. Clearly defined and enforced water rights reduce uncertainty and assure that the benefits of water are captured. Transferable rights force users to face the full cost of water, including its value in other uses. If alternative uses are more valuable, then current users have the incentive to reallocate scarce water by selling or leasing it.

Unfortunately, well-specified and transferable water rights are often conspicuously absent from the legal institutions that govern water resources. Governmental restrictions produce uncertainty of ownership, stymie water transfers, and promote waste and inefficiency in water use. By removing these governmental restrictions and adhering more closely to the prior appropriation doctrine, water marketing can provide a mechanism for improving efficiency and environmental quality.

The prior appropriation doctrine evolved on the western frontier, where water was scarce and agricultural and mining operations required users to transport water considerable distances from the stream. Responding to the special conditions in the West, early California gold miners devised their own system for allocating water. They recorded each claimant's right to divert a specific quantity of water from a stream and assigned it a priority according to the principle of "first in time, first in right." Under this system, a market for water quickly evolved in the late nineteenth century, but it was short-lived.[4]

In 1902, the system for managing water in the West changed dramatically. The Newlands Reclamation Act ushered in massive subsidies for the storage and delivery of water and sent signals, especially to the agricultural sector, that water was cheap. The act established funding to construct and operate projects that would deliver water to arid western lands. Initially, western irrigators were to repay the construction costs within ten years of project completion. However, interest-free repayment schemes, together with deferrals and extensions of the period of repayment—and a dramatic rise in interest rates during the 1970s and 1980s—raised the value of the subsidy to as high as 95 percent of the actual costs.[5] In addition, the irrigation subsidy is not limited to free interest on repayment of construction costs.[6] . . .

As if the fiscal implications were not enough, subsidized water projects encourage inefficient use and excessive demand. Paying only a fraction of the cost, irrigators have no incentive to consider alternative technologies and crops that would save water. In addition, many irrigation systems use less than half of the water that flows to them. The rest runs off fields, carrying with it pesticides, herbicides, and soil nutrients; evaporates as it moves through open canals; or percolates into the ground through un-lined ditches. Lands can become waterlogged as farmers apply copious amounts of water to their crops.

These conditions can lead to serious environmental problems, as evi-denced by what happened at the Kesterson National Wildlife Refuge. For years, California's Central Valley Project provided water to Westlands Water District farmers who paid only a fraction of the actual cost of de-livery. This encouraged them to irrigate even marginally productive lands. Wastewater from these lands drained into nearby Kesterson refuge via a drainage system built by the federal government.[7]

In 1983, the U.S. Fish and Wildlife Service noticed grotesque defor-mities in the birds and fish living in Kesterson. The toxic culprit was sele-nium that had leached from the soil and carried out to the refuge in the irrigation drainage from Westlands Water District. In small doses, sele-nium is necessary for life, but it can be a deadly pollutant when concen-trated, as it was at Kesterson.

Stopping the flow of wastewater into Kesterson by shutting off water to the irrigation district might have been a solution, but Westlands' farm-ers and the banks who held the debt on their farms would have none of that. Instead, taxpayer-funded pollution control costing millions of dol-lars was implemented to solve an environmental travesty caused by water subsidies.[8]

Some of the problems could be eliminated if water were tradeable, but reclamation laws have generally restricted transfers because they would allow farmers to make windfall profits on their subsidized water. As a re-sult, there are many questions about whether reclamation-project water can be sold or leased for a profit, whether it can be transferred away from the lands to which it was originally assigned, and whether it can be used for non-irrigation purposes. In 1988, the Bureau made an effort to re-move some of these barriers to transfers by declaring itself a "water mar-ket facilitator" and by outlining procedures to govern transfers of feder-ally supplied water. These types of reforms suggest that water policy is moving in a direction that will get the incentives right by allowing mar-kets to play a greater role in water allocation.

Since the 1980s, when economists and policy analysts began to recognize that water markets could help allocate water, we have come a long way. Trades between cities and agriculture have become more commonplace. Witness the trade between the Metropolitan Water District (MWD) and the Imperial Irrigation District (IID) in southern California. MWD constantly faces future water shortages because of the arid climate and growing population. For years, MWD could not acquire water from nearby agricultural sources because of restrictions on water transfers under California and federal reclamation law. A change in the California water code coupled with Bureau of Reclamation policy becoming favorable to water transfers in the region led to the 1989 Water Conservation Agreement. Under the agreement, MWD pays for ditch lining and other conservation projects within HD in exchange for the 106,100 acre-feet of water per year that is salvaged. The agreement is in effect for 35 years.[9] . . .

Even at the Bureau of Reclamation, home of subsidized water use, the focus now is on transferring full ownership of federal water projects to local water users. Not only do current users through their local water districts assume complete responsibility for project operation, they also stand to gain directly from water trades with cities and other potential water customers willing to pay them a premium for any surplus water they generate. This cannot help but improve prospects for expanding water markets down the road. As of April 1999, Congress has passed two pieces of legislation designating title transfers of project water. The first (S. 538, P.L. 105-351) was enacted to convey the South Side Pumping Division of the Minidoka Project, located in Burley, Idaho, to the Burley Irrigation District. The second (HR. 3687, P.L. 105-316) was enacted to convey the Canadian River Project to the Canadian River Authority in Texas, pending prepayment of the district's debt on the project. Other good prospects for transfer in the near term include the Clear Creek Unit of the Central Valley Project in California and the Pine River Project in Colorado.[10]

The market revolution in water is not confined to the United States. Chile, known for its application of market solutions to a variety of social problems, implemented a market-oriented water policy in 1974. The constitution of Chile, passed in 1980 and modified in 1988, reversed the expropriation of water rights by the state begun in 1966 and established secure, transferable water rights. The constitution states, "The rights to private individuals, or enterprises, over water, recognized or established by law, grant their holders the property over them."[11] Chile's market-oriented water policy is credited with giving farmers greater flexibility in selecting crops to respond to market demand, producing greater efficiency in urban water and sewage services, and allowing growing cities to buy water from farmers without having to buy land or expropriate water.[12]

Australian states have carried their water reforms a step further with interbasin water transfers. In 1992, the first interbasin water transfer involved a five-year lease of 7,982 acre-feet from a property on the Murrumbidgee River in New South Wales to a cotton farm on the lower Darling River in South Australia. Since then, the interbasin water market has developed incrementally through a series of temporary water transfers.[13]

The steady development of transborder water trading in Australia is the type of approach that is needed in North America. Unfortunately, proposed water transfers between the United States and Canada entail massive projects to deliver water from remote regions of Canada to populated areas of the United States. For example, the infamous North American Water and Power Alliance would have delivered 250 million acre-feet of water from northern Canada to the southern United States. The construction cost alone was estimated as high as $380 million in 1990 dollars. Projects like this encounter strong resistance from Canadian citizens who gain little or nothing as individuals. If such resistance is to change, trades will have to be scaled down and carried out incrementally, as was the case in Australia.[14]

While the push for grandiose schemes stymies international water trading, the prospects for water trades between states are looking up. Referring to prospects for water trades between Arizona, California, and Nevada, Interior Secretary Bruce Babbitt noted that "we are on the threshold of a new period in which the three lower division states together will regularly be using that full apportionment." He believes this will necessitate "encouraging conservation in use, voluntary transfers of water, and managing our storage and delivery systems so that we can meet the growing demands that the new century will bring."[15] At least with respect to individual states, the future of transborder water trading may be here.

Expanding Water Markets

The same insights that have helped to refocus the debate on the efficacy of markets in the allocation of surface water can be extended to the more complex tasks of allocating instream flows and groundwater. America's environmental awakening and burgeoning demand for recreational facilities, coupled with the declining quality of many streams, have drawn attention to the importance of instream flows. In many areas of the West, the depletion of groundwater supplies and water contamination due to toxic wastes have raised new concerns about groundwater. Both instream flows and groundwater are thus prime candidates for free market environmentalism.

Instream Flows

At one time, the management of instream flows was restricted to the maintenance of flow levels sufficient for navigation and power generation; today, however, water must meet a broader range of instream uses. For example, adequate instream flow levels must be maintained to sustain fish and wildlife habitats. Maintaining adequate flow levels can assimilate pollutants that remain a threat to many inland water bodies. And there is a growing demand for instream recreational opportunities such as fishing and floating. With the value of instream flows rising, the problem is to facilitate reallocation from off-stream to instream uses, but most states have laws that significantly limit the option for this reallocation.

A major stumbling block to the private provision of instream flows are state laws that link diversion to beneficial use. In frontier mining camps, an appropriation could be made by anyone who was willing to use the water by diverting it from the stream. Claiming water for instream flows is further complicated by the "use it or lose it" principle.[16] According to this principle, if a water user is not diverting his water, it is available to others for appropriation. Therefore, if an environmental group were willing to pay a farmer to reduce irrigation diversions, the conserved water left instream would be subject to diversion by other irrigators.

Courts have generally made it clear that private appropriations for instream flows are not valid. In a 1917 ruling against a claim to appropriate water for a duck habitat, the Utah Supreme Court concluded that it was

> utterly inconceivable that a valid appropriation of water can be made under the laws of this state, when the beneficial use of which, after the appropriation is made, will belong equally to every human being who seeks to enjoy it. . . . We are decidedly of the opinion that the beneficial use contemplated in making the appropriation must be one that inures to the exclusive benefits of the appropriators and subject to his domain and control.[17]

In 1915, *Colorado River Water Conservation District v. Rocky Mountain Power Company* also emphasized diversion. The conservation district had sought to establish the right to appropriate instream flows for the propagation of fish, but in 1965 the Colorado Supreme Court found that there was "no support in the law of this state for the proposition that a minimum flow of water may be 'appropriated' in a natural stream for piscatorial purposes without diversion of any portion of the water 'appropriated' from the natural course of the stream."[18] As recently as 1979, instream flow claims in California were even denied to a state agency and a nonprofit public-interest corporation.[19] In both cases, the California Supreme Court argued that there was no evidence that there would be a diversion of or physical control over the water.

Having been denied the option of private appropriations, states have undertaken to reserve flows by other means. States have traditionally chosen to maintain instream flows by reserving water from appropriation, establishing minimum stream flows by bureaucratic fiat, conditioning new water permits, directing state agencies to acquire and hold instream flow rights, or using the public trust doctrine to establish that existing diversion rights do not trump the state's responsibility to maintain instream flows. . . .

Given the problems with political water allocation, it is appropriate to ask whether water markets could do better.[20] Though traditional water

rights have not allowed for instream flows, the rising demand for instream uses and new technologies for monitoring water use and water
quality are putting evolutionary pressure on water rights. As law professor
James Huffman explains, "Sophisticated technologies of stream flow
monitoring can serve the law of instream flow rights just as the technology of barbed wire served the nineteenth-century law of private rights in
grazing land. Defining the parameters of a right to instream flows is no
more difficult than defining the parameters of a right to divert water for
agriculture or industry.[21] . . .

Environmental or recreational groups wanting more instream flows
argue that allowing such market transactions still may not provide
enough instream flows because it is too costly to prevent free riders from
enjoying benefits such as scenic values, fishing experiences, and improved
wildlife habitat. Nonpayers could reap the existence value, the critics
point out; that is, they would have the satisfaction derived from simply
knowing that an amenity exists, even if they do not consume or use it.
For example, a Bostonian might be happy knowing that the Snake River
in Idaho is free flowing and providing salmon habitat, even if she has no
intention of looking at it, fishing in it, or rafting on it.

Of course, all goods have some potential for free riding, but the free-
rider problem has not precluded the private provision of some instream
flows. With increasing frequency, private groups and small communities
have moved to secure protection and enhancement of instream flows.
During the winter of 1989, for example, irrigators, the Nature Conservancy, the Trumpeter Swan Society, and the city of Grand Prairie, Alberta
(Canada) contributed to such an effort on the Henry's Fork of the Snake
River in Idaho. The resident population of trumpeter swans on the river
was near starvation, its aquatic food supply cut off by river ice. Additional
water from the upstream dam was desperately needed to clear a channel
and allow the birds access to their food. A series of deals were struck between swan supporters and irrigators to increase flows to 400 cfs (up
from 100 cfs), enough to break up the ice jam. To prevent recurrence, a
long-term contract was also signed that guarantees a flow of 200 cfs, the
amount necessary to prevent freeze-up.[22]

The market process can foster solutions to the free-rider problem
because free riders represent opportunities for entrepreneurs who can

devise ways of collecting from them. Environmental entrepreneurs in the Nature Conservancy, Trout Unlimited, and other private organizations play an important role in creating private rights and capturing the benefits of instream flows. With the right incentives, entrepreneurs in ranching and farming can accomplish similar results. Suppose that a rancher who owns riparian land is deciding whether to increase cattle grazing, which in turn would reduce fish habitat by destroying bank vegetation and causing siltation. Motivated by profit, the rancher is unlikely to give up grazing to preserve fish habitat unless he can profit from fishing. . . .

Groundwater

As with past handling of instream flows, there has been practically no opportunity for the market to play a role in allocating groundwater in the United States. Free market environmentalism helps explain what has hindered market application and how markets could alleviate problems in the allocation of that resource.

Like so many of our natural resources, concern is growing that groundwater sources are being depleted by increasing groundwater demands. In 1970, 19 percent of the water used in the United States came from groundwater sources. By 1985, groundwater accounted for 25 percent of the water used and provided drinking water for more than half the population.[23] Due to the rising demand, extraction now exceeds natural recharge in many key groundwater basins. One of the most dramatic cases of depletion is occurring in the Ogallala Aquifer, which underlies 174,000 square miles of the High Plains from South Dakota to Texas. Withdrawals from the Ogallala irrigate 15 million acres and account for 30 percent of total U.S. groundwater used for irrigation. Overdraft (withdrawals in excess of recharge) occurred in 95 percent of the Ogallala, sparking forecasts that the aquifer would be 23 percent depleted by 2020.[24]

In many parts of California, aquifers are overdrawn. Statewide, average annual groundwater withdrawals exceed average annual replenishment by 2 to 2.5 million acre-feet per year. The state has identified 11 critically overdrafted groundwater basins and 42 more basins where overdraft has taken place but is not considered severe.[25]

Land subsidence and saltwater intrusion are two problems that can result when water tables fall excessively. Pumping in the Floridan aquifer has drawn saltwater from the seaward edge of the aquifer along the coasts of South Carolina, Georgia, and Florida. In the area of Kingsville, Texas, pumping from numerous wells has led to saltwater intrusion in the Evangeline aquifer. Overdraft in the Houston–Galveston region has caused subsidence up to 8.5 feet in a 4,700-square-mile area. Intensive groundwater pumping in California's San Joaquin Valley has resulted in an area the size of Connecticut subsiding by as much as 30 feet in some places. In parts of Arizona, heavy pumping has resulted in land subsiding by as much as 12 feet and earth fissures that damaged property.[26]

Does such groundwater depletion make good economic sense? From an efficiency standpoint, the answer may be yes.[27] Mining a groundwater basin, as it is called when withdrawals exceed inflows, is appropriate if the future value of the water is expected to be lower than current value and there are no third-party impacts such as land subsidence.

A major difficulty in allocating groundwater, however, is that the future value of water left in a basin may not be available if there is open access to pumping. Water left for the future is often subject to the tragedy of the commons. Suppose that an individual must decide whether to leave water in a basin in order to offset future shortfalls in precipitation or surface water availability. Even if he believes that the current consumption value is less than the discounted future insurance value, his incentive to leave water in the basin is reduced by the knowledge that other users can pump the water immediately. Each individual realizes that anything he leaves behind may be consumed by others. And if others pump enough to lower the level of water in the basin, future pumping costs may be higher too. In the absence of secure ownership claims, future value gets zero weight in the calculus.

Groundwater users cannot optimize the rate of extraction unless the rights to water in a basin are clearly defined by water institutions and the courts. Only then can users accurately calculate the current and future value of groundwater supplies. Thus, the first step in solving the problem of depletion is to secure well-defined rights to groundwater use, which in turn will facilitate market transfers.

To gain an understanding of the present property rights structure, it is important to realize that the underpinnings of groundwater law are found in English common law. Because little was known about the hydrology of groundwater, rights to groundwater were assigned to the owners of the overlying land. As Frank Trelease has pointed out, "It was in the light of this scientific and judicial ignorance that the overlying land-owner was given total dominion over his 'property,' that is, a free hand to do as he pleased with water found within his land, without accounting for damage."[28] When groundwater rights either are not assigned or are as-signed on the basis of overlying land, the common pool problems can be-come severe. Each individual achieves the greatest net benefits by pump-ing water earlier than the others, because the lift costs increase as the level is lowered. The tragedy of the commons occurs because each individual has an incentive to pump water earlier than everyone else, so the supply is rapidly depleted.

Such poorly defined rights were harmless as long as there was little de-mand for groundwater; but as demand has increased, changes have oc-curred in the institutions that allocate groundwater, but these have not led to efficient use. For example, owners of overlying land have been granted rights to groundwater on the basis of reasonable use. The prob-lem with the rule of reasonable use is that the interpretation of reason-ableness has been subjected to the whims of judges and administrators, which has made the tenure of rights uncertain. In addition, the equal rights provision has usually been interpreted to mean that water use is re-stricted to overlying land and cannot be transferred elsewhere. . . .

Conclusion

Dire predictions that the blue planet will face global water shortages may unfold if we cannot supplant water politics with water markets. Growing demands for consumption, pollution, dilution, and environmental amen-ities will put pressure on limited resources. But those pressures need not create a water crisis if individuals are allowed to respond through market processes. Perhaps more than with other natural resources, water alloca-tion has been distorted by politics under the notion that water is differ-ent. Some would say that water cannot be entrusted to markets because it is a necessity of life. To the contrary, because it is a necessity of life, free market environmentalism argues that water is so precious that it must be entrusted to the discipline of markets that encourage conservation and innovation.

In order to reap the benefits of water markets, policy makers must stay the course. They must continue to find ways to define property rights in water, enforce them, and make them transferable and then guard against doctrines that erode these principles. The prior appropriation doctrine supports these principles, but the public trust doctrine erodes them. By limiting the application of the public trust doctrine, by extending the application of the prior appropriation doctrine to instream flows, by instituting clearly defined property rights to groundwater basins, and by reducing the impediments to exchange for nontraditional uses such as instream flows, policy makers will vastly improve water allocation.

Notes

1. Originally published in: T. Anderson and D. Leal, *Free market environmentalism*, 2nd edition (New York: Palgrave, 2001), 89–105. Reprinted with permission.

2. Thomas J. Graff, "Future water plans need a trickle-up economizing," *Los Angeles Times*, June 14, 1982, V-2.

3. Rodney T. Smith, *Trading water: the legal and economic framework for water marketing*. (Claremont, CA: Claremont McKenna College, Center for Study of Law Structures, 1986), 26.

4. Terry Anderson, "Institutional underpinnings of the water crisis," *Cato Journal* 2 (Winter 1983): 759–92.

5. Richard W. Wahl, *Markets for federal water: sibsidies, property rights, and the Bureau of Reclamation*. (Washington, DC: Resources for the Future, 1989), 33.

6. Ibid., 27 and 46.

7. Ibid., 198–205.

8. Terry Anderson, "Water Options for the Blue Planet," in *The true state of the planet*, ed. Robert Bailey (New York: Free Pres, 1995), 269.

9. Terry Anderson and Pamela S. Snyder, *Water markets: priming the invisible pump*. (Washington, DC: Cato Institute, 1997), 104–5.

10. Testimony before the Subcommittee on Water and Power, House of Representatives, by the Honorable Eluid Martinez, Commissioner, Bureau of Reclamation, February 2, 1999.

11. Constitucion Politica de la Republica de Chile, chapter 3, article 24, final paragraph: "Los derechos de los particulares sobre las aguas, reconocidos o constituidos en conformidad a la ley, otorgaran a sus titulares la propiedad sobre ellos."

12. Renato Gazmuri Schleyer, "Chile's Market-Oriented Water Policy: Institutional Aspects and Achievements," in *Water policy and water markets*, ed. Guy Le Moigne et al., World Bank Technical Paper 249 (Washington, DC: World Bank, 1994), 76.

13. Anderson and Snyder, 1997, 195.

14. The focus on the Colorado River, where California and Nevada face shortages and high costs for alternative supplies and where Arizona is awash in subsidized water from the Central Arizona Project. See Anderson and Snyder, 1997, 197–98.

15. Quoted in *Water Intelligence Monthly*, "Babbitt Endorses Water Markets and Places High Premium on Political Consensus," January 1996, 2–3.

16. For a more detailed discussion of the "use it or lose it" principle, see Anderson and Snyder, 1997, 59, 87–88, and 115.

17. *Lake Shore Duck Club v. Lake View Duck Club*, 50 Utah 76, 166, 309 (1917).

18. 158 Colo. 331, 406, P. 2d 798 (1965).

19. *Fullerton v. California State Water Resources Control Board*, 90 Cal. App. 3d 590, 153 Cal. Rptr. 518 (1979); *California Trout, Inc., v. State Water Resources Control Board*, 90 Cal. App. Ed 816, 153 Cal. Rptr. 672 (1979).

20. Terry L. Anderson and Ronald N. Johnson, "The Problem of Instream Flows," *Economic Inquiry* 24 (October 1986): 535–54.

21. James Huffman, "Instream Uses: Public and Private Alternatives," in *Water rights: scarce resource allocation, bureaucracy, and the environment*, ed. Terry L. Anderson (San Francisco: Pacific Institute for Public Policy Research, 1983), 275.

22. Terry L. Anderson and Donald R. Leal, *Enviro-capitalists: doing good while doing well* (Lanham, MD: Rowman and Littlefield Publishers, 1997), 98–99.

23. Richard W. Guldin, *An analysis of the water situation in the United States: 1989–2040*, USDA Forest Service General Technical Report RM-177 (Washington, DC: U.S. Government Printing Office, 1989), 13.

24. Jean Margat, "A Hidden Asset," *UNESCO Courier* 15 (1993): 15.

25. Gregory S. Weber, "Twenty Years of Local Groundwater Export and Legislation in California: Lessons from a Patchwork Quilt," *Natural Resources Journal* 34 (summer 1994): 660.

26. Terry L. Anderson and Pamela S. Snyder, "A Free Market Solution to Groundwater Allocation in Georgia," *Issue Analysis* (Atlanta: Georgia Public Policy Foundation, 1996); David Todd, "Common Resources, Private Rights and Liabilities: A Case Study on Texas Groundwater Law," *Natural Resources Journal* 32 (summer 1992): 233–63; and Guildin, 1989, 15.

27. Terry L. Anderson, Oscar Burt, and David Fractor, "Privatizing Groundwater Basins: A Model and Its Applications," in Huffman, 1983.

28. Frank J. Trelease, "Developments on Groundwater Law," in *Advances in groundwater "mining" in the southwestern states*, ed. Z. A. Saleem (Minneapolis: American Water Resources Association, 1976), 272.

Chapter 10

Surface Water and Groundwater Regulation and Use: An Ethical Perspective[1]

Steven E. Kraft

EXISTING CASE LAW, statutory regulation, and legal writing on water resources is a pastiche of themes derived from common law, economic theory, legal theory, and descriptive ethics informed by past and present social mores. As such, water resources law tends to reflect where society has been rather than being sympathetic to its future needs. This is especially true if we consider that existing laws and regulations controlling the allocation and utilization of water resources are informed by an ethic largely based on utilitarianism and reflecting a worldview dating back at least to Greek antiquity. While utilitarianism and a worldview in which nature is seen as immutable has become ingrained in our legal foundation, technology now raises ethical problems and economic issues that undermine at least part of this legal foundation. In this paper, I will attempt to describe some of these ethical problems and economic issues while relating them to existing and emerging water resources law and litigation. In doing so, I will be drawing extensively on the seminal works of Hans Jonas, *The Importance of Responsibility: In Search of an Ethics for the Technological Age* (1984), and John Rawls, *A Theory of Justice* (1971). As opposed to utilitarians who justify actions based on the intrinsic goodness or badness of the end(s) resulting from the action, both Jonas and Rawls are ethical formalists seeking rules of conduct that all agents perform as a matter of principle.[2]

The distinction is not just of academic interest. Rather, the difference has import for economics, the laws of society, and our notions of justice.

Indeed, utilitarianism implicitly underlies much of contemporary economic theory providing the justification for benefit–cost analyses and the determination that specific water uses are "beneficial," that is, the uses result in ends that are intrinsically good.[3] Basically, the economic assumption has always been that as individuals act to maximize their utility, i.e., act so as to secure ends which they deem to be intrinsically good, society will also achieve a maximization of its intrinsically good ends. Boulding, Kelso, and others question this assumption.[4]

Alternatively, many advocates of an environmentalist approach to issues of natural resources tend to adopt ethical formalism, i.e., a rule of right conduct.[5] Indeed, recent federal environmental legislation implicitly reflects this ethical approach, i.e., the adoption of rules of conduct specifying how resources will be used, e.g., best management practices under the Federal Water Pollution Control Act Amendments of 1972. There is an inherent conflict between case law and common law with their utilitarian orientation and recent environmental statutes that represent an approach of ethical formalism. Given the differences between the two approaches, the courts are going to become increasingly a battleground for advocates using one approach or the other to further their ends. Since justice is based on distribution, ethical formalism implies that a distribution of valued things is just if it is considered to be fair by every person. Alternatively, utilitarianism is an aggregative concept. Consequently, one situation is judged better than another if more good, intrinsically valued ends exist regardless if some persons consider themselves to be unfairly treated,[6] i.e., in the language of the economist, "more is better." Consequently, utilitarianism and ethical formalism give rise to divergent sets of criteria to use in evaluating the "correctness" of a proposed use of either surface water or groundwater. In the case of the utilitarianism, as long as it could be demonstrated that potential benefits outweighed potential costs, the proposed use would be cast in a favorable light. However, the same proposed use might be judged unacceptable from the perspective of ethical formalism if it could be demonstrated that individuals now or in the future would be adversely affected by the change even though the benefits were potentially greater than the costs.

Jonas asserts that Western society has developed ethics prescribing human actions vis-à-vis other humans in an interhuman framework that ignores the surrounding natural world.[7] Jonas traces these ethical roots into classical antiquity showing the development of ethics regulating human actions towards other humans and the development of the perception of the natural world as an immutable source of material for crafting a human society. These ethics of human interactions gradually became codified in the laws and institutions of evolving Western civilization.

In parallel fashion, nature was raped and pillaged as humans embarked on becoming civilized. However, in this process of exploiting nature, people's impact on it was seen as essentially superficial and non-disruptive to its functioning,[8] that is, all the benefits and ills associated with people's inventive capacity to exploit nature are realized within the human enclave and do not touch the natural world in any lasting way. In other words, the good and bad resulting from human actions lie close to the actions both spatially and temporally. Since the ends were immediate, there was little need for planning with respect to either the distant places or the future. "Ethics accordingly was of the here and now, of occasions as they arise between men, of the recurrent, typical situations of private and public life."[9] From these origins derived our ethical rules as codified in laws for dealing with each other and the larger natural world. While technology was relatively benign in terms of the natural world, this situation posed few problems. However, as technology has become more powerful, humankind has acquired the techniques to alter the natural world either purposely or accidentally and while doing so alters the qualitative basis of human existence and human interrelationships within the human enclave.[10]

Jonas traces the development of a set of social institutions regulating human actions that is informed primarily by utilitarianism and a view of nature as immutable. Two such social institutions are law and business enterprise. In the case of water resources law, the preponderance of case law and legal theory is closely tied to the concept of beneficial use, which is generally specified in utilitarian terms: uses are beneficial if they result in generally remunerative activities, i.e., domestic use, agriculture, mining, manufacturing, and power. Uses that result in monetary gain to individuals are generally seen as beneficial. A recent departure from this approach has been forced on state decision makers and the courts through the Endangered Species Act of 1973.[11] In short, water resources law whether from the perspective of riparian rights or prior appropriation is closely tied to utilitarian ethics: the means or actions are judged suitable if they result in ends which are either intrinsically good or which minimize intrinsic badness. In the case of prior appropriation, this utilitarian approach is modified by the effects of historical accident: water rights go to those first in time, i.e., the familiar dictate, "first in time, first in right." Beyond the traditional caveats of reasonable use and the peculiarities of each system of water allocations, both riparian rights and prior appropriation rest on an assumption that beneficial uses can be generally determined by signals sent by the economic system, i.e., prices as determined by product and factor markets.

If we borrow some concepts from land economics,[12] we can look at water-use capacity and the highest and best use of water. By water-use capacity, we basically mean the capacity of water to yield a level of return and/or satisfaction over and above the costs of utilization. If a given use of water results in a positive use capacity, we mean that the returns or satisfactions from the use are greater than the costs incurred through use. Implicitly, we are assuming that the relevant costs and returns are determined by price signals sent from our system of "competitive" markets. Basically, we follow the rule in water allocation that uses are beneficial if they have a positive use capacity. Similarly, uses for given water resources can be rank ordered based on their relative use capacity with the use with the largest net return labeled the highest and best use of the water. The key element in both the determination of use capacity and highest and best use is the assumption that markets capture the relevant costs and benefits inherent in given uses consequently providing the data necessary for the utilitarian calculus. Similar assumptions underlie the use of benefit–cost analyses in assessing the appropriateness of water development projects and in ranking alternative projects.[13]

However, given the actual functioning of markets, this assumption is relatively naive. There is an extensive literature documenting the problems of market failure: externalities, indivisibilities in consumption, nonexclusiveness, congestible public goods, and natural monopolies. In many instances, at least in terms of natural resources and specifically water, the models of the competitive economy and the free market system are not closely approximated by reality. What should inform water resources law and regulation are not idealized models, but the realities of economic life within an institutionalized social environment.[14] Given the thrust of the present paper, of particular interest are the failures generally called contemporaneous and intergenerational technical externalities. Additionally, many of the inherent benefits and costs associated with the use of water resources are intangibles or incommensurables[15] and are not reflected in market activity and hence become difficult to factor into utilitarian analyses of beneficial use. Those implicit benefits and costs that cannot be readily translated into monetary terms tend to be ignored or evaluated through bureaucratic protocols and judgmentally integrated into the overall evaluation of the proposed change. Finally, the market analysis tends to be rooted in the present and in the case of prior appropriation in the past. In a very real sense, the use of market results is a tyranny of the present over the economic future of society. The markets do not capture the potential value of resource use in the future; prices reflect the interaction of supply and demand in the present. Consequently, when dealing with uses of water resources that result in either quantitative reductions in the availability of future water supplies and/or in the degradation of the quality of these supplies, these future negative effects are discounted by present decision makers using a utilitarian approach.

The literature on user costs[16] explains how ignoring the value of resources in the future when carrying out analyses in the present using a utilitarian perspective leads to unrealistically low current values for resources and excessively high rates of use in the present. In summary, the reliance on markets to determine beneficial use results in society using what Soderbaum has called monetary reductionism to make decisions with respect to the present utilization of water resources.[17] The resulting decisions are not necessarily efficient from a societal perspective; they may be from the perspective of private individuals at the present time.

Given the use of market information to determine beneficial use, the extent of humankind's technological prowess, and the lack of complete information of future occurrences, we run the risk that contemporary use of water resources, as sanctioned by current law and custom, will result in irreversible changes in the quantity and quality of service flows from the same resources in the future. In many instances, these changes will be translated into extensive alterations in the form and quality of human life. Depending on how the particular water resources are specified,

one or more of McInerney's four basic models of natural resources are
applicable in analyzing the impact of current use on the present and future viability of the resources.[18] It is the possibility of ignoring the future
consequences of present and in some cases past action with respect to
water resources that has led some thinkers to urge the adoption of the
ethical formalism of Rawls and Jonas in dealing with issues of resource
utilization.[19] Both writers have proposed ethical systems that implicitly
force the consideration of uncertain future impacts on society when
making decisions in the present.

The utilitarian worldview and its accompanying ethic is mute on
questions of actions or uses of water deemed appropriate in the present
that have negative consequences in the future for the same generation;
actions or uses deemed appropriate by the present generation that have
negative consequences for future generations; present actions resulting in
apparent irreversible degradation of the environment; and procedures resulting in changing bureaucratic and legal institutions in light of new scientific information and emerging cultural goals. Consequently, given
technological advances since antiquity, the resulting mutability of nature,
and potential long-term consequences of actions taken in the present,
some writers would argue that our existing ethical principles as a society
and as reflected in our laws and institutions are inappropriate for informing individual and social behavior vis-à-vis the allocation and utilization
of surface water and groundwater resources to say nothing of natural resources in general.[20]

Rawls' theory of justice can be interpreted meaningfully for questions
of water resource use.[21] Given the negotiations taking place among societal members behind the Rawlsian veil of ignorance, his allowance for
the just savings principle, and the implicit presence of future generations
in the negotiations, we can infer that the decisional structure for using resources will be based on the desires of society conceived as a continuum
extending into the future. Consequently, the needs of future generations
for adequate supplies of undegraded water will not be trampled on by
the existing generations clamoring for the maximization of net benefits
from water use in the present. Rawls' two principles of justice for institutions are the following:

First principle: Each person is to have an equal right to the most extensive total system of equal basic liberties compatible with a similar system of liberty for all.

Second principle: Social and economic inequalities are to be arranged so that they are both: (a) to the greatest benefit of the least advantaged, consistent with the just savings principle, and (b) attached to offices and positions open to all under conditions of fair equality of opportunity.[22]

The just savings principle basically forces upon the negotiations behind the veil of ignorance a concern for the allocation of natural primary goods, including natural resources, across the whole course of society. Indeed, the elimination of some of these goods or the irreversible degradation in their qualitative nature due to over use or abuse would negate Rawls' second principle. Furthermore, we can argue that just as the uneven distribution of natural primary goods is an undeserved circumstance that should not be used to the unfair advantage of luckily endowed individuals, so is the generation of birth. One generation, i.e., the present, due to its existence cannot take unfair advantage of other, future generations through unjustly exploiting the resources they find around them. Consequently, given the difference principle (the second principle) it would be unjust for one generation to use water resources in such ways as to deprive succeeding generations of the use of the resources, unless the action helped to raise the level of other subsequent generations.

In the case of water resources, this demands the use of laws that protect the use rate of these resources across time, encourages the development of recycling options, and assures the maintenance of the desired qualitative nature of the service flow from the resources. Uses or negative externalities that do not permit these alternatives would be judged unjust since they deprive the future of essential equal access to the same resources, even though such uses might be justified under the existing utilitarian criterion. In short, from Rawls' perspective, questions such as those raised earlier about actions with negative consequences would not be permitted unless it could be shown that the future would not be adversely affected. Under the utilitarian approach, such actions would be permitted as long as it could be shown that the overall net effect would be an increase in intrinsically good ends over bad.

Coming from a different perspective, Jonas arrives like Rawls at the conclusion that actions taken in the present cannot be made based on utilitarianism such that the future is disadvantaged.[23] Given that "ethics is for the ordering of actions and for regulating the power to act," Jonas attempts to find an imperative or principle to use for ordering actions and regulating the power to act appropriate for our technological age.[24] Positing that the consequences of actions are no longer limited to the immediate temporal and spatial realm of the actor but can be far reaching in time and space, he argues that the essential imperative regulating human action is a responsibility to the continuance of human existence and a minimum quality of life similar to what now exists. Actions with the potential to either threaten the continuance of human existence or significantly lessen the quality of human life are not acceptable regardless of their potential short-run benefits to the existent population. Since we lack complete information as to the full range of potential outcomes from actions contemplated during the present, he asserts that societal actors must consider in detail the distant contingencies associated with today's actions. This must include a consideration of both the good effects and the bad. The potential bad effects include what is at stake in terms of possible losses. If these bad effects are such that either human existence is threatened or the quality of human life degraded, the contemplated action is unacceptable. This potential of doom associated with the acceptance of the imperative that the present cannot endanger the future results in the selection of technologies and uses of resources that do not have any potential threat to the future of humankind or the quality thereof. Accepting Jonas' categorical imperative based on an ontological ideal results in resource uses and technology which are essentially benign towards human existence.

Gradually at the federal level through legislation and legislative initiatives,[25] we are seeing the emergence of a policy perspective vis-à-vis water resources, toxic substances, and the environment in general that encompasses the ethical formalism of Rawls and Jonas, imperatives that speak to the requirement not to adversely damage the future in search of short-run gain. As these efforts continue and are implemented in laws, the utilitarian confrontation between utilitarian informed decisions to utilize resources now and the consideration of future consequences will heighten. A preview of this confrontation has already been seen in the watering down of the Endangered Species Act in response to protests that its implementation adversely circumscribed the potentially profitable use of water resources in the present.

In summary, Jonas argues that the ethics of the past are inappropriate for decision making in the present and future because of the impact of today's decisions on the future. A basic ethical component of contemporary society informing the use of water resources is utilitarianism. Utilitarianism also informs much of the case law and legal writing used in the litigation of water related issues. This core of tradition is in potential conflict with recent legislation that embodies a gradual departure from utilitarianism and the acceptance of an ethical view calling for actions taken in the present which do not degrade future human life. The reconciliation of these two perspectives within the judicial and legislative arenas is a challenge not only for those of us interested in water but also for society as a whole.

Notes

1. Originally published as: S.E. Kraft, "Surface water and groundwater regulation and use: an ethical perspective," in *Water resources law: the proceedings of the National Symposium on Water Resources Law*. (Chicago: American Society of Agricultural Engineers, 1986), 198–206. Reprinted with permission.

2. P. Taylor, *Principles of ethics: an introduction*. (Belmont, CA: Wadsworth Publishing, 1975).

3. See *State Dept. of Parks v. Idaho Dept. of Water Administration*, 530 P. 2d. 924 (1974). Also see statutory summary in, D. Getches, *Water law in a nutshell*. (St. Paul, MN: West Publishing, 1984).

4. K. Boulding, "The economics of the coming spaceship earth," in *Environmental Quality in a Growing Economy*, ed. H. Jarrett (Baltimore: Johns Hopkins University Press, 1966), 3–14; M. Kelso, "Natural resource economics: the upsetting disciplines," *American Journal of Agricultural Economics* 59 (1977): 814–823.

5. R. Manning, "Environmental ethics and John Rawls' theory of justice," *Environmental Ethics* 3 (1981): 155–166.

6. See Taylor, 1975.

7. H. Jonas, *The imperative of responsibility: in search of an ethics for the technological age*. (Chicago: University of Chicago Press, 1984); H. Jonas, "Technology and responsibility: reflections on the new tasks of ethics," in *Philosophical essays: from ancient creed to technological man*. (Englewood Cliffs, NJ: Prentice-Hall, Inc., 1974), 3–20.

8. Jonas, 1974.

9. Ibid., 7.

10. See, *Environmental Defense Fund v. Environmental Protection Agency*, 598 F. 2d. 62 (1978); R. Carson, *Silent spring* (Greenwich, Conn: Fawcett Publishing, 1962). Regrettably, contemporary examples abound in which technology employed in "beneficial" uses has resulted in extensive damage to the natural world with the effects visited upon humanity. Examples include the fear of carcinogens and mutagens in the wake of the toxic polluting of groundwater at Love Canal, New York, and dioxin contamination at Times Beach, Missouri. Other examples capture the effects of groundwater overdraft and the accompanying problems of subsidence, aquifer compaction, and salt water intrusion (California Dept. of Water Resources, "Sea-Water Intrusion," *California Bulletin* (1968) 63:15–87; R. Ford, "Groundwater use in California," *California Geology* 31 (1978): 247–249; K. Knapp, and H. Vaux, "Barriers to effective ground-water management: the California case," *Ground Water* 20 (1982): 61–66). The devastating aftermath of the Chernobyl nuclear accident underscores these potential impacts. These effects often result in irreversible changes in the qualitative nature and quantity of the service flows of the affected resources (see the type III and type IV resources of J. McInerney, "Natural resource economics: the basic analytical principles," in *Economics of environmental and natural resources policy*. (Boulder: Westview Press, 1981), 30–58). McInerney (1981) presents a framework useful to understanding natural resource economics which is relevant to the present discussion. First, he distinguishes among the physical stock of the resource, i.e., the unrefined physical amount of the resource, the resource stock. i.e., the resource refined and ready for use, and the service flow of the resource, i.e., the services the resource provides when Combined with other productive inputs.

11. *Endangered Species Act of 1973*, 16 U.S.C. sec. 1531–1543 (1982); A. Tarlock, "The Endangered Species Act and western water rights," *Land and Water Law Review* (1985) 20: 1–30; *Riverside Irrigation District v. Andrews*, 788 F. 2d. 508 (1985).

12. R. Barlowe, *Land resource economics: the economics of real estate*, 4th ed. (Englewood Cliffs, N.J.: Prentice-Hall, Inc., 1986).

13. Water Resources Council, "Principles, standards, and procedures for water and related land resource planning," *Federal Register*, Part III, 1973, 38–174.

14. K. Kapp, "The nature and significance of institutional economics," *Kyklos* 29 (1976): 209–232; G. Myrdal, "Institutional economics," *Journal of Economic Issues* 12 (1978): 771–783.

15. P. Sassone and W. Schaffer, *Cost–benefit analysis: a handbook*. (New York: Academic Press, 1978).

16. McInerney, 1981; A. Scott, "Notes on user cost," *Economic Journal* 63 (1953): 368–384.

17. P. Soederbaum, "Economics in relation to ecology: discussion on development concepts" (paper presented at the 19th Int'l Conf. of Ag. Economists, Malaga, Spain, 1985).

18. McInerney, 1981.

19. See Boulding, 1966; Kelso, 1977.

20. See Boulding, 1966; Kelso, 1977; Jonas, 1974.

21. J. Rawls, *A Theory of Justice*. (Cambridge: Harvard University Press, 1971); see Manning (1981) for such a development.

22. Rawls, 1981, 302.

23. Jonas, 1974, 1984.

24. Ibid., 23.

25. See, Office of Technology Assessment, Congress of the United States, "Technologies and Management Strategies for Hazardous Waste Control" (Washington, DC: U.S. Government Printing Office, 1983); Office of Technology Assessment, Congress of the United States, "Protecting the Nation's Groundwater from Contamination" (Washington, DC: U.S. Government Printing Office, 1984); Office of Technology Assessment, Congress of the United States, "Superfund Strategy" (Washington, DC: U.S. Government Printing Office, 1985).

Chapter 11

Understanding Transfers: Community Rights and the Privatization of Water[1]

Joseph L. Sax

IN A RECENT REPORT, the National Research Council observed that water markets cannot be expected to resemble more conventional markets for a variety of reasons, including the long-held tradition that water resources support a wide variety of public uses.[2] Transfers can impose significant third-party effects, which must be accounted for in any reallocation. If transfers are to achieve their potential, the report said, the decision-making process should bring all relevant third parties into the deliberations. This broad participation is necessary because water is a unique resource, different from other commodities. Markets alone cannot accurately reflect all the relevant values of water. I share these conclusions.

In testifying before the study commission that wrote the report, I noted the common inclination to think of transfers as a contract, with two parties only—a buyer and a seller. I believe that a more appropriate model would be a diplomatic negotiation with a number of parties, each with important and legitimate interests that need to be accommodated, but without clearly defined rights. The future of water transfers will be jeopardized unless something like that broader and more inclusive model is embraced.

The question of who has, and who ought to have, what rights in water raises an issue that has received very little recognition in our legal system: the rights of communities. A companion issue is the limit on privatization of water as a commodity. Unlike almost every other form of property, which we allow to be entirely privatized, water has always been viewed as something in which the community has a stake and which no one can fully own. The complexity of this point is usually embraced in the phrase "third-party effects" when talking about water transfers.

Although third-party effects exist wherever significant resources are allocated or reallocated, they are usually ignored. Years ago, when O'Hare Airport in Chicago was opened, Midway Airport—at that time the busiest airport in the world—was entirely closed down. Many of the businesses located around the airport, and dependent on it, went broke. When a theater next to a restaurant is sold and turned into a warehouse, the restaurant may go out of business. When General Motors closes a factory in Michigan and opens one in another state or another country, workers may be left in a lurch. These are all third-party effect problems. With rare exceptions, they have no standing in our legal system. But water is and always has been different—certainly in theory, and to some extent in practice.

Reallocations of resources, such as a factory relocation, usually generate a variety of costs to the export community, such as increased welfare payments, more unemployment compensation, and fewer public services as tax revenues decline. At worst, reallocations result in the creation of a permanently depressed Appalachian-type community. However, positive effects also occur. A new community may prosper, products may be produced more efficiently, and obsolete industries phased out.

Legal History of the Issue

Concerns about the de-watering of the Owens Valley by Los Angeles gave rise to the area of origin law in California legislation stating that people in the area where water arises have first claim to it.[3] This is not solely a California phenomenon; the same issue has arisen elsewhere in the West. It has been played out between the western slope of the Rockies in Colorado and the more populous and urbanized eastern slope; the western slope people have had their rights recognized as water was removed from the area of origin.[4] The same is true in the Great Lakes area, where states and Canadian provinces bordering the lakes have fought and won, through Federal law, the right to keep other states from drawing on the water there.[5] The intense sense of loss was not diminished by the fact that in the Great Lakes region, water is measured not in acre-feet but in cubic miles.

Sometimes, the state itself asserts a right in water. Many years ago, a New Jersey company diverted water from the Passaic River in order to transport it to New York and sell it there. The State of New Jersey prohibited the exports, and the U.S. Supreme Court sustained the state by rejecting the property claims of the putative exporter.[6] The Supreme Court described water as something that could not be fully privatized, something in which there was a residual and inalienable interest in the community of origin. In effect, the Court stated that water was a heritage resource, which the community could control and keep for itself. This may be the earliest example of court action holding that ordinary contract principles were not sufficient to govern water marketing. The Supreme Court more recently recognized a similar public right in groundwater. In that case, the State of Nebraska wanted to prevent water from being pumped there and exported to Colorado. The court recognized that—at least where there was a demonstrable need for the water in the area of origin—the state could override property claims, or claims that water was simply a commodity.[7]

The situation involving water is very unusual, and it applies to virtually nothing else. For purposes of interstate commerce, for example, all other state resources may be privatized fully, and freely shipped away from the area of origin as ordinary commodities—even though states have often tried to keep such resources within their own boundaries to benefit their own residents. Such efforts have routinely and repeatedly been held unconstitutional by the courts.[8] The only other common example where things are treated like water—that is, as community resources and not as ordinary salable commodities—arises with cultural properties, antiquities for example, where the nation of origin often asserts a national claim on the property in order to prevent exports.[9]

Community claims on water do not arise solely in the context of interstate commerce. They are also found in state law. The area of origin protection that California and other states employ in a variety of forms already has been mentioned. California has a law that limits rights to transfer if there are unreasonable impacts on the local economy or on natural resources.[10] Some states have an even broader test of compatibility, with the public welfare as a condition of transfer, or requiring consideration of economic loss to the community, although the content of these so-called "public interest statutes" has been given very little interpretation.

As is well-known, California has applied the public trust doctrine in the Mono Lake case to limit the removal of water from its natural setting.[11] Of course, the traditional theory of riparian law was that water must be kept for use on land riparian to its native stream and within its watershed. At least in theory, this is still the law in California.

In addition, there is a tradition, both in some western states and also under the original federal reclamation program, to keep water appurtenant to the land on which it was first used—that is, to keep it within the community as a community resource.[12] Appurtenance is a very strong tradition in other cultures, such as Hispanic water law, where community is valued far more than efficiency.[13]

Lack of Legal Doctrine

Thus, to treat water purely as a commodity, and transfers as two-party transactions only, is to depart from a very deeply rooted tradition in the water field and from consistent intuitions about water as a community resource. But community right is such an unusual idea in our law that, despite its history and despite its strong intuitive power, we have little experience in giving it content. For example, we may say that in general an owner may not sell more water than his or her consumptive use; but we have no theory about whether even that should be salable. We have virtually no legal doctrine to describe the relation between an owner who wants to sell water and the community from which that water will be exported.

Nor is there any clear concept of a "community" entitled to protection against the effects of export transfers. There are all kinds of different communities whose claims could lead, depending on how the community is described, to very different sorts of limitations on water transfers.

If the state is the relevant community, then a review of transfers by a state agency might be seen as fulfilling the community claim. But if the community is the local economy, then the state may not—and to some extent almost certainly will not—fully reflect that community's interests. Another relevant community may be the water institution, the water district, for example, which certainly has interests of its own. If the district is the relevant community, it may not fully overlap the local economy that may be affected by a sale of water. There also are the so-called "natural communities" or "in-stream value communities."

Because of strong desires to facilitate transfers, efforts have been primarily directed toward empowering individual sellers as against community claims in order to promote transfers. Almost all recent legislation dealing with transfers looks in this direction. This is understandable. If enough interests are involved and each has something like a veto power, transfers will be so weighted down that the whole enterprise is likely to collapse under its own bureaucratic weight and increased transactional costs.

Redistribution of Wealth

My observations are based on two premises: (1) that the claim for a community stake in water is legitimate and is reflected in a wide range of responses to water problems over a very long time; and (2) that legitimate community claims have been neglected in the effort to facilitate water transfers.

First, water in place is a type of wealth. That wealth accrues not only to the owner of a water right, but to many other people in the place where the water is located—in the form of employment, direct and indirect; in lower prices for water because of its relative abundance; and in natural values, such as recreation and fisheries, that arise as a result of water's presence.

Second, when water is sold as a mere commodity, only the formal owner of a water right is compensated. For that individual, there is a transformation of wealth from one form to another—from water to cash. Indeed the seller is likely to be significantly enriched, particularly in agricultural-to-urban transfers, since water has usually been under-priced. Payments for water frequently exceed the profits that sellers could have obtained from using the water for irrigation.

Third, while such sales are, for the owner-sellers, transformational—wealth is transformed from water to cash—for everyone else who has

been benefiting from the presence of that water, the sales are redistribu-
tional. That is, others in the community who have up to that point ben-
efited from wealth in the form of water in place will be made worse off,
since the water is gone and they receive nothing in return. Moreover, it is
likely that the redistribution will be especially adverse to (1) people who
have salaried jobs that depend on the presence of the water and are likely
to be the first to lose work if economic activity is reduced, and (2) poorer
people in the communities, since they are often the least mobile residents; they are unlikely to move and find equivalent work and amenities
elsewhere.

It may be true that aggregate losses resulting from agricultural-to-
urban water transfers are relatively small because agricultural employment is a small percentage of total state employment, and because the
economic contribution of the low value crops that are the most likely to
decline is small. Nonetheless, to those in the community who are the losers, the losses are likely to be very significant.

All this suggests to me the existence of a first order conflict between
user-sellers—that is owners of water rights who have been in a position
to reap the benefits of a sale—and other interests, natural, economic, and
social, who have hitherto been enriched by the presence of water and
will obtain no benefit from its sale. The relevant community is composed
of those who would be made poorer by the sale of a particular amount of
water.

To avoid wealth redistribution in transfers, the following precepts
would apply: first, transfers should not be redistributive to the disadvantage of those in the selling area, in both human and natural terms. Second, the price of the water to those acquiring it should take into account
all the benefits the water has produced, not just those that have flowed to
the holders of formal water rights.

Approaches to Mitigation

There are several practical ways to promote such goals. One is to favor sales that minimize disadvantages to the community. The most obvious are those that free up water by applying water-saving techniques,
so that the same amount of economic activity continues in the selling
community.

Another device is the provision of community compensation through a transfer tax. Where sales generate a general decline in the wealth of the community, the concern ought to be for those who remain—those who are least able to leave, rather than for those who can shift and leave the community. Transfer taxes benefit those who remain in the community. A tax on water sales, depending on the nature of the sale and its redistributive impact, would be the easiest means to mitigate the redistributive tendency of export sales. A similar approach could be taken to mitigate natural losses—losses to waterfowl habitat for example.

It is true that much of the water likely to be sold does not come from the original place of origin, but rather from a place to which water has been imported. That fact should not affect the conclusion as long as a community has been established—whether it is a human settlement or a natural habitat, such as a wildlife refuge. Once such uses are established, the removal of water constitutes a disruption in that community, even if the community is only a few decades old, and thus also constitutes wealth redistribution.

The more one enlarges the interests that need to be accounted for, and the more complex or extensive the arrangements to evaluate transfers become, the more transfers will be discouraged. This is a serious problem, but there are ways around it. The best way to deal with this issue is to adopt generally applicable formulae that are meant to approximate the losses to the community caused by various types and sizes of transfers. Formulae for taxes on transfers, compensation to in-stream uses, and prioritization of favored and disfavored types of transfers can be employed to assure mitigation without making transactional costs unduly burdensome. Large and pervasive impacts can be treated differently from small and ephemeral ones; and different standards can be imposed for in-basin and out-of-basin transfers.

Reducing all these concerns to some kind of workable formulae can promote transfers by reducing transaction costs while taking account of the most important third-party effects: reductions in existing wealth. Of course, a formulaic approach is a second-best solution, and will not produce the appropriate result in every individual case. But the alternative—extensive participation and elaborate public interest hearings—while theoretically appropriate, threatens to make all but the largest water transfers uneconomic and untimely. Certainly some review process is necessary, but the goal should be to make it largely a fall-back device for especially hard cases. For the most part, some sort of formulaic approach will have to be adopted, or the whole system is likely to sink from its own weight.

Most discussion of water transfers has been focused on what are seen as obstacles—legal, institutional, and psychological. In my view, we need to encourage some transfers, but not by commodity theories that lead to reverse wealth redistribution. The solution to inadequate water transfers in California is not to ignore community interests in water, but to institutionalize them as part of the price of water, rather than letting all the benefits flow to the formal owners of water use rights and to the buyers of the water.

Notes

1. Originally published as: J. Sax, "Understanding transfers: community rights and the privatization of water," *West Northwest Journal of Environmental Law and Policy*, 1 (1994): 13–16. Reprinted with permission.

2. Committee on Western Water Management, National Research Council. "Water transfers in the West: efficiency, equity and the environment" (1992).

3. E. g., CAL WATER CODE § 11460 (West 1992).

4. E.g.. COLO. REV. STAT. § 3745-1 18(b)(iv) (West 1990).

5. 42 U.S.C. § 1962 d-20 (1988).

6. *Hudson County Water Co. v. McCartler*, 209 U.S. 349 (1908).

7. *Sporhase v. Nebraska ex rel. Douglas*, 458 U.S. 941 (1982).

8. Laurence Tribe, *American constitutional law*, 2nd ed. (New York: Foundation Press, 1988), 409–10.

9. See. e.g., Jeanette Greenfield, *The return of cultural treasures.* (New York: Cambridge University Press, 1989).

10. E.g. N.M. STAT. ANN. § 72-5-23 (1990), WYO. STAT. § 41-3-104(A).

11. *National Audubon Society v. Superior Court*, 658 P2d 709 (1983).

12. 43 U.S.C. § 372 (1988).

13. Arthur Maas and Raymond Anderson, *And the desert shall rejoice: conflict, growth and justice in arid environments.* (Cambridge: MIT Press, 1978), 41.

Chapter 12

A Basis for Environmental Ethics[1]

Augustin Berque

The Caohu "Ecological Migration"

The region of Xinjiang ("New Frontier"), China's Far West, contains the majority of the planet's forests of *huyang* (*Populus diversifolia*): 360,000 hectares, or more than two-thirds. This tree is a miracle of nature, able to withstand the worst ecological conditions. It tolerates salt, which it gives off through its bark. It tolerates drought, with its roots that seek water almost 20 metres down; but it tolerates as well several months' flooding during the Tarim's high-water season in the summer months, for this interior river—which is as powerful as the Danube but peters out in the Lob Nor sands—has a current fed by the Karakorum, Pamir, and Tianshan snow and ice melt in summer. This combination of high water and heat, which favours vegetation, has turned the banks of the Tarim into a corridor of life that stretches more than 2000 km across the desert. In its natural state the area is characterized by the primal *huyang* forest. Among the tree's extraordinary properties there is also the appearance of its foliage with its changing forms, which has given it its scientific name *Populus diversifolia*: a single tree can have on it leaves so different—some as wide as an aspen's, others narrower than a willow's—that at first you would think you were looking at two trees. Last but not least, the profile of the *huyang*, with its massive trunk, which is said to take a thousand years to grow, a thousand to die, and yet another thousand to decompose once it has fallen, stamps its characteristic mark on the land both when it

125

is alive—for example those incredible watery landscapes visible on the Tarim's middle reaches, recalling Louisiana bayous in the middle of the desert—and when it is dead and its tortured forms, like an army of skeletons, rise up among the dunes or *yardangs*, where the shifting riverbed has given way to desert. Hence its amazing ability to stabilize sand, which has given it the nickname *yingxiong shu*, "the defender tree": it protects oases against the Taklamakan.

The *huyang's* ecosystem is so remarkable and so valuable both for human life and for biodiversity that in 1983 an area of nature reserve (*ziran baohu qu*) was created on the Tarim's middle reaches, taking in parts of Luntai and Korla municipalities and covering more than 5.8 million *mu* (3924 km^2). According to the official literature[2] this creation was decided upon not only to "protect positively" (*jiji baohu*) the species but also to "restore the resources of the *huyang* forest" (*huifu huyanglin ziyuan*). In China this notion of "resources" (*ziyuan*) has a high status. For instance it appears in the titles of many bodies that in the West would simply mention a scientific discipline; as an example, the "Institute of Geography and Research into Resources" (*Dili kexue yu ziyuan yanjiusuo*) of the China Academy of Sciences. And when you mention "resources" you naturally imply "resources for human beings" and more specifically "for the economy." Thus there is a fundamental ambiguity in a policy of protecting nature that at the same time claims to be restoring a resource, since the first objective focuses on nature itself (for instance, preserving biodiversity) and the second centres on human beings' interests.[3] There can be a contradiction between these two objectives, which is evidenced by many controversies thrown up by the rise in ecological concerns since the 1960s; but it appears that China's environmental policy does not see the issue in that light. Here the central idea, repeated everywhere, is that protecting nature is achieved through developing the economy and society.[4] And this is not in the least unusual, since history shows that a certain degree of prosperity is needed for a society to acquire the distance to instigate an environmental policy; for below a certain threshold all that counts is day-to-day survival, with no consideration for ecological balance. In particular peasant poverty has always been the enemy of forest policies.

In the area in question the way of life of the locals—known as the

"Lob Nor folk" (*Luobu ren*)—depended on fishing, hunting, and a subsistence polyculture with a strong pastoral element. Cut off by the desert, they lived without electricity, running water, or telephone, in a situation of "low cultural quality" (*wenhua suzhi jiao di*).[5] It seems that one day this situation did not fit in with the "great development of the west" (*Xibu da kaifa*)[6] promoted by the central government. In a subtle twist of political thinking a link is also made between that situation and the drop in the quantity of water flowing down from the upper reaches of the Tarim, which was jeopardizing the *huyang*'s whole ecosystem as well as irrigation opportunities using the river. And so part of the protected section was made a no-access area, and it was decided to move the inhabitants out. Thus it was that, "for the mother river" (*weile muqin he*),[7] the Caohu people—758 households comprising 3420 individuals—were made "ecological migrants" (*shengtai yimin*). The government resettled them in a new village higher up in the Tianshan foothills and nearer to the town of Luntai, with modern amenities, all the equipment needed for controlled irrigation and the job of working there in an agriculture focusing on apricots, jujube, and cotton. Starting on 16 November 2002, the operation was completed in a few months. However, the agreement between the inhabitants and the authorities allows for them to be able to return to their old land if cotton does not do well on the new land within three years.

I visited the area in June 2004. The Caohu lakes had dried out and the Tarim was almost completely dry too, though this had never been seen in the high-water season.[8] The obvious cause of the shortfall is the overexploitation of the river upstream. In this respect the "ecological migration" forced on the "Lob Nor folk" seems ineffective; but that is not the point I want to make with this example. It is to ask on what ethical basis a decision can be made that is painful for human beings—involving exile and giving up a way of life—but is in theory intended to bring benefit to nature; in this case the health of a river (the Tarim) and an ecosystem (the *huyang* forest).

The Limits of the Quantifiable Dimension

It is interesting that in administrative and even scientific vocabulary an operation such as the Caohu "ecological migration" is classified in the category of *gongcheng*, or "engineering," like public works and building. Thus, in a summing-up article on the Tarim works,[9] we find the following list under the heading "Engineering activities in the overall works" (*Zonghe zhili gongcheng cuoshi*):

> In order to radically improve the ecological environment in the Tarim river basin there are used in conjunction: engineering work for emergency hydraulic transfer into the main stream,[10] ecological salvage engineering,[11] ecological migration engineering, which is still in progress in the Tarim basin, dam-building engineering, engineering work to return agricultural land to forest (or grassland),[12] sand-stabilizing engineering work, engineering work to protect natural forests, engineering work to improve and extend retaining banks, irrigation systems engineering (construction, etc.).

This series of techniques used in the overall works in the great river's basin includes, as we can see, operations affecting the society itself. So the question arises as to how it is possible to measure in the same way, an engineer's way, phenomena associated with the science of nature and phenomena associated with the human sciences; a connection of which technical control is presupposed in the idea of engineering. The reality of these operations, apprehended via their effects, makes us think that not only technical control but even representation of the processes involved is far from perfect, even simply at the level of ecology. In fact a recent study[13] applying the Constanza evaluation methods[14] to the area that was cleared on the lower Tarim at the time of the Great Leap Forward (*Dayuejin*)[15] came to the conclusion that "ecosystem services" (*shengtai xitong fuwu*) were seriously underestimated there. Because of this the clearance carried out had unforeseen negative effects which can be summarized as an encroachment of desert at the expense of the Tarim's "green corridor" (*lüse zoulang*) oases. Now the river does not reach Lob Nor; it hardly flows at all beyond the Daxihaizi dam, which was built when the clearing was done. Between 1986 and 2000 the *huyang* forest in the area studied died back by 50% (14% of the surface area in 1986, 8% in 1990, 7% in 2000), as did the grasslands (36% of the surface area in 1986, 22% in 1990, 19% in 2000). As far as arable land is concerned it seems relatively stable (4%, 3%, and 3%, respectively, for the same three years),[16] but this proportion is deceptive: in fact it is the result of gradual migration since agriculture has cleared land here and then left it behind because it has become unusable due to salination, pollution, etc., the overall outcome of this development being of course an absolute deterioration in the ecological potential. The authors of a general assessment of the "oasis crisis" (*lüzhou de weiji*)[17] summarize it in a disturbing phrase: "As a result of the effect of human activity the evolution of the Tarim basin's ecological environment is tending to 'take two steps forward and four steps back' (*liang kuoda, si suoxiao*), meaning that the oases and the desert are growing simultaneously."[18]

Hazarding a quantification—which in any case is only partial—of these environment "services" (*fuwu*) that had not been taken account of, the authors of the earlier case study estimate they declined by an annual average of 1.5 million yuan between 1986 and 2000.[19] These figures speak volumes, since they enable us to express in a common language, the language of the economic system, what previously remained in the external world of the market. For this reason studies of that type may carry some weight in defining and implementing planning policies, where in practice financial considerations play a predominant, even overwhelming, role. Nevertheless it is impossible to conceal the fact that they depend on a simulation, since the "services" concerned are in fact never on the open market. Of course the purpose of this kind of research is precisely to avoid the reductive effect of commercial accounting, which is dragging the contemporary world—of which the Xinjiang oases are like a microcosm on a scale 1/n—towards blindly overexploiting the planet's resources, eventually destroying the ecological foundations of human life (see below). We do need to rectify this blindness. However, it remains the case that translating into commercial terms is by definition limited to a field—the economy—whose relevance is immediately cancelled out by the simulation that makes the translation possible. In this case the authors of the aforementioned study in fact acknowledge that they have only been able to quantify part of the ecosystem, leaving out, for instance, "services" such as those provided by the snow and glaciers from the surrounding mountains, or even by the desert itself; but this limitation does not affect the principles of the method adopted. And it is indeed a question of principle. The Constanza method in fact brings problems of the environment down to a dimension which is itself inherent in a system—the market—that, as history shows, leads to the destruction of the planet's environment. It seems more logical to question the relevance of that referent, and look for a more fundamental one.

Bringing the Human Down to Earth Itself

Since the rise of awareness in the 1960s there has developed, as we know, a field of study called environmental ethics, which is now part of our intellectual landscape. There are some excellent books on the topic;[20] I shall not trace its history here, nor shall I go into the range of positions that have been expressed on the subject. As I see it[21] these positions extend between two theoretical extremes, one of which would be humanity's subordination to the biosphere, and the other subordination of environmental issues to humanity's interests. In general the first set of views is labeled *holism* and the second *anthropocentrism*. In addition, though its history contains plenty of strictures and stereotypical simplifications, environmental ethics also comes up against a basic aporia as soon as it is developed a little further: at one and the same time acknowledging that in a sense the human transcends nature and that in another sense the second subsumes the first. Indeed expecting the human race to behave ethically and respect the interests of other species means *ipso facto* giving it a separate status, since we cannot reasonably attribute to them a reciprocal duty towards us. In other words the fields of ethics and ecology remain fundamentally heterogeneous.

In practice this aporia can only be resolved in the political area via the interplay of power relations between the supporters of one or the other of the aforementioned views: holism or anthropocentrism. But "resolution" depends on concealing, consciously or not, the above aporia using various metaphors or simulations and bringing the issue down to a common field of reference. We saw an example of this earlier with the Constanza evaluation method. Some of the routes worked out in this area are aimed explicitly at a "cosmopolitics," where the interests of both nature and humanity would be discussed according to the same measures.[22] Nevertheless they do not overcome the stubborn obstacle raised by the fact that non-humans do not speak and that, when every metaphor has been exhausted, the political arena is actually monopolized entirely by *Homo sapiens'* soliloquy.

Personally I see as dead-ends the constructions that are designed to place humans and non-humans on the same footing. In fact the right method seems to me to take as a basis the obvious fact that the human situation is unique. So that uniqueness should be put into a genuinely cosmological perspective; that is, rather than reducing it, as above, to the same level, envisaging instead an ontological depth to the general order (the *kosmos*)[23] of the phenomena we can know. Once again this implies that we should not bring everything (both human and non-human) down to the same scale, whether it is in the end a human or non-human one, but on the contrary that we should try to define the relationship of different things to the human; and vice versa, the relationship of human things to nature.

Let us first take a simple example. As we have seen, the Constanza method reduces the environment's existence to "services" that the market needs to take into account, whereas it normally does not do so, since these are external matters. This reduction to a similar level, that of services that are quantifiable just like others (those between humans), is indeed a way of calculating the importance of the environment, but it rests on a fiction; a tenacious fiction since it is in fact the same one that Marx ironically upbraided Ricardo for in a note in *Capital*:

> Ricardo himself has his Robinson stroke. For him the primitive hunter and fisherman are traders who exchange fish and game in relation to the duration of the work represented by their value. Here he commits this exceptional anachronism that in order to calculate the instruments of their work hunter and fisherman look up the annuity tables used in the London Stock Exchange in 1817.[24]

And which he countered, as we know, with his own theory of goods, based on analysis of the socio-political relations of production. Indeed, like Ricardo, Constanza brings down to the "London Stock Exchange" (that is, market values) phenomena that of their essence have no connection with it. That is the fiction (the Robinson stroke). Instead what we need to do is define the relationship between ecological and economic phenomena via an appropriate scale, that is, one that accounts for their respective identities instead of misrepresenting the first in the second.

If we acknowledge that ecological phenomena are associated with the planet Earth and economic phenomena with human life on it, the simplest measure in this regard is to assess what Wackernagel and Rees have called the "ecological footprint," in other words to express in units of surface area the impact on ecosystems of a particular way of life.[25] Some relatively simple conversions enable one to calculate the area for any natural resource. For instance, the area of carboniferous forest needed to produce one tonne of coal is estimated, and by relating that value to the productive capacity of the present biosphere the consumption of that tonne of coal is converted into square metres. There are no metaphors here since we remain within the same ontological order, that of ecosystems. But the capital consumed by our way of life is visible in very concrete terms, as is the degree to which it exceeds, or not, the planet's ability to reproduce that capital. And so it appears that around the turn of the century human consumption exceeded that ability by a third; in other words, we would need 1.3 planet Earths to sustain our way of life over the long term. With a constant population our ecological footprint should be substantially below 2 ha per person to maintain that balance; but it is approaching 3 ha. The most disturbing aspect is that this is only a worldwide average. In fact rich countries' lifestyle, which, through international bodies in particular (World Bank, IMF, etc.), is becoming the model in development scenarios for poor countries, produces a far larger footprint. If we all lived like Californians, we would need not one but a dozen blue planets (again with a constant population) to make maintaining that lifestyle possible. It is obvious that such a way of life is not ecologically sustainable.

Using equally simple conversions we can see that lifestyle is also unsustainable from a moral point of view. Indeed—since we have only one Earth—it implies on the one hand that the poor consume less to the extent that the rich consume more, and on the other that the capital in resources our descendants will have at their disposal will be reduced to the extent that we exceed our capital's ability to renew itself. So there is a double injustice.

Being Human on the Earth

If arguing in terms of an ecological footprint makes it possible to highlight the fact that our way of life is unsustainable—ecologically limited and morally unjustifiable—nonetheless that does not clarify the aporia noted earlier. In particular it does not explain why a reasonable being—the human being—is tending to live in an increasingly unreasonable manner. There must be a fundamental gap in our cosmology: we find it impossible rationally (in accordance with a coherent *kosmos*) to make our behavior fit with our knowledge. And that gap is specifically a modern one. In fact all traditional societies have had the ability to integrate within a *kosmos* their representations of nature and their moral rules. We moderns lost that ability from the moment when things turned into morally neutral *objects* for us, ontologically distinct from us as moral *subjects*. Indeed that was the assumption—what is called *dualism*—that made modern science possible; and that dualism brought about what Heidegger denounced as a loss of world, or "deworlding" (*Entweltlichung*). Personally I prefer to say "decosmizing"; or loss of *kosmos* as order binding together the being of things and our own, in particular, connecting the representation we have of our existence with the one we have of the basis that makes it possible: the Earth or nature. For us the former relates to what I call[26] the modern ontological *topos*: the "individual person: individual body" identity; the latter relates to objects external to that ontological *topos*. But this duality denies the condition *sine qua non* for an environmental ethics, for moral rules can only be applied to self-conscious subjects. We cannot reasonably expect them to be observed by objects (we come back to that aporia I pointed to earlier), nor in the relations between subjects and objects, except through fictions that see those relations as similar to the ones between subjects (such as the "services" envisaged by Constanza).

However, effective though it may be, the above-mentioned ontological *topos* is nothing more than a mental representation. It characterizes the *classic modern Western paradigm*, Descartes' and Newton's, whose cosmology and physics have been out of date for a century.[27] On the ontological level that *topos* was also radically questioned by Heidegger, who put up against it a *Dasein*: a "being-there" which is "being-in-the-world," "being-with-things," etc.; in short a "being-outside-oneself" (*Ausser-sich-sein*) that goes beyond the *topos* in question. These views, which overturn modern (and especially Cartesian) ontology, entail a consequence unforeseen by Heidegger himself: they provide a reason to extend the field of ethics to that "outside" (*Ausser*), which is now part of our being and no longer part of the objective—or, I should say more precisely, *objectal* (related to the object)—world. For me this reason is the essential condition that allows us to transcend the aporia the modern ontological *topos* entails for environmental ethics.

Nevertheless Heidegger did not follow the logic of *Dasein* through to the end. As Watsuji Tetsurô[28] noted, it remains limited by an individual horizon: one's own death (in other words the temporal limit of the modern ontological *topos*). Indeed Heidegger writes:

> Death as the end of *Dasein* is the most specific, non-relative possibility of *Dasein*, certain and as such indeterminate, insurmountable. Death as the end of *Dasein* is in the being of this existing towards its end.[29]

For this reason the ontology of Heidegger's *Dasein* is that of a "being towards death" (*Sein zum Tode*), a vision that Watsuji radically criticizes. Indeed for him human existence (*ningen sonzai*) is that of a "being towards life" (*sei e no sonzai*):

> Historicity structures social existence. Here too one can see the dual nature, finite–infinite, of human existence. People die, their between-link (*aida*) changes, but even though they constantly die and change, people are alive and their between-link goes on. It is in this fact of constantly ending that it is constantly continuing. What is *being towards death*, from the individual's viewpoint, is *being towards life* from society's point of view.[30]

We can see that for Watsuji the human being is composed inseparably of an individual dimension and a social dimension: and the link—the "between-link", *aida*—from one to the other goes well beyond Heidegger's "being-with" (*Mitsein*), which ceases with the individual's death. For Watsuji death does not put an end to the social part of our existence (and, we might add, it even confirms it).[31] Furthermore he is the first to have clearly spelt out that this between-link is also the basis for our relationship with the environment, and that consequently the latter is no less a part of our being than the *aida* that connects us to others. Thus human existence is constituted by the dynamic of the relationship between an individual dimension and a socio-environmental dimension, a relationship that Watsuji defines as the "structural moment of human existence" (*ningen sonzai no kôzô keiki*).[32]

So in my view Watsuji, whose writing in fact chiefly concerns ethics, has opened up the possibility not only of radically transcending the modern ontological *topos*, but also in particular of going beyond the aporia that it placed in the way of creating a genuine ethics of the environment.[33] This aporia arose from the fact that a being limited by the individual horizon of the Cartesian "I", and even Heidegger's *Dasein*, cannot structurally operate a moral rule requiring that one take account of what is beyond that horizon: the *environment* (or *fûdo* in Watsuji's vocabulary), which, in time as well as space, goes beyond the modern individual's ontological *topos*. However, seeing this context not as external to our being (in the form of the objectal environment), but as constituting it no less fundamentally than the identity of our *topos*, allows us to carry out a decentring process that is as decisive as the one that inaugurated modern times—the Copernican revolution. The first of these decentring moments was the source of enormous progress; but at the same time it was to bring about a decosmization that, as we know today, could only be fatal in the shorter or longer term and is now unsustainable. Avoiding that outcome is the challenge of the second decentring, the revolution that will replace the modern individual's being towards death with the being towards life of what is the true basis of our existence: *being human on the Earth*.[34]

Notes

1. Originally published as: A. Berque, "A basis for environmental ethics," *Diogenes* 52(207) (2005): 3–11. Translated from the French by Jean Burrell. Reprinted by permission of SAGE Publications.

2. In this case the highly orthodox book by Su Haofa and Mai Xueshen (2003), *Luntai gu jin* [Luntai Yesterday and Today], Urumqi, Xinjiang Renmin Chubanshe, p. 164.

3. We shall see below that there are profound ontological reasons behind this ambiguity: the things in our environment are not objects but relative entities conditioned by our existence and in turn conditioning it. So it is inseparable from them.

4. This is the position claimed in particular in Song Yudong, Fan Zili, Lei Zhidong, and Zhang Fawang (eds.) (2000), *Zhongguo Talimu he shui ziyuan yu shengtai wenti yanjiu* [Research on the Ecological Problems and Water Resources of the River Tarim, China], Urumqi, Xinjiang Renmin Chubanshe.

5. Su and Mai, op. cit., p. 164.

6. This ubiquitous theme is the first word in *Xinjiang shouce: Zhongguo xibu* [Xinjiang Manual: China's West] by Hu Wenkang et al. (2000), Urumqi, Xinjiang Renmin Chubanshe, which opens as follows: "The great development of the West is currently the hottest topic of conversation throughout the country" (p. 1). *Kaifa* can also be translated as "exploitation." Indeed "great exploitation of the West" would seem to me closer to the fact, but the phrase is used by its promoters in the sense of "development."

7. The title of the chapter about this operation in Su and Mai, op. cit., pp. 321 et seq.

8. More precisely the start of the season, since high water used to begin in June and reach its height in August.

9. Wang Ranghui et al. (2004), "Zhongguo Talimu he xiayou shengtai zhili gongcheng ruogan wenti de sikao" [Thoughts on Some Engineering Problems in the Ecological Works on the Lower Reaches of the River Tarim, China], in *Zhongguo xibu huanjing wenti yu kezhixu fazhan guoji xueshu yantaohui lunwenji* [Contributions to the International Scientific Conference on Environmental Problems and Sustainable Development in the Chinese West], ed. Li Peicheng, Wang Wenke and Pei Xianzhi (Beijing: Zhongguo Huanjing Kexue Chubanshe), 57–60.

10. From Lake Bosten, which is well supplied by the Kongqi, four similar transfers (*yingji shushui*, or emergency pumping) were carried out between 2000 and 2004, the biggest (400 million cubic metres) between 1 April and 17 November 2001.

11. *Shengtai zhili qiangqiu gongcheng.* This refers to a series of hydraulic works designed to restore an adequate supply of water for ecosystems.

12. *Tuigeng huanlin (cao) gongcheng.*

13. Xu Yingqin, Wu Shixin, Liu Zhaoxia, Yan Xinhua, Maier. "Talimu he xia you ken qu lüzhou shengtaixi fuwu de jiazhi" [Value of Ecosystem Services in the Oases of the Cleared Areas on the Lower Tarim], *Ganhanqu dili*, 26(3) (2003): 203–216.

14. R. Constanza, R. De Groot, et al. "The value of the world's ecosystem services and natural capital," *Nature*, 387 (1997): 253–260.

15. This refers mainly to works carried out between 1957 and 1960 and where the population rose to 38,000 by 1981 and 40,800 by 2001. Op. cit., p. 209.

16. Op. cit., p. 214.

17. The title of chapter IV of Guojia huanjing baohu zongju xuanchuan jiaoyu bangongshi [Education and Propaganda Bureau of the National Office for the Protection of the Environment] (2003), *Zhongguo shengtai huanjing jingshi* [Warning Signs for the Ecological Environment in China], Beijing, Zhongguo huanjing kexue chubanshi, pp. 94–122. In the same publication reference is made to "the desertification caused by artificial enlargement of the oases" (*rengong lüzhou guangda suo dailai de huangmohua*, p. 101) and without resorting to euphemisms the "ecological migrants" (*shengtai yimin*) mentioned elsewhere are here quite straightforwardly "ecological refugees" (*shengtai nanmin*, p. 105).

18. Op. cit., p. 98.

19. Xu et al., op. cit., p. 215. In real terms this is roughly equal to the same amount in euros (1 euro = 10 yuan in 2004).

20. To quote just one, I refer readers to Catherine and Raphaël Larrère, *Du bon usage de la nature. Pour une philosophie de l'environnement.* (Paris: Aubier, 1997).

21. I have discussed these positions and suggested my own in, *Être humains sur la terre. Principes d'éthique de l'écoumène.* (Paris: Gallimard, 1996).

22. See Bruno Latour et al., *Cosmopolitiques I. La nature n'est plus ce qu'elle était.*(La Tour d'Aigues: l'Aube, (2002).

23. We should remember that the Greek word *kosmos* has the threefold meaning "order", "world" and "decoration." The Latin *mundus* also has these three meanings whose origin signifies that there is an order to the things making up the world, and this order is positive in terms of human values (*kalos k'agathos*, both beautiful and good). On the other hand the universe of modern physics is axiologically neutral. In other words it is no longer a *kosmos*.

24. Karl Marx (1867), *Capital*, Book I.

25. Mathis Wackernagel and William Rees, *Our ecological footprint: reducing human impact on the earth.* (Gabriola Island, BC, New Society, 1996).

26. Here I am brusquely summarizing views I expounded in detail in (2000), *Ecoumène. Introduction à l'étude des milieux humains*, Paris, Belin.

27. This is said schematically, with Einstein's relativity and quantum mechanics in mind; but more profoundly still, non-Euclidean geometries had already rendered outdated the Euclidean space that is the basis for the paradigm in question.

28. In the normal Japanese order the patronym precedes the "first" or "Christian" name.

29. "Der Tod als Ende des Daseins ist die eigenste, unbezügliche, gewisse und als solche unbestimmte, unüberholbare Möglichkeit des Daseins. *Der Tod ist als Ende des Daseins im Sein dieses Seienden zu seinem Ende.*" Martin Heidegger (1993), *Sein und Zeit* [Being and Time], Tübingen, Niemeyer, pp. 258–259. Originally published in 1927. Heidegger's emphasis.

30. Watsuji Tetsurô (1979), *Fûdo. Ningengakuteki kôsatsu* [Environments. A Humanological Study], Tokyo, Iwanami shoten, pp. 19–20. Originally published in 1935.

31. Which is illustrated by, among other things, funeral rites observable throughout the human race.

32. Reusing the formulation I have shown in *Écoumène* that this structural moment ("moment" to be understood here in the sense German philosophy derived from mechanics, that is, a dynamic coupling) is specifically human because the environment that constitutes "half" of our being—the other "half" being the modern ontological *topos*—is not only ecological (which would not distinguish us from non-humans) but also technical and symbolic: it is eco-techno-symbolic. This theory leans in particular on the notion of "social body" in Leroi-Gourhan (1964), who (in *Le Geste et la parole*, 2 vols, Paris, Albin Michel) detailed the processes of "exteriorizing" and developing into technical and symbolic systems the initial functions of our "animal body" over the evolution of our species. This exteriorizing has made every human environment a system of relative entities—*resources, constraints, risks* and *pleasures*—that it is radically impossible to consider, in the modern manner, as a collection of objects: it is inseparable from our very being.

33. *Environment* translates here the French *milieu*, which translates the Japanese

fûdo. Watsuji distinguishes *fûdo* (phenomenal environment, supposing the existence of the human subject) from *kankyô* (objective environment). This distinction was inspired by Heidegger's categories, which themselves were inspired by Jacob von Uexküll's distinction between *Umwelt* (the phenomenal environment of a given species) and *Umgebung* (objective environment, as analysed by the scientist).

34. This brief presentation could not go further than a few principles; more arguments will be found in *Être humains sur la Terre* and especially in *Écoumène,* op. cit.

Part Four

Water as a
Community Resource

Chapter 13

Editors' Introduction

> Ruin is the destination toward which all men rush, each pursuing
> his own best interest in a society that believes in the freedom of the
> commons. Freedom in a commons brings ruin to all.
>
> —Garrett Hardin[1]

SOME ELEMENTS OF EARTH'S life support systems are such that individuals can behave in a manner that benefits them as individuals, while the costs of their actions are spread over an entire group. These are often called commons, or more accurately, open access systems—where there are no barriers to use. Many of Earth's freshwater systems have these characteristics. A factory located by a river may discharge its wastes into the stream, capturing the benefits of getting rid of the pollution while perhaps sharing the polluted water with all the other users. Depletion of an aquifer can have the same characteristics: the one person withdrawing the water gets all the benefits while the whole community has less at its disposal. Establishing ways for governing and managing resources held in common requires ethical principles and behaviors that work to preserve the commons. In essence, these systems convert open access systems to those managed by the community. This section considers different ways of conceptualizing community-based decision making.

There is a long history of how societies have organized themselves to resolve conflicts and promote cooperation through formal or informal agreements. At local, national, and international scales these ethical issues are often dealt with through contracts of various shapes and sizes that may vary from handshakes to international treaties. Different tenure systems have evolved over decades, centuries, and even millennia and have been modified over time to accommodate changes in population size, climate, and other factors.

Common-pool resource systems vary on a spectrum from long-term, experimental and community efforts to principle driven, explicitly regulatory attempts to influence resource practices. Typically, common-pool management exercises and decisions draw on ideas, moral principles, and traditions from numerous sources. For instance, in international treaties on water four different factors highlight how cooperation over common-pool resources often works out:[2] First, water needs, for purposes such as irrigation or local subsistence, are prioritized over the strict enforcement of water rights. Second, historically, prior uses of water and the institutions built upon them are shown considerable respect in negotiations between upstream and downstream users. Third, there are considerations of both direct and indirect economic benefits. Finally, and very importantly for this discussion, the unique local setting of the treaties often results in clauses that are flexible and not intended to establish precedent. These mixed and open agreements have led previous commentators to argue for a range of positions from explicit, economically driven priorities, to considerations of what a "river needs" as the baseline for achieving optimal outcomes in common-pool decision making.[3]

In 1990, Elinor Ostrom developed a very influential theory about how principles for common-pool resource management are chosen. Ostrom argued in *Governing the Commons* that an essentially game-theoretic model explained the nature of trade-offs, gains, and losses that made local common-pool resource institutions successful.[4] In many regards, Ostrom's theory undermined that of Garrett Hardin, quoted in the epigraph, who had argued that individuals are locked into rational, selfish behavior that would eventually overexploit shared resources and cause the commons to collapse.[5] However, Ostrom argues that from the perspective of game theory, individuals are involved in different games where they attempt to balance risks against returns in an effort to secure a system of resource use they conceive to be best in the long run. Sometimes this involves choosing a less advantageous position for oneself so that the community is better off on the whole. Such is the case in Thailand, where researchers report that a mixture of contracts recognizing both communal and private water tenure systems coexist and protect common interests at some points and private interests in others.[6]

However, there are reasons to question Ostrom's reliance on game theory. First, in actual community decision making, the "individualistic person who inhabits game *theory* gives way to the relational person *who lives* in successful, often thriving communities."[7] Hence, game theoretic approaches miss the fact that the individuals who live in communities define themselves as members—not merely rational economizers—so a hard distinction between the self and the community is misleading. There are complex sets of relationships, beliefs, norms, and interests of resource users that influence actual decisions regarding common-pool resources.[8] By excluding these factors from the analysis, game theoretic explanations do not provide many of the terms necessary for evaluating the ethical obligations or social relationships affecting common-pool resources.

At the other end of the spectrum, in regulatory theory and especially water law, a common assumption is that increased regulation is necessary as resource scarcity increases. That is, a failure of common-pool arrangements requires some firmer system of norms to constrain individual use. However, as several legal scholars point out, legal remedies are often premised on protecting existing values, such as economic development, rather than on curtailing negative resource uses per se.[9] In fact, legal regulations have often legitimated certain activities that, en masse, exploit and degrade the water commons. Such has been the case with the Western models of sanitation that protect the flushing of copious amounts of wastewater every year based on criteria such as "reasonable" or "beneficial" uses of water.[10] In these cases, regulations may result in the degradation of the commons rather than its protection.

While Ostrom's theory of common-pool resource management has been quite influential, other accounts of community management exist. One currently gaining momentum is known as environmental pragmatism. As a tool for managing community resources, environmental pragmatists promote such things as value pluralism, deliberative dialogue, and experimental environmental policies.[11] The philosophical heritage of environmental pragmatism draws on the American pragmatist movement of the 19th and early 20th centuries and philosophers such as C. S. Peirce, William James, and John Dewey.[12] From this perspective, institutional success in resource management takes place at the community level. Hence, rather than trying to limit personal behavior solely or primarily through regulatory enforcement, pragmatism takes a pluralist view of values and attempts to incorporate, in an open manner, the positions of those affected by resource decisions.[13] In the current literature, UNESCO's series on water and ethics takes a pragmatist view in its promotion of democratic decision making and its attempt to incorporate as many perspectives as possible in a democratic decision model.[14]

Contents

This section offers a range of perspectives regarding water as a community resource and the different ethical principles that may influence community-based decisions. The first essay, by Elinor Ostrom, Paul C. Stern, and Thomas Dietz, considers some of the main lessons gleaned from literature on common-pool resource theory. These authors respond to a set of governance and institutional challenges by offering perspective on the main issues when treating water as a commons. The second essay, by Paul Trawick, details the principles that have led to the success of common-pool irrigation systems in Peru and elsewhere. He considers the institutional and economic principles that enable long-term community survival and those that may contribute to institutional instability. The third essay, by Madeleine Cantin Cumyn, considers the civil law concept of *res communis*, which states that water cannot be either personal or common property. She explores the governance pressures in the Canadian province of Quebec to make water property of individuals, firms, or the state for increased economic development. The fourth essay, by Bryan G. Norton, presents a pragmatist view of environmentalism. Norton argues against traditional environmental ethics by drawing on the work of environmental ethicist and manager Aldo Leopold. He concludes with suggestions for how community-based management might take a place-based, pluralist, and experimental view of watershed indicators in community management.

Notes

1. G. Hardin, "The tragedy of the commons," *Science* 162 (1968): 1243–1248. At 1244.

2. See, M. Giordano and A. Wolf, "Incorporating equity into international water agreements," *Social Justice Research* 14 (2002): 349–366.

3. Contrast, for instance, C. Sadoff and D. Grey, "Beyond the river: the benefits of cooperation on international rivers," *Water Policy* 4 (2002): 389–403; J. Kolars, "The need for a river ethic and river advocacy in the Middle East," in *Water in the Middle East: a geography of peace*, ed. H. Amery and A. Wolf (Austin: University of Texas Press, 2000), 244–261.

4. E. Ostrom, *Governing the commons: the evolution of institutions for collective action.* (New York: Cambridge University Press, 1990).

5. Hardin, 1968.

6. A. Neef, L. Chamsai, M. Hammer, A. Wannitpradit, C. Sangkapitux, Y. Xyooj, P. Sirisupluxuna, and W. Spreer, "Water tenure in highland watersheds of northern Thailand—tragedy of the commons or successful management of complexity?" in *Land use, nature conservation, and the stability of rainforest margins in Southeast Asia*, ed. G. Gerold, M. Fremerey, and E. Guhardja (New York: Springer-Verlag, Berlin, Heidelberg, 2004), 367–389.

7. P. Brown, *The commonwealth of life: economics for a flourishing earth*, 2nd ed. (Montreal: Blackrose Books, 2008), 182. Emphasis in original.

8. M. Zwarteveen and R. Meinzen-Dick, "Gender and property rights in the commons: examples of water rights in South Asia," *Agriculture and Human Values* 18 (2001): 11–25.

9. C. Rose, "Energy and efficiency in the realignment of common-law water rights," *Journal of Legal Studies* 19 (1990): 261–296; C. Stone, *Should trees have standing? Towards legal rights for natural objects.* (New York: Avon Books, 1974).

10. J. Benidickson, *The culture of flushing: a social and legal history of sewage.* (Vancouver: UBC Press, 2007).

11. See, A. Light and E. Katz (eds.), *Environmental pragmatism.* (New York: Routledge, 1996).

12. L. Menand, *The metaphysical club: a story of ideas in America.* (New York: Farraf, Straus and Giroux, 2001).

13. J. Habermas, *Moral consciousness and communicative action.* (Cambridge, MA: MIT Press, 1990); see also, J. Habermas, *Between facts and norms: contributions to a discourse theory of law and democracy.* Translated by William Rehg. (Cambridge: MIT Press, 1998); J. Habermas, *The theory of communicative action.* Translated by Thomas McCarthy. 2 vols. (Boston: Beacon Press, 1981).

14. J. Priscoli, J. Dooge, and R. Llamas, *Water and ethics: overview.* (Paris: UNESCO, 2004).

Chapter 14

Water Rights in the Commons[1]

Elinor Ostrom, Paul C. Stern, and Thomas Dietz

Scarcities of usable, fresh water resulting from demographic change, industrialization, and agricultural expansion elevate water to the rank of a major resource policy issue of the 21st century for both developing and developed countries.[2] Policymakers in many countries are trying to understand how best to cope with increasing water scarcity. Two "solutions" are frequently proposed—giving responsibility to government agencies to act on behalf of all citizens or privatizing water so as to utilize market systems for allocation. Decades of research and public policy experience have shown the limits of making a strict distinction between government and the market and have led to a more nuanced understanding of the possibilities for effective management of water and other natural resources.[3] Much of this research has been brought together in a new book from the National Research Council, *The Drama of the Commons*.[4] Drawing on an earlier report by Stern and others, we highlight some of these major lessons.[5]

Lesson 1: There Is No One Best System for Governing Water Resources

Researchers usually distinguish four basic types of governance systems, defined in terms of who controls access to resources: private property, government property, common property, and open access (i.e., no one's property). Research has consistently shown the inefficient outcomes of open access since open access almost always leads to destruction of any resource that is in great demand. This is the problem identified in Hardin's famous essay, although he called open access "commons," which led to substantial subsequent confusion.[6] The other three systems, however, have mixed records in terms of sustaining water resources, including both great successes and massive failures. Thus, the ability of a type of ownership to enhance sustainable resource management depends on a number of other factors discussed below.

Lesson 2: Many More Viable Options Exist for Resource Management Than Envisioned in Much of the Policy Literature

Successful community resource management is not only possible but commonplace. Contrary to the presumption that only external coercion constrains individual selfish appetites, throughout history communities have used informal social controls, often complementing them through modest use of formal enforcement, to manage their water.[7] Among the most important is the use of indigenous knowledge of the characteristics of the resource system and culturally acceptable ways of restricting the use of commonly held assets. Such commons management has often achieved long-term sustainability. Irrigation systems around the world have been built, maintained, and used by farmer associations for centuries.[8] In the contemporary U.S., farmers create special districts to manage irrigation and drainage. Many disasters of resource management during the 20th century have been caused by replacing effective community management with ineffective or corrupt government management.

A substantial body of research shows that a variety of governance systems—many of them hybrids of the basic types—can be effective. For example, in southern California, water users developed tradable rights to ground water through a series of court decisions.[9] But the development of rights to ground water does not turn the ground water basin into a privately owned resource. Instead, the total allowable withdrawals were determined by a state court and are monitored by a watermaster appointed by the court. Further, southern California water users have created multiple special districts to manage a series of injection wells along the coast (effectively building a "dam" against salt-water intrusion). These districts levy substantial pump charges on all ground water extractors in a basin to pay for replenishing the basin. The resulting water-rights system cannot be classified as purely private or government management. It is a unique system that has been in operation for almost 50 years and has protected a series of ground water basins underlying the Los Angeles metropolitan area. The tradable water rights system combines features of private and government property in novel and effective ways. Such hybrids are appealing on theoretical grounds and are sometimes, though not always, highly successful.[10] Further, multiple ways exist to establish such systems. For example, Arizona has adopted a policy of specifying ground water rights as a matter of state policy, thus reducing many of the transaction costs faced in the basin-by-basin adjudication system adopted in southern California.[11]

Current knowledge provides more subtle and nuanced insights into sustainable management than the simple models of pure government, market, commons, or open access. We are moving toward an approach to resource management that resembles medical practice. Diagnosis and treatment are based on hard science as well as many individual case histories and meta-analyses of accumulated evidence from cases. However, because every case has unique aspects, an effective practitioner draws both on established principles and on knowledge of the specific case in facing the challenges of diagnosing problems and prescribing courses of action.

Lesson 3: It Helps To Think of Resource Management as a Problem of Designing a Management System to Meet a Set of Ongoing Challenges

From this perspective, the best system of control is one that meets the most critical challenges of the situation at hand. The reason each type of control system sometimes succeeds and sometimes fails is that the challenges of resource management vary with the type of resource; characteristics of the resource users; and the environmental, social, economic, and political context of resource use—most of which change over time. Water managers can use current research to diagnose their situations and find the most likely set of management strategies for meeting particular challenges.

In its concluding chapter, *The Drama of the Commons* identifies seven key challenges of resource management (see right side of Figure 14-1).[12]

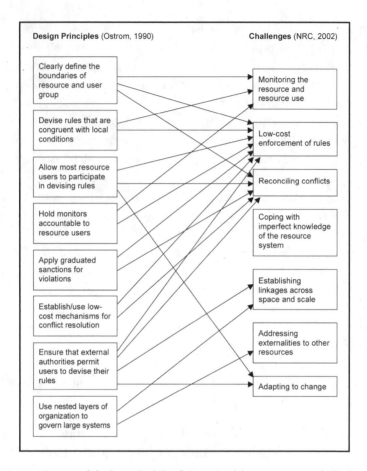

Figure 14-1 Proposed design principles for commons management, challenges of management, and linkages between the two.[13]

These are: (1) monitoring the resource and resource use, (2) low-cost enforcement of rules, (3) reconciling conflicts, (4) coping with imperfect knowledge of the resource system, (5) establishing linkages across space and scale, (6) addressing externalities to other resources, and (7) adapting to change. These challenges are not equally important in all situations. For example, monitoring the resource is a more difficult challenge for rivers than for lakes. Reconciling conflicts is a bigger challenge when the resource users live far away from each other (e.g., when water users live hundreds of miles away from the source of their water supply, like Los

Angeles, San Francisco, Boston, and New York City) than when they all live in the same community and interact on a regular basis.

How should management systems be designed to meet these challenges? Some researchers have proposed sets of design principles for resource management systems (one set, from Ostrom,[14] is listed in the left half of Figure 14-1). The hope is that the use of these will increase the chances of success. The principles are based on empirical and theoretical evidence about what works under different circumstances.[15] Although most of the emerging design principles probably constitute good general advice, they do not constitute a rigid blueprint. Examples of sustainably managed resources exist that deviate in some ways from the suggested principles. Practitioners will still need to exercise judgment to place a particular situation into its appropriate category.

It is worth noting that each design principle addresses only a subset of the challenges, as suggested by the arrows in Figure 14-1. Thus, in situations where a particular challenge is especially critical (for example, linking authorities at different levels or in different jurisdictions), some design principles may offer little help while others are especially worth trying to apply (such as using nested layers of organization).

It is also the case that some of the challenges are closely interlinked in many situations: Conditions that make one of them problematic tend to have a similar effect on others. Further, interventions that help with one challenge often also help with others. Monitoring, enforcement, and conflict resolution, for example, are linked in several ways. Small, stable, isolated groups that subsist on local resources (a small lake or river) often share a number of characteristics that make it possible for groups of resource users to solve problems at low cost. They are collectively dependent on a clearly defined resource base, and they have strong incentives to maintain it. In addition, they often have well established community norms and procedures of conflict management that operate in many areas of local life.

These social characteristics, sometimes described as strength of community or social capital, greatly reduce the incremental costs of monitoring, rule enforcement, and conflict resolution because much of the necessary activity is already going on. Where resource users do not constitute strong communities, the challenges of monitoring, enforcement, and conflict resolution may also be linked in the sense that it may be possible to design mechanisms, perhaps learning from those of small, stable communities, that meet all the challenges together.

For example, participatory processes for decision making and monitoring have been suggested as a promising strategy for meeting several challenges and also for building the capacity (or social capital) needed for effective resource management in groups that are not already strong communities. In a review of World Bank water projects, for example, Watson and Jagannathan found that projects where participation had been built into the design of the project made more efficient investment decisions and water use was monitored more closely.[16]

Lesson 4: Complexity, Uncertainty, and Conflict Are Inherent Attributes of Many Water Management Systems

Many water resources are complex systems not adequately described by simple deterministic models, but neither are they wholly chaotic or unpredictable. As a result, outcomes of particular use strategies can be projected only with considerable uncertainty. Using uncertain projections of rainfall or other resource characteristics without highlighting the likelihood of error often leads to resource collapse, especially as uncertainty interacts with political and economic pressures to produce unsustainable levels of resource extraction—the most optimistic forecasts are often chosen to meet immediate needs and reduce short-term conflict.[17] Since projections of resource availability at the high end of the uncertainty range will be wrong more often than they are right, such politically motivated optimism can easily lead to systematic overexploitation of resources.

This combination of scientific uncertainty and the resulting political dynamics ensures that resource management is typically conflictual. In any social arrangement in which there is some play for politics, conflict will arise around water management. Rather than seeing conflict as a pathology to be avoided, it may be better to see it as an inevitable feature of human use of resources and to build institutions to manage conflict as well as manage the resources. Indeed, sometimes conflict over resource management is just one manifestation of broader and deeper conflicts.

Lesson 5: Water Management, Notwithstanding Its Technical Aspects, Is Largely a Problem of Governance

Research on conflict in resource management is still emerging, but at least one lesson seems to hold across many types of environmental policy. In democratic societies, conflict about the commons is best managed via effective deliberative processes.[18] Such processes not only suggest compromises around immediate issues but also build cultures of understanding and trust that can be critical to devising management systems that can change as conditions change. This is the essence of adaptive management. Research shows that adaptive management is as much about broad discourse among all those affected by resources as it is about understanding resource dynamics.

Lesson 6: Successful Resource Management Depends on Integrating the Human Sciences

Many water resource managers are trained in the basic natural sciences or engineering. Managers know that they must rely on approximations and experience on a day-to-day basis, but those trained in the physical and biological sciences take pride that management integrates good science with practical constraints in the field. We suggest that exactly the same approach is required for understanding the human and institutional dynamics—the governance problems—of water resource management. Resource managers should learn enough of the basic ideas and methods of research on resource management institutions to be active and skeptical readers of this literature as well. One goal of *The Drama of the Commons* is to provide a starting place for obtaining that literacy, which is at least as important to sustainable resource management as literacy in hydrology, ecology, or the other relevant natural sciences.

Notes

1. Originally published as, Elinor Ostrom, Paul Stern, Thomas Dietz, "Water Rights and the Commons." American Water Resources Association, Water Resources IMPACT 2003. Reprinted with permission.

2. M. Shirley, *Thirsting for efficiency: the economics and politics of urban water system reform.* (The Netherlands: Pergamon Press, 2002); W. Blomquist, E. Schlager, and

T. Heikkila, *How institutions matter: conjunctive water management in Arizona, California, and Colorado.* (Under review at the University of Arizona Press, forthcoming).

3. R. M. Saleth and A. Dinar, "Evaluating water institutions and water sector performance," World Bank Technical Paper No. 447. (Washington, DC: The World Bank, 1999).

4. NRC (National Research Council), *The drama of the commons.* National Research Council, Committee on the Human Dimensions of Global Change. Ed. E. Ostrom, T. Dietz, N. Dolsak, P. Stern, S. Stonich, and E. Weber. Division of Behavioral and Social Sciences and Education (Washington, DC: National Academies Press, 2002).

5. P. Stern, T. Dietz, and E. Ostrom, "Research on the commons: lessons for environmental resource managers," *Environmental Practice* 4(2) (2002): 61–64.

6. G. Hardin, "The tragedy of the commons," *Science* 162 (1968):1243–1248.

7. See, M. Lubell, M. Schneider, J. Scholz, and M. Mete, "Watershed partnerships and the emergence of collective action institutions," *American Journal of Political Science* 46(1) (2002): 148–163.

8. W. F. Lam, *Governing irrigation systems in Nepal: institutions, infrastructure, and collective action.* (Oakland: ICS Press, 1998).

9. W. Blomquist, *Dividing the waters: governing groundwater in Southern California.* (San Franciso: ICS Press, 1992).

10. T. Tietenberg, "The tradable permits approach to protecting the commons: what have we learned?" in *The drama of the commons.* National Research Council, Committee on the Human Dimensions of Global Change, ed. E. Ostrom, T. Dietz, N. Dolsak, P. Stern, S. Stonich, and E. Weber, Division of Behavioral and Social Sciences and Education (Washington, DC: National Academies Press, 2002), 197–232.

11. Blomquist et al.

12. NRC, 2002.

13. Figure from Stern et al., 2002.

14. E. Ostrom, *Governing the commons: the evolution of institutions for collective action.* (New York: Cambridge University Press, 1990).

15. A. Agrawal, "Common resources and institutional sustainability," in *The Drama of the Commons.* National Research Council, Committee on the Human Dimensions of Global Change, ed. E. Ostrom, T. Dietz, N. Dolsak, P. Stern, S. Stonich, and E. Weber, Division of Behavioral and Social Sciences and Education (Washington, DC: National Academies Press, 2002), 41–86.

16. G. Watson and N.V. Jagannathan, "Participation in water and sanitation," Participation Series Paper No. 002. (Washington, DC: The World Bank, Environment Department Papers, 1995).

17. J. Wilson, "Scientific uncertainty, complex systems, and the design of common-pool institutions," in *The drama of the commons.* National Research Council, Committee on the Human Dimensions of Global Change, ed. E. Ostrom, T. Dietz, N. Dolsak, P. Stern, S. Stonich, and E. Weber, Division of Behavioral and Social Sciences and Education (Washington, DC: National Academies Press, 2002), 327–360.

18. T. Dietz and P. Stern, "Science, values and biodiversity," *BioScience* 48 (1998): 441–444.

Chapter 15

Encounters with the Moral Economy of Water: General Principles for Successfully Managing the Commons[1]

Paul Trawick

The Theory of Tragedy

Few works in social science have had as much impact on policy as Garrett Hardin's attempt, in "The Tragedy of the Commons," to explain the tendency of people to overexploit the resources that they hold in common in terms of an irresolvable conflict between the interests of the individual, said to be inherently selfish, and the cooperative needs of the group.[2] The results of such a tragedy are, of course, evident today in many parts of the world in the use of common-property resources. Yet many authors have strongly criticized the theory, based on numerous examples of communities where local people have managed such resources cooperatively, and done so quite effectively, over a long period of time. This rebuttal has turned attention toward the task of devising an alternative theory to explain how people have been able to overcome their conflict of interest, escape the "commons dilemma," and pursue the common good.[3]

Progress toward this goal has been especially noteworthy with regard to one vital resource, irrigation water, which is particularly significant given the impending water crisis that threatens nearly every country in the "developing" world. Recent research, however, lends new support to the effort and promises to allow a thorough refutation and revision of the conventional theory. It indicates that local people in a great many communities in several different parts of the world long ago arrived, quite independently, at the same solution to the commons dilemma, creating a set of principles for sharing scarce water in an equitable and efficient manner that minimizes social conflict. Wherever communities have managed a scarce resource autonomously, and done so effectively over a long period of time, the principles of distribution and use appear in many cases to be highly similar if not exactly the same. This generalization appears to hold for a great many systems based on communal ownership, but it also applies to some systems referred to as "markets," where a significant portion of the resource is privately owned.

Such a finding could have a major impact on the policies of institutions such as the World Bank and the various regional banks with which it is affiliated. Their development programs continue to be strongly shaped by the conventional theory, and they have long advocated water privatization—along with state ownership and control, one of Hardin's proposed solutions to the commons dilemma—on a massive scale.[4] My research indicates that water markets do not work in the manner that they are widely thought to work, at least not in the small-scale systems that typify most of the developing world, since it reveals heretofore unrecognized commonalities in the dynamics of successful communal and market systems.

Scholars and scientists have made steady and important progress in critiquing and revising the theory of the tragedy, most notably Ostrom and Tang, who have led the way in identifying, through comparison of a large number of case studies in different countries, basic design principles that all effective locally run irrigation systems seem to share.[5] Their focus has tended to be on small-scale canal systems of 1000 hectares or less,[6] the kind of "indigenous" or peasant community system found throughout much of the globe, since such limited scale, and the kind of intensive face-to-face interaction among water users that this makes possible, seems to be a critical thing that the systems have in common.[7] However, most of the principles identified thus far remain rather abstract, more suitable for predicting the general conditions under which people will be able to come up with a solution than for showing them how, in concrete terms, to manage water effectively in situations where they have failed or lost the ability to do so on their own.

The Principles Underlying Success

The effort to revise theory and make policy has been hindered by the limitations of the primary data, which are typically thoroughly *etic*, that is, objective, scientific, and descriptive at the system level, but without incorporating much of the *emic* point of view, the more subjective and culture-bound perspective of the water user. Analysts have also tended to emphasize the diversity that exists among local irrigation systems, while not giving enough attention to the one important feature that nearly all of them do have in common, at least at certain times of the year, and that is water scarcity. All of this has obscured the fact that the keys to local success in dealing with water scarcity—that is, *operating principles* which together instill a strong positive incentive in people to obey the rules and conserve the resource, rather than a negative one that merely rests on punishing infractions—appear to be highly similar if not exactly the same in many parts of the world. Once the principles are identified ethnographically, and the way that they work together from the water users' point of view is understood, the parallels in other countries become evident, and a striking pattern is revealed.

The following are principles for successful management of scarce water at the local community level, as identified through extensive fieldwork in several villages in the Peruvian Andes:[8]

1. *Autonomy:* The community has and controls its own flows of water.

2. *Contiguity:* During each distribution cycle, water is given to fields in a fixed contiguous order based on their location along successive canals, starting at one end of the system and moving systematically across it.

3. *Uniformity* [one component of equity] *among rights:* Within each sector of irrigated land serviced by a given source or canal flow, all plots of land are watered with the same frequency, so that the scarcity is shared on a single schedule; *in technique:* everyone irrigates in the same basic way.

4. *Proportionality* [the other component of equity] *among rights:* No one can use more (*equity*) water than the proportional amount to

which the extent of their land entitles them, nor can they legally get it more often than everyone else; *among duties*: people's contributions to maintenance of the canal system must be proportional to the amount of irrigated land that they have.

5.   *Regularity*: Things are always done in the same way under conditions of scarcity; no exceptions are allowed, and any unauthorized expansion of irrigation is prohibited (boundary maintenance).

6.   *Transparency*: Everyone knows the rules and has the capacity to confirm, with their own eyes, whether those rules are generally being obeyed, and to detect and denounce any violations that occur.

The principles, taken together, are distinctive in depicting irrigation as a social problem, in which scarce water is distributed among households according to criteria of equity or fairness, rather than as a technical and agronomic problem wherein the central concern is with meeting the water "needs" of crops. Close examination of the published data suggests that this same basic solution to the problem of sharing a scarcity has been worked out independently by peasants and indigenous people in many parts of Peru, as well as Mexico, Spain, India, Nepal, Bali, and the Philippines.[9] Although the evidence for this is not entirely conclusive and requires one to read between the lines of these works, it is compelling enough to show that some of these local irrigation systems badly need a second look.[10]

The foregoing studies do reveal the existence of some of the principles in a manner that logically implies, or at least strongly suggests, the presence of others, although they have not been explicitly recognized and discussed. Autonomy, for example, is invariably mentioned, since that is basic to the "indigenous" systems—the traditional community-based systems—that have been so extensively studied. Another widely noted principle is proportionality, both among "individual" household water rights (all of which have the same land-to-water ratio) and between people's rights and their corresponding maintenance duties.[11] However, proportionality also implies uniformity in the watering frequency within each user group, since without it there can be no real proportionality among people's rights. It also requires a significant degree of uniformity in people's technique of water use, or at least some limits on the nature or extent of such use, for the same reason.

It is possible, through this kind of logical inference, to confirm the likelihood that all of the aforementioned principles are present in many of the systems described in the literature. One of the virtues of the comparative analyses that have been done to date, particularly those of Ostrom[12] and Tang,[13] is that they show how widespread the principle of proportionality is, and thereby reveal this possibility.[14] The pattern, however, must ultimately be confirmed firsthand through fieldwork if it is to help in the effort to reformulate theory and if it is ever to have an impact on resource management policy. The principles must be shown to be recognized and understood by the water users themselves, and to be motivating their cooperation and minimizing the temptation to cheat or "free-ride."

Water Markets and the Incentive to Conserve

The results of my research, both as an ethnographer and as a consultant on water reform for the World Bank, show that a strong motive for conservation will not materialize as a result of privatization and the creation of markets alone, either in the Andean highlands or in other geographically similar parts of the world. The solution to the water crisis does not appear to lie in the "invisible hand" of the market, in the profit motive and the law of supply and demand, at least not in the small-scale systems that typify most parts of the developing world. Rather, as I have argued elsewhere,[15] it seems to lie in a clearly defined and secure set of individual or household water rights, according to which everyone irrigates on the same schedule, so that any prevailing scarcity of the resource is equitably shared. This fundamental equality creates a direct and obvious link—established by the aforementioned principles and clearly recognized by the irrigators themselves—between the efficiency and orderliness of water use and the duration of the irrigation cycle. The logic of such a system is that, by irrigating frugally and obeying the rules, people are maximizing the frequency of irrigation for themselves and everyone else, responding to a close correspondence between individual self-interest and the common good that cannot be achieved through any other institutional arrangement. The effectiveness of the principles does not, I think,

in any way depend on water being worth money, although that can be
and is a feature of some of the systems where the principles appear to be
in place today.

An intriguing example of the latter is the community of Alicante in
Spain, formerly the oldest water market in the world and one of the few
places where peasants had privatized the resource and adopted a market
approach to its management.[16] Although it is not widely known, the famous "water market" of Alicante collapsed in 1983, partly due to chronic
and persistent scarcity that was attributable to long-term drought, and it
was formally disbanded in 1989, after having virtually ceased to function
for almost a decade. In any case, my own analysis of the published data on
Alicante strongly suggested that the same set of basic principles was formerly operating in Alicante as in the neighboring districts of Valencia and
Murcia, and that these were the same principles that I had encountered
in my ethnographic research in Peru. The hypothesis was tested in fieldwork done in the region in 2003–2004. The latter communities are successful systems of communal water management, originally studied by
the same authors, which also stand out in the literature as examples of
success.

Alicante is widely thought by economists to demonstrate the effectiveness of the profit motive in giving farmers an incentive to use the resource efficiently and with minimal conflict. Close inspection, however,
revealed that its "market" system, while it still existed, had not been well
described nor well understood from the water users' point of view. Given
that the system had collapsed and been reorganized, this study relied
heavily on archival research and a review of previous historical studies[17]
along with interviews with the few individuals still alive who had detailed knowledge of how the original system had worked.

These efforts, which can only be discussed briefly here, revealed two
key points. First, the only water sold was the private and essentially feudal
water—the so-called old water, consisting of approximately half of the
total amount available within the community in each distribution round,
which was in the hands of a wealthy minority of approximately 400
households—contrary to what the original published accounts indicated.
Small farmers, who numbered roughly 2000 households with propor-

tional rights to tiny shares of the other half of the total flow—the so-called new water, created when the Tibi dam was built in 1597—did not engage in buying and selling water to each other. Rather, they were continually forced, by the great inadequacy of this fully communal water, to buy portions of additional "old" or private water from the local "water-lords" in order to alleviate the scarcity that always prevailed. Peasant farmers had to buy this commodified water in order to supplement their allotments of communal water, which were far from adequate in every case, no matter how often the farmers' turns came around in the general cycle. Secondly, the private water that was constantly being transferred between the two types of owner–users was always delivered on the same schedule, and in the same fixed contiguous order of turns, as people's regular communal water allotments, so that it was only available to small farmers with the same frequency, as part of the general irrigation cycle. The famous market of Alicante in fact rested on a communal foundation, without which it could not have continued to exist, a set of cooperative institutions that had the effect of defining individual water rights—both communal and private—clearly and making them secure, so that the private water could be transferred reliably. But the transfers went in only one direction, from the rich to the poor, a basic inequity that ultimately played a major role in the system's demise.

The existence of a highly similar set of operating principles in such seemingly different kinds of systems, under property regimes that at first glance seem diametrically opposed, can only mean that the way that successful market systems, in particular, work has been sometimes widely misunderstood. The following is a list of the principles that are either explicitly mentioned or at least well described in the published accounts of Valencia, Murcia-Orihuela, and Alicante, as well as other principles, shown in parentheses, whose existence can be logically inferred from that information.

- Valencia, a *turno* system consisting of eight user communities: proportionality, contiguity (uniformity, regularity, transparency)

- Murcia, a *tanda* system consisting of forty user communities: proportionality, contiguity (uniformity, regularity, transparency)[18]

- Alicante, formerly a "market" system consisting of three user communities: proportionality, contiguity (uniformity, regularity, transparency)

The presence of such similar or even identical principles in the two kinds of institutional settings can only indicate that the monetary incentive to conserve water, where it exists—as it formerly did in Alicante—must be of secondary importance. In this general kind of system, by using the resource wisely, obeying the rules, and respecting tradition, people are optimizing (and stabilizing as much as possible) the frequency of irrigation for themselves and everyone else, responding to a close correspondence between individual self-interest and the common good that cannot be achieved through any other kind of institutional arrangement. And transparency is achieved, and effective mutual monitoring ensured, in the same way in each case, by applying the simple principle of spatial contiguity in the order of water distribution.

Equity and the Moral Economy

A final example worthy of mention are the peasant communities in northern Chile, the only country in the world that has fully privatized its water and the only one that supposedly has a "national" water market. Again, Chile is widely cited by economists as an example of the efficiency of such markets, which are thought to function effectively even in the small-scale canal systems of the Andes and other parts of the so-called Third World.

During work as a World Bank consultant in 1993 through 1995, I was able to find out from Chilean colleagues that, contrary to what Bank publications suggest, there had in fact been no significant sales of water between households within that country's peasant communities since the current water law was implemented in 1981, a pattern that has since been verified in several published studies.[19] Instead, the reason for the efficiency of local water management in those cases seems to lie in a process called regularization, according to which, as described in preliminary but reliable accounts, the national government either implemented or endorsed practices that manifested the same set of principles previously described. This was seen as a necessary first step in regularizing water use and clarifying individual rights in communities that were being integrated into the market system. However, it was often discovered that such use was already quite regular in such cases and that individual rights were often clearly defined, in an equitable way, under customary or "indigenous" systems of water use. It seems likely, from what I have been able to learn, that the aforementioned principles already existed locally in many cases (the twelve indigenous communities of San Pedro de Atacama are one clear example) and are in fact a survival of the much older Andean tradition of water management that I encountered in Peru.

This tradition, which I call "the moral economy of water," rests on the principle of *equity*, a concept that is often mentioned in the literature but has proven notoriously difficult to define, in concrete terms, for most natural resources. In the field of irrigation and water rights, however, the concept seems easy to define and appears to have been widely defined by people in the same way, wherever they have been allowed to do this on their own. It necessarily encompasses both uniformity and proportionality. This hypothesis, if ultimately confirmed more widely through fieldwork, will be pivotal in the effort to build more powerful theories of collective action, and to devise policies that strongly encourage such action by local communities to take place.

At a time when governments throughout the developing world are having to get out of the business of managing water and tighten their belts financially, under the impact of programs of "structural adjustment" and, more recently, by the ongoing worldwide recession, the need for such a new direction for policy is especially great. If the hypothesis is correct—and the evidence for it is already quite strong—this will indicate that water management may be one of the few domains of human life where a highly effective and widely applicable solution to a major social problem exists, one based on a moral principle that has been recognized and continuously affirmed by people from widely different cultures and backgrounds, and upon which they seem generally able to agree. Such a finding, in both communal and "market" systems, would surely find an important place in the efforts of many scholars and scientists to find ways of creating a more equitable, sustainable, and secure world than the one in which we now live.

Notes

1. A previous version of this paper was published in the journal *GAIA*, Volume 11/3 (2002): 191–194; revised by the author and published with permission from the journal *GAIA* and the author, who thanks the John D. and Catherine T. MacArthur Foundation for generously supporting his research.

2. G. Hardin, "The tragedy of the commons," *Science* 162 (1968): 1243–1248.

3. National Research Council (NRC), *Proceedings of the Conference on Common Property Management* (Washington, DC: National Academy Press, 1986); B. McCay and J. Acheson eds., *The question of the commons: the culture and ecology of communal resources.* (Tucson: University of Arizona Press, 1987); D. Bromley (ed.), *Making the commons work: theory, practice and policy.* (San Francisco: Institute for Contemporary Studies, 1992); E. Ostrom, *Governing the commons: the evolution of institutions for collective action.* (New York: Cambridge University Press, 1990); World Bank, *Peru: a user-based approach to water management and irrigation development.* Report No. 13642-PE. (Washington, DC: World Bank, 1995).

4. World Bank, 1995.

5. E. Ostrom, 1990; E. Ostrom: "Institutional arrangements for resolving the commons dilemma," in *The question of the commons: the culture and ecology of communal resources*, ed. B. McCay and J. Acheson (Tuscon: University of Arizona Press, 1987), 250–265; E. Ostrom, *Crafting institutions for self-governing irrigation systems.* (San Francisco: Institute for Contemporary Studies Press, 1992); E. Ostrom and R. Gardner, "Coping with asymmetries in the commons: self-governing irrigation systems can work," *Journal of Economic Perspectives* 7/4 (1993): 93–112; E. Ostrom, "Reformulating the commons," in *The commons revisited: an Americas perspective*, ed. J. Burger, R. Norgaard, E. Ostrom, D. Policansky, B. Goldstein (Washington, DC: Island Press, 1998), 1–26; E. Ostrom, J. Burger, C. Field, R. Norgaard, and D. Policansky, "Revisiting the commons: local lesson, global challenges," *Science* 284 (1999): 1–10; S.Y. Tang, *Institutions and collective action: self-governance in irrigation.* (San Francisco: ICS Press, 1992).

6. J. Mabry and D. Cleveland, "The relevance of indigenous irrigation: a comparative analysis of sustainability," in *Canals and communities: small-scale irrigation systems*, ed. J. Mabry (Tuscon: University of Arizona Press, 1996), 227–260.

7. Ostrom, 1987, 1998.

8. P. Trawick, "Successfully governing the commons: principles of social organization in an Andean irrigation system," *Human Ecology* 29/1 (2001a): 1–25; P. Trawick, "The moral economy of water: equity and antiquity in the Andean commons," *American Anthropologist* 103/2 (2001b): 361–379; P. Trawick, "Comedy and tragedy in the Andean commons," *Journal of Political Ecology* 9 (2002): 35–68; P. Trawick, *The struggle for water in Peru: comedy and tragedy in the Andean commons.* (Palo Alto, CA: Stanford University Press, 2003a); P. Trawick, "Against the privatization of water: an indigenous model for local success in governing the commons," *World Development* 31(6) (2003b): 977–996; P. Trawick, "Going with the flow: the state of contemporary studies of water management in Latin America," *Latin American Research Review* 40(3) (2005): 443–456; P. Trawick, "Scarcity, equity, and transparency: general principles for successfully governing the water commons," in *Mountains: Sources of Water, Sources of Knowledge*, ed. E. Wiegandt (The Netherlands: Springer Press, 2008), 43–61.

9. Ostrom, 1990, 1992, 1998; J. Treacy, *Las Chacras de Corporaque: Andeneria y Riego en el Valle del Colca.* (Lima: Instituto de Estudios Peruanos, 1994); D. Guillet, "Canal irrigation and the state: the 1969 water law and irrigation systems in the Colca Valley of Southern Peru," in *Irrigation at high altitudes: the social organization of water control systems in the Andes,* ed. W. P. Mitchell and D. Guillet. Society for Latin American Anthropology Publication Series, vol. 12. (Washington DC: AAS, 1994), 167–188; R. Hunt and E. Hunt, "Canal irrigation and local social organization," *Current Anthropology* 17 (1976): 129–157; A. Maass and R. L. Anderson, *And the desert shall rejoice: conflict, growth and justice in arid environments.* (Cambridge, MA: MIT Press, 1978); E. W. Coward, "Principles of social organization in an indigenous irrigation system," *Human Organization* 38/1 (1979): 28–36; R. Wade, "Common property resource management in South Indian villages," in National Research Council (NRC), *Proceedings of the Conference on Common Property Management.* (Washington, DC: National Academy Press, 1986), 231–258; R. Wade, *Village republics: economic conditions for collective action in South India.* (Cambridge: Cambridge University Press, 1988); R. de los Reyes, *47 communal gravity systems: organizational profiles.* (Quezon City, Philippines: Ateneo de Manila University, Institute of Philippine Culture, 1982); R. Y. Siy, *Community resource management: lessons from the Zanjera.* (Quezon City, Philippines: University of the Philippines Press, 1982); N. Sengupta, *Managing common property: irrigation in India and the Philippines.* (New Delhi: Sage Press, 1991); W. F. Lam, *Governing irrigation systems in Nepal: institutions, infrastructure, and collective action.* (Oakland: ICS Press, 1998).

10. Trawick, 2008.

11. Ostrom, 1987, 1990, 1992, 1993, 1998; Ostrom et al., 1999; Tang, 1992; Guillet, 1994.

12. Ostrom, 1987, 1990, 1992, 1993, 1998; Ostrom et al., 1999.

13. Tang, 1992.

14. Maass and Anderson, 1978; Wade, 1986, 1988; Sengupta, 1991; Lam, 1998.

15. Trawick, 2001a, b; 2003a, b; 2005, 2008.

16. Maass and Anderson, 1978; Trawick, 2001a, b; 2003a, b; 2005, 2008; for an excellent example and a primary historical source, see A. Alberola Romá, *El Pantano de Tibi y el Sistems de Riegos en la Huerta de Alicante* (Alicante: Instituto de Cultura "Juan Gilbert" and Fundacion Cultural CAM, 1994).

17. See Alberola Romá, 1994.

18. Note that two categories of user groups formerly existed, one of which was privileged and irrigated significantly more often than the other under the traditional system; that system has since been modified, however, mainly because of its inability to cope successfully with drought, and it now conforms closely to the Valencia model.

19. See e.g., A. Dourojeanni, A. Jouravlev: "El Codigo de Aguas de Chile: Entre la Ideologia y la Realidad," *Debate Agrario,* No. 29–30, (Lima : CEPES, 1999), 138–185.

Chapter 16

The Legal Status of Water in Quebec[1]

Madeleine Cantin Cumyn

THE AVAILABILITY, QUALITY, AND PERENNITY of freshwater are undoubtedly the primary concerns of any environmental analysis or policy, since no life is sustainable without water. Water is not simply a resource to be dealt with like any other mineral, plant, or animal resource. The concept of *res communis*, which applies to water and air in the civil law tradition, embodies this reality and is the juridical recognition of their exceptional nature. The Civil Law of Quebec adheres to the concept of *res communis* as formulated by Roman law, and whose origin is undoubtedly more ancient. Before discussing the meaning and the consequences which attach to such a legal category, I shall briefly situate the legal discourse within its wider social and political context.

The Politics of Water in Quebec

Issues related to water tend to receive extensive coverage in the Quebec press and they are the object of great interest and some concern amongst the population. There is a vigorous public debate around such questions as the pollution of water ecosystems by modern agricultural practices as well as the preservation of public control of water supply infrastructures, water purification and distribution systems, and their related services. The provision of running water for human use and consumption is presently the responsibility of municipalities in urban areas. However, major economic interests are exerting increasing pressure on public authorities to consider water as an object of commerce, to be supplied privately like any other commodity. That water is a sensitive subject in Quebec may come as a surprise, given the impressive quantity of freshwater that Nature has endowed the province. The real situation is somewhat different, however, when one considers actual access to these freshwater resources. Quebeckers occupy less than 10% of the territory of the province, essentially in the south, where climatic conditions make agriculture possible. Quebec's northern climate discourages the establishment of large settlements above the fiftieth parallel. Because of the concentration of population in a small portion of the territory and the pollution affecting some rivers and underground bodies of water, freshwater available to Quebeckers living in the south is not abundant, and in some areas, there is even a scarcity of freshwater of suitable quality.

Preoccupation with the preservation and management of water resources has led the Quebec Government to create two commissions of inquiry, the first in 1970–72[2] and the second in 1999, in order to clarify legal questions and to gain a more precise knowledge of the quantity, quality, and present uses of available freshwater. The report of the most recent Commission sur la gestion de l'eau au Quebec (the Beauchamp Report), published in 2000,[3] contains a wealth of information providing an up-to-date picture of the situation as well as reserving an appropriate place for the concerns expressed by the public during the hearings. The main focus of the Report was to correct the present piecemeal approach to water issues and the incoherent and incomplete character of the existing legislation. It recommended the adoption of an official policy for freshwater, wetlands, and aquatic ecosystems as well as the drafting of an outline for a water charter, which would clarify the legal status of water and constitute the Law of water. This would be done through a revision and consolidation of previous dispositions dealing with water, which are presently found in various pieces of legislation. The Beauchamp Commission also recommended the adoption of a separate integrated decision-making and water management process for the watershed of each major watercourse. The government that set up the inquiry started to implement the recommendations of the Beauchamp Report in 2002 by publishing an official policy (la Politique nationale de l'eau[4]) based on the explicit recognition that water, whether surface or under ground, is a *res communis*. It also adopted a statute creating a segregated fund to provide the financial resources to implement the policy.[5] However, the government of the Parti Quebecois was defeated in the 2003 provincial election that brought to power the Quebec Liberal Party, intent on transforming the style of government and reviewing all of its programs. Although the new government officially endorsed the Politique nationale de l'eau, it has not shown the same interest in proceeding with its implementation. Therefore, since the previous piecemeal legislative approach remains unchanged, it is more appropriate to consider the regime applicable to freshwater under the Code civil du Quebec.

The Legal Concept of *Res Communis*

Article 913, para.l, of the present Civil code of Quebec (C.c.Q.), as did article 585 of the previous Civil code of Lower Canada (C.c.L.C.),[6] acknowledges that the notion of *res communis* is part of the law.[7] As a *res communis*, freshwater cannot be property. It cannot be appropriated or owned by anyone, either a private person or the State. As a *res communis*, water is intended for the general use of all. Ownership of land does not carry with it a right of ownership of the water that runs through the land or underground. The treatment the law reserves for water is different from the legal regime applicable to the minerals found underground and to animals in the wild. Minerals are, in principle, owned by the owner of the land, although they may be the object of an exclusive right, distinct from ownership of the land, which may be attributed to another. The Province has, in fact, retained extensive mineral rights under land transferred in ownership to private persons.[8] Wild animals and aquatic fauna are susceptible to ownership, although they are *res nullius* until they are captured.[9]

In the examination of the legal regime applicable to water, it is useful to consider separately the different uses that may be made of lakes and rivers as watercourses and the use of water itself. In addition, an accurate understanding of Quebec Law requires that the nature of the right of ownership be taken into account. In 1854,[10] Quebec abolished the tenure system under which land was initially granted to individuals. Estates in land were replaced by a full title based on the Roman law model of the dominium. The owner of private land in Quebec has therefore the ultimate title. No eminent or overriding domain remains with the State as regards land owned by private persons in the Province. Neither the State's power to expropriate land nor its power to regulate its use derives from any title in the land, but rather from its mission as public authority to ensure the peaceful enjoyment of private property, public order, and the common good.[11]

Rights Pertaining to a Watercourse

Watercourses may be used for various purposes such as commercial transportation and recreational navigation, fishing, the removal of surface mineral substances from the river bed, the construction of wharves or other works, and the development of hydraulic power. Issues related to these activities were, until recently, the main object of legislation and litigation. In Canada, the constitution grants to the Federal Parliament exclusive powers to legislate over navigation and shipping.[12] Other uses are within the competence of the Provincial Legislatures. In Quebec, ownership of the bed of a watercourse carries certain ancillary rights—the right to fish, to incorporate a structure, to take gravel or sand from the banks, etc., subject however to environmental constraints. The same rule would apply to hydraulic power if this activity had not been reserved almost exclusively to Hydro-Quebec, a company whose sole shareholder is the provincial State.[13] Generally, the Province is the owner of the bed of navigable watercourses. It also owns the bed of non-navigable rivers or lakes unless the land bordering such watercourse was first transferred to a private person before 1918.[14] The bed of a watercourse extends to the high water mark. Private persons who do not own the bed of a river or a lake may nevertheless exercise the activities mentioned above if a permit has been issued to them under the appropriate statute. Various statutes provide for such permits.[15] Early court decisions dealing with the rights to the bed of a watercourse may have relied in some way on the concept of water as a *res communis*. However, upon further analysis, it becomes clear that the concept is not relevant in determining whether a private person may lawfully exercise ancillary rights attached to the bed of a river.

The Legal Status of Water Itself

The characterization of water as *res communis* is stated in general terms in the Civil Code. The courts have had the opportunity to confirm authoritatively that the water of a lake or a river is a *res communis*, regardless of its status as a navigable or non-navigable watercourse.[16] The situation is somewhat different with respect to groundwater and water that springs naturally above ground. Their characterization is a matter of controversy. Some are of the view that the status of *res communis* applies only to surface running water and not to groundwater and water from a spring that is not the head of a watercourse. This would imply that they can be appropriated. According to this view, it follows that groundwater and water from a spring are, in law, owned by the owner of the land above which such water is found. The debate has not yet been brought directly before the courts.

The point of view that attributes a different legal status to water depending on where it appears in nature relies primarily on the text of the Code stating that the owner of land may use and dispose of a spring on his land.[17] It infers ownership from what may effectively be the exclusive use of a spring or body of water since no one other than the owner of the land can legally gain access to it. However, the text of the Code can be read simply as the recognition by law that, in the particular situation of a spring, general access to the *res communis* cannot be allowed without destroying the owner's exclusive right to the land. When the owner of the land alone has access to a spring, the water remains a *res communis* to be used to satisfy his needs, even though his use may consume it entirely.[18] The interpretation that reconciles the exclusive use of a spring with the notion of *res communis* is strengthened by the argument that the distinction between surface and groundwater being put forward is outdated and contradicted by current scientific knowledge. Today's hydrological knowledge amply establishes that the physical state of water does not support the establishment of a legal distinction between water on the surface and groundwater or spring water. Since there is continuity in nature between surface water and groundwater, water must receive a single legal characterization in the absence of a clear contrary provision. It is unlikely that judges would entertain an artificial distinction where scientific expertise points to a different conclusion.[19]

The Debate over Water as a *Res Communis*

The recognition that water, as a *res communis*, forms, with air, a distinct legal category firmly establishes the authority of the State to act as custodian of the resource in the common interest of present and future generations. The State is empowered to put in place appropriate measures for the preservation of the quality and the quantity of water, the determination of the legitimate uses that can be made of the *res communis* and of the best structure to provide for the management of the resource. Since 1972, Quebec has addressed most of the problems of air, water, and soil pollution in a particular statute.[20] As a consequence a significant reduction in pollution originating from municipal, domestic, and industrial sources has been achieved. Today, the main source of water pollution that remains to be controlled is agriculture. Raising the standards of agricultural practices is a political and an economic issue, since effective measures of preservation of water quality increase the costs to the producer and the consumer.

The concept of *res communis* implies that the object so classified is reserved for the common use of everyone. This general principle, independent of rights of ownership, acknowledges that whatever the modes of distribution in place in the province, its residents must all have sufficient access to this vital resource. In addition the concept must be further clarified with respect to the uses that may legitimately be made of water. These two sets of questions about public access and legitimate uses are identified as strategic in the 2000 report of the Commission sur la gestion de l'eau. They were directly or indirectly the object of most testimony before the Commission and of reports submitted to it. We have noted earlier that municipalities generally own and operate the waterworks that distribute water to their inhabitants. The concerns expressed in this respect relate to the improvements to be made to municipal infrastructure and services and whether to maintain public control. The determination of what uses are acceptable and how to resolve conflicts between users awaits consideration. There is some urgency in addressing these issues as they are currently causing confrontations between the population of certain rural areas and commercial interests.[21] The Government has been hesitant, appearing to pursue conflicting objectives. It is clearly tempted by a joint Public/Private ownership of water infrastructures, and legislation has been enacted to permit municipalities to adopt this model.

What uses of water may be considered normal or legitimate within the meaning of a *res communis*? Traditionally, the legitimate uses of water are firstly those that satisfy human needs, including alimentary and sanitary requirements. These needs, which ought to take precedence, are met, in most urban areas, by the public waterworks tapping surface or groundwater. Those who do not have access to a municipal aqueduct may draw directly from a body of surface water or from underground sources. Water is also taken for agricultural purposes. The legitimacy of this use is not questioned, although modern industrial agriculture and the growing practice of irrigation for crops create a new context to be taken into account. The use of water in industrial processes is also legitimate but should not have priority over agriculture. The three sets of uses so far identified share the feature of not permanently removing substantial quantities of water from the hydrographic basin of origin. Certain activities such as intensive pig production and irrigation of crops and fruit trees may be a source of conflict because they alter the quality of the water in the area where they are located or because they require such large quantities of water. As was advocated in the Beauchamp Report, an order of priority between legitimate uses and a mechanism to resolve conflicts between users need to be established to complement the concept of *res communis*. Ultimately, when the quantity of available renewable freshwater cannot meet all legitimate demands, the approach of governance by watershed should be adopted in order for the choice of preferred activities to be made locally, by the representatives of the inhabitants in each hydrographic basin.

Successive Quebec governments have professed to adhere to the principle that water is a *res communis*. However, the public administration's actions are not always consistent with that affirmation, and are sometimes plainly in contradiction with it. For a few decades, the Province has condoned a practice that is in direct conflict with the concept of *res communis*: commercial water bottling. A regulation adopted pursuant to the Environmental Quality Act sets the procedure to be followed for the capture of groundwater for human consumption with the stated objectives of promoting its protection, preventing the withdrawal of excessive quantities, and minimizing the negative impact of catchments on watercourses and bodies of water on persons entitled to use them and on the ecosystem.[22] The legislative intent thus enunciated appears to coincide with the notion that water is a *res communis* and to recognize the natural connection between surface water and groundwater. Besides setting norms applicable to all extraction to ensure that the water withdrawn is safe for human consumption, the Regulation submits projects intended to supply more than twenty persons and those of a capacity of seventy-five cubic meters or more to a specific authorization by the Minister of Environment. Among the projects requiring such authorization are "groundwater catchment projects intended to be distributed or sold as spring water or mineral water."[23]

In a number of cases, commercial projects have been authorized under the Regulation. As a general rule, a *res communis* can neither be owned nor sold as a good. The bottling of freshwater would be compatible with water's *res communis* status if it were set up as a publicly owned alternative way of providing water to the general population. However, the water bottling operations presently in business cannot be justified on that basis. They are strictly commercial ventures and constitute an activity that contradicts the current legal definition of water. The sale of bottled water for profit is not a legitimate use of a *res communis*. On the contrary, it supposes that the operator has ownership of the water sold. Such a right could have only one of two grounds: either ownership of the water is acquired by the sole action of appropriating it, the mode of acquisition of a *res nullius*, or it is derived from ownership of the land, that is to say, acquired by accession.[24] Neither of these modes of acquiring ownership applies to a *res communis*. The public authority's position must be viewed for what it is: the satisfaction by the government of the commercial objectives of major players in the water business.

Such activities have a number of negative consequences besides being illegal. The water bottled and sold on the open market is irretrievably lost to the hydrographic basin of origin. Secondly, the bottling activities, which are presently carried out mostly in the populated part of the province, are prejudicial to the other owners of land who use the same body of water. The hydrogeological impact studies on users and on the environment, required by the regulation, are more and more frequently criticized, both for the manner in which they are conducted and for the reliability of their conclusions.[25] One may also question the equitability of a governmental practice that gives one landowner authority to make a profit from the commercialization of groundwater, but cannot grant the same authority to all neighboring landowners, even if they have an equal claim to it, without unduly depleting the resource.

Another instance of government inconsistency is the Water Resources Preservation Act, which prohibits the transfer outside of Quebec of surface water or groundwater taken in Quebec, unless it is packaged in containers of twenty liters or less.[26] In formulating its official water policy in 2002, the Government had identified this Act as one of the measures introduced in conformity with the idea that water is common to all Quebeckers.[27] It is strange that water should lose its status as a *res communis* and be freely exported, provided it is placed in small containers!

Conclusion

The recent public inquiry has shown that in Quebec a significant portion of the population is ahead of its government in understanding the necessity of preserving freshwater resources. The traditional concept of *res communis* is an optimal legal tool to achieve that goal. However, it needs to be further articulated in legislation and adapted to present circumstances. If it is accepted that water is not owned by anyone and that, in nature, there are no real surpluses of water, then the indispensable role of water in sustaining other forms of life is more likely to be taken into account when deciding which practices to allow and which developments to pursue.

Notes

1. The editors gratefully acknowledge permission to reprint "The legal status of water in Quebec," which originally appeared in *Quebec Studies* 42 (2007): 7–15.

2. Commission d'etudes des problemes juridiques de l'eau, whose reports were published in 1975.

3. L'eau, ressource a proteger, a partager et a mettre en valeur, also referred to as Rapport Beauchamp, Bureau des audiences publiques sur l'environnement (or BAPE), 2 vols. (Quebec, 2000). For a description of the situation in Canada generally, see David R. Boyd, *Unnatural law: rethinking Canadian environmental law and policy.* (Vancouver: U British Columbia P, 2003) 13–63.

4. L'eau, La vie, L'avenir (Quebec: Bibliotheque nationale du Quebec, 2002).

5. An Act to establish the Fonds national de l'eau, Revised Statutes of Quebec, chapter F-4.002. Section 1 describes the object of the fund as follows: "The fund shall be dedicated to the financing of measures taken by the Minister of the Environment to ensure water governance and in particular, to the financing of measures conductive to the protection and development of water resources and to ensuring a

sufficient quality and quantity of water in a perspective of sustainable development."
Quebec Statutes and Regulations are accessible on the Web at www.publicationsdu
Quebec.gouv.qc.ca/accueil.en.

6. The Civil Code of Quebec replaced the Civil Code of Lower Canada in
1994.

7. Article 913 C.c.Q. reads: "Certain things may not be appropriated; their use,
common to all, is governed by general laws and, in certain respects, by this Code.
However, water and air not intended for public utility may be appropriated if
collected and placed in receptacles." Former Article 585 C.c.L.C. read: "There are
things which have no owner and the use of which is common to all. The enjoyment
of these is regulated by laws of public policy."

8. See section 1 of the Mining Act, Revised Statutes of Quebec, Chapter
M-13.1, which excludes water from its definition of mineral substances.

9. The relevant texts of the code, articles 914, 934 and 935, read as follows: 914:
Certain other things, being without an owner, are not the object of any right, but
may nevertheless be appropriated by occupation if the person taking them does so
with the intention of becoming their owner. 934: Things without an owner are
things belonging to no one, such as animals in the wild, or formerly in captivity but
returned to the wild, and aquatic fauna, and things abandoned by their owner. . . .
935: A movable without an owner belongs to the person who appropriates it for
himself by occupation.

10. An Act respecting the General Abolition of Feudal Rights and Duties, (also
called the Seigneurial Act), 18 Victoria, chapter 3.

11. Article 952 C.c.Q. dictates: "No owner may be compelled to transfer his
ownership except by expropriation according to law for public utility and in consideration of a just and prior indemnity." Private property is also protected in the Charter of Human Rights and Freedoms, Revised Statutes of Quebec, chapter C-12, section 6.

12. Constitution Act, 1867, section 91, paragraph 10.

13. Hydro-Quebec Act, Revised Statutes of Quebec, chapter H-5. and Watercourses Act, Revised Statutes of Quebec, chapter R-13, section 3.

14. See article 919 C.c.Q.

15. The Watercourses Act, Revised Statutes of Quebec, chapter R-13; An Act respecting Agricultural Lands of the Domain of the State, Revised Statute of Quebec,
chapter T-7.1; An Act respecting the Lands in the Domain of the State, Revised
Statute of Quebec, chapter T-8.1 and the Mining Act, above note 2, are the main
pieces of legislation under which rights in State Land are granted to private persons.

16. See the most recent decision at *Morin v. Morin*, (1998) Recueil de jusrispru-
dence du Quebec 23, judgment of the Court of Appeal.

17. Article 980 C.c.Q. reads as follows: "An owner who has a spring on his land
may use it and dispose of it. He may, for his needs, use water from the lakes and ponds
that are entirely on his land, taking care to preserve their quality."

18. The quantity of water provided by a spring is, by inference, limited, the
spring which is the headwater of a watercourse being treated as such in article 981
C.c.Q. Its status as a common thing is not questioned. See also article 982 C.c.Q.

19. For a more complete argument against a double characterization of freshwater, see our submission prepared for the 1999 Commission sur la gestion de l'eau which is substantially reproduced in Madeleine Cantin Cumyn, Michelle Cumyn, and Claire Skrinda, "L'eau, chose commune: un statut juridique a confirmer," *Canadian Bar Review* 398 (2000).

20. Environmental Quality Act, Revised Statutes of Quebec, chapter Q-2. The first statute is found in the Statutes of Quebec, 1972, chapter 49. It is noteworthy that the Act does not distinguish between surface water and groundwater: see section 1.1.

21. See the 2000 Rapport Beauchamp cited in footnote 2, in particular volume 1, pages 16 to 23.

22. See the Groundwater Catchment Regulation, Chapter Q-2, r.1.3, in particular section 1.

23. Section 31 of the same regulation.

24. Section 32 of the regulation requires that the application for an authorization contain the titles of ownership of lots located within a thirty meters radius from the intended site of catchment.

25. See the 2000 Rapport Beauchamp, cited in footnote 2, volume 1, p. 18.

26. Statutes of Quebec 1999, chapter 63 as amended by Statutes of Quebec 2001, Chapter 48.

27. L'eau, La vie, L'avenir, cited in footnote 3, p. 83.

Chapter 17

The Rebirth of Environmentalism as Pragmatic, Adaptive Management[1]

Bryan G. Norton

We conservationists . . . have many ideas as to what needs to be done, and these ideas quite naturally conflict. We are in danger of pounding the table about them, instead of going out on the land and giving them a trial. The only really new thing which this game policy suggests is that we quit arguing over abstract ideas, and instead go out and try them.

—Aldo Leopold from *A Sand County Almanac and Sketches Here and There*, 1949.[2]

The cowman who cleans his range of wolves does not realize that he is taking over the wolf's job of trimming the herd to fit the range. He has not learned to think like a mountain. Hence we have dust bowls, and rivers washing the future into the sea.

—Aldo Leopold from *The American Game Policy in a Nutshell*, 1930.[3]

Introduction: The Rhetorical Legacy of Early Conservation and the Age of Ideology

If you have visited an environmental website lately—practically ANY environmental website, that is—you are well aware that we are gathered here, at best, for a memorial service. The death of environmentalism has been announced, the obits have been written and published on websites and in print—environmentalism's wake has been held. An odd wake it was, as some celebrated the life of the movement, or even protested that the reports were exaggerated, even as the Limbaughs and the right-wing bloggers celebrated its proclaimed death. According to Shellenberger and Nordhaus, those of us who are here to discuss environmentalism and its future are just family members who continue for awhile to speak in the present tense of their lost loved one.[4] All that remains for environmental pundits like us, apparently, is to turn to history and try to understand how a once-rich and powerful movement could go moribund, even as our environment suffers insult after insult before our eyes.

In this essay, I offer an alternative account of this death by re-identifying the corpse, and by telling a story whereby death sets the stage for rebirth in the form of a new generation of environmental thinking, what I am calling the "Age of Adaptive Management," and for a new way of talking about and thinking about "environmental" problems and the values they threaten. What died, I hope, is not the sentiment that favors protecting our natural landmarks, biological diversity, and systems productive of vital resources. No, what ended was not the life of the environmental viewpoint or activity of committed environmentalists. What died was what I call the "Age of Ideology" in environmentalism. My purpose is to sketch the broad outlines of the new Age, by celebrating the rebirth of environmental concern as a commitment to learning by doing. . . .

I will begin my sketch of adaptive management by emphasizing one important aspect of the thoughts and actions of Aldo Leopold—his pragmatic commitment to experimentalism in management. I believe that Leopold was the first adaptive manager—that he identified and developed the essentials of a post-ideological approach, guided by Darwinian analogies, to environmental decision making and management, even though the phrase, "adaptive management," was invented decades later by C. S. Holling. By emphasizing this aspect of Leopold's thought—which involves (1) a temporally sensitive, multiscalar interpretation of Thinking Like a Mountain, and (2) Leopold's activism and experimentalism, I believe I can demonstrate that Leopold deserves, despite the tardiness of the label, to be called the "first adaptive manager." . . .

Here, in Part II, I will summarize my reasons for thinking that ideological environmentalism, and the value theories that support the polarized ideologies essential to it, are bankrupt; I hope they are also dead. Then, in Part III, I will take a look at the bigger picture in resource evaluation, challenging the reader to question the usual assumptions about the nature of environmental problems, arguing that a pluralistic understanding of environmental values is more realistic, and also more functional. In Part IV, I present an overview of the approach to adaptive management that emerges if one rejects positivist science and if one rejects, simultaneously, the ideological commitments to *a priori* ontological positions about the nature of environmental value. Once a pluralistic value system is articulated, and problem formulation is freed from dogmatism about the one right way to characterize environmental value, it is possible to formulate environmental problems so that we can move toward cooperation and compromise.

II. Ideology in Environmental Ethics and Environmental Economics

Environmental ethics and environmental economics, at least insofar as we understand them as sub-disciplines of philosophy/ethics and of mainstream economics, emerged in the 1970s as academic sub-fields devoted to understanding the ethical and economic relationships between the human and nonhuman worlds.[5] What emerged, however, was that these subfields came to embody the rhetorical positions of Muir and Pinchot as practitioners embraced assumptions and commitments exemplified by the ideological thinking just mentioned. The two disciplines have followed Muir and Pinchot into the same blinding rhetoric: humans and nature are in a struggle; Pinchot opted to protect and enrich humans, with regard only for sustaining consumption,[6] while Muir threatened to sign up on the side of the bears in the war of humans against nature.[7] In this section, I will caricature the two ideological approaches to environmental value, briefly surveying where the ongoing battle between environmental ethicists and environmental economists stands today.

Most writing on environmental ethics concerns the dichotomy between humans and nonhumans, and much of the work in the field has been motivated by the effort to escape "anthropocentrism" with respect to environmental values. Resulting debates about whether to extend "moral considerability" to various elements of nonhuman nature have been inconclusive, to say the least, and writings in this vein have had no discernible impact on the development of sustainability theory or on public policy more generally.[8] Discussions in the field of environmental ethics, which emerged as a separate sub-field of ethics in the early 1970s, have thus turned on defining and explaining key dichotomies.[9] This trend originated with the 1967 publication by the historian Lynn White, Jr., of an influential essay, The Historical Roots of Our Ecologic Crisis.[10] White declared that Christianity "is the most anthropocentric religion the world has seen," setting the stage for a spate of responses by ethicists who questioned the longstanding ethical divide between humans and nonhumans.[11] Environmental ethicists have, accordingly, focused on the dualisms of Modernism: humans vs. nonhumans, moral exclusivism (the view that all and only humans have intrinsic value), and the underlying dichotomy between matter and spirit.[12] From 1970 until the early 1990s, these dichotomous formulations dominated environmental ethics because the question of where to draw the line between those beings that are morally considerable and those that are morally irrelevant seemed so seminal a question that the field could not proceed without some resolution of it, and yet discussions of "intrinsic" or "inherent" value shed little light on practical questions about what to do.

Worse, emphasis on these dichotomies created an unresolvable conflict with environmental economists, blocking any integration of philosophical and economic discourse.[13] Because economists insist that all values are values of human beings (consumers), they are in ontological disagreement with environmental ethicists, who wish to shift the line of moral consideration to include nonhumans and their interests. It is difficult to see what would resolve this disagreement. . . .

By the 1990s, a few philosophers began to see that this unfortunate stalemate between economic approaches and environmental philosophy rested mainly on ideological commitments and a priori theories, theories that for non-empirical reasons attempt to force all environmental value into a single valuational currency. As noted above, no empirical evidence can be brought to bear upon whether nature has intrinsic value, and commitments to valuing objects as consumable items with a price are likewise based on a priori assumptions. Worse, the categorical nature of the debate has encouraged all-or-nothing answers to complex management problems and a conceptual polarization that leads to direct oppositions and an inability to frame questions as open to compromise.

If one instead adopts pluralism, accepting the fact that humans value nature in many ways, and considers these values to range along a continuum from purely selfish uses to spiritual and less instrumental uses, it is unclear—and not really very important—where to "separate" value into "human" and "nonhuman."[14] If we think of natural objects as having many kinds of value, arguments about why we should protect nature slide into the background and the focus moves to protecting as many of the values of nature as possible for the longest time that is foreseeable. Leopold, Rachel Carson, and all of the great second-generation conservationists have believed that protecting nature is protecting the future of mankind, and that protecting the future requires protecting nature. By defining humans as ecological beings, it was obvious to them that the destruction of nature would be the destruction of humans. Conservationists have always seen the values of protection of nature as additive; Muir, in choosing to fight on the side of the bears, of course believed that the humility enforced by a victory of the bears would also be just the right prescription for human arrogance. From Muir to Leopold to adaptive managers, what has been constant is a commitment to a convergence on a set of policies that would serve both the goals of saving humankind in the long run, and of saving present elements and processes of the natural world. Of course there will be disagreements about priorities and immediate objectives, but if policies are devised to protect as much of nature as possible for the use and enjoyment of humans for as long into the future as possible, then it is perhaps not crucial whether those values preserved are counted in one theoretical framework or another. Remaining disagreements are more likely to be formulated as testable hypotheses about possible effects of actions, or as disagreements about priorities in the expenditure of resources to pursue various goals. Unlike ideological and ontological disagreements, these latter disagreements are open to test or to negotiation.

The viewpoint advanced here is referred to as environmental pragmatism, which is a philosophy of environmental action that begins with real-world problems, not with abstract, theory-dependent questions regarding what kind of value nature has.[15] Environmental pragmatism bypasses the theoretically grounded questions of environmental ethics and focuses on learning our way out of uncertainty in particular situations. Adaptive management is social learning; and pragmatism provides an epistemology adequate to support social learning through experimental adaptation.

Further, pragmatism complements the search for sustainable development because it is a forward-looking philosophy, defining truth as that which will prevail within the community of inquirers in the long run. This feature makes it a natural complement to the theory of sustainable development and acts as the unifying thread in the justification of preservation efforts at all scales. This forward-looking sense of responsibility and commitment to learning our way to sustainability can be thought of as pragmatism's contribution to the theory of sustainable development.[16]

In the remainder of this essay, I will propose one approach to a new environmental philosophy, a philosophy that is more geared to learning to live sustainably than in defining what kind of good nature has. This philosophy emphasizes social learning and community adaptation, and it derives its method more from the epistemology of pragmatism than from theoretical ethics.

III. Adaptive Management

Adaptive management, which can be understood as a search for a locally anchored conception of sustainability and sustainable management, sets out to use science and social learning as tools to achieve cooperation in the pursuit of management goals.[17]

Three characteristics can be taken to define a process of adaptive management:

1. *Experimentalism*: Adaptive managers respond to uncertainty by undertaking reversible actions and studying outcomes to reduce uncertainty at the next decision point.

2. *Multi-scalar Modeling*: Adaptive managers model environmental problems within multi-scaled ("hierarchical") space–time systems.

3. *Place-Orientation*: Adaptive managers address environmental problems from a "place," which means problems are embedded in a local context of natural systems but also of political forces.

By profession, most adaptive managers are ecologists and most discussions to date have emphasized learning our way out of scientific uncertainty; these ecologists have paid less attention to developing appropriate processes for evaluating environmental change and for setting intelligent goals for environmental management. I incorporate the ideas of these ecologists and expand them to include learning about social values as an integral part of the adaptive management process.

The adaptive management approach that I wish to defend rests on three intellectual pillars.

A Commitment to a Unified Method: Naturalism

Attempts to separate factual from value content in the process of deliberation are rejected; there is only one method for evaluating human assertions, including assertions with all kinds of mixes of descriptive and prescriptive content, and that is the method of experience—active experimentation when possible, but careful observation otherwise. The scientific method is embraced as the best approach to evaluating hypotheses about cause and effect, but it is also considered the best way to evaluate hypotheses about what is valuable to individuals and cultures.

A more realistic—and less theory-driven—view of the relation between factual and evaluative discourse is advocated by B. A. O. Williams, who argued persuasively that, in ordinary discourse, fact-discourse and value-discourse are inseparable; when philosophers separate them, they do so on the basis of a specialized theory, such as logical positivism.[18] To insist on partitioning policy discourse into fact-discourse (positivistic science) and value-discourse is to artificialize the public discourse in which policy must be discussed. There is an alternative, of course. Following pragmatists such as C. S. Peirce and John Dewey, one can advocate a pragmatic epistemology for environmental science and policy discourse, a discourse conducted so as to maximize social learning among participants.[19] This epistemology insists upon a single method—the method of experience—and this method applies equally to factual claims and to evaluative ones. Following Dewey, assertions that something or some process is valued are taken as a hypothesis that the thing or process is valuable. Pursuing that value, and acting upon associated values, provides communities with experience that can support or undermine the claim that the thing or process is indeed valuable.

So, rejecting non-naturalism, the first pillar of my proposed approach is a form of methodological naturalism. This method, while not expecting deductions from facts to values, relies on the open-ended, public process of challenging beliefs and values with contrary experience. From these challenges, we expect attitudes, values, and beliefs to change—but the changes cannot be justified by deductive arguments flowing one way from facts to values. The changes needed to support a new conservation consciousness are usually reorganizations and re-conceptualizations of facts, not deductions from value-neutral facts. The specific means by which assertions of value are connected will be through the development and refinement of measurable indicators that reflect values articulated by the stakeholders who represent multiple positions within the community. Pluralism is operationalized in process as communities participate in choosing multiple indicators, as will be discussed in the next two sections.

An Emphasis on Process

The term "methodological naturalism" describes the form of naturalism I adopt because it replaces abstract principles of right and good, which are thought by some naturalists to be derivable from observation of nature, with an emphasis on a process of deliberation and learning. Process-oriented approaches are not burdened with the need to defend a general principle that is to be applied to particular cases; process approaches emphasize the way problems get formulated and addressed across time by participants in public discourse, and provide heuristic guidance to encourage the asking of the right questions. The process approach, to put it in the terms of decision science—while it may make use of optimizing models as part of simulations or broader inquiries— does not seek optimal outcomes or expect real-world problems to be "solved" by algorithms. It seeks, rather, to improve the "rationality" of the process. Here, however, rationality does not refer to computational "solutions" to optimization problems, but to heuristic attempts to make the management process more open, and to make the process one that is conducive to cooperative action. In my book, I endorse a way of talking about how to accomplish such improvements—called "social learning" by Dewey—that relies heavily upon the work of Jurgen Habermas and his work on "communicative ethics." While time does not permit a full discussion of this endorsement here, its mention may give some idea of the kind of discourse and decision processes that might be favored.

Having forsaken the hopeless goal of algorithmic solutions to complex problems, pragmatists and adaptive managers analyze processes and offer heuristics to help communities—in as democratic and open a process as possible—remain focused on the right questions, the questions that will lead to plans to protect their place and the values it embodies in their own culture.

A New Approach to Scaling and Environmental Problems

Building on this Empirical Hypothesis, scalar choices in modeling environmental problems, if made a topic for open public discussion, might provide insight into the temporal and spatial "horizons" over which impacts will be measured and processes of change monitored. In policy, they direct the formation of effective administrative strategies for addressing problems; scientifically, careful attention to the dimensions and models developed in response to environmental problems might clarify problem formulation and illuminate public discourse. . . .

IV. Scaling and Environmental Problem Formulation

Environmental disputes are so problematic, among other reasons, because it is so difficult to provide a definitive problem formulation. This feature was explained well by Rittel and Webber, who distinguished "benign" and "wicked" problems.[20] Benign problems, they said, have determinate answers, and when the solution is found the problem is uncontroversially "solved."[21] Mathematics and some areas of science exemplify benign problems. Wicked problems, on the other hand, resist unified problem formulation because of controversy regarding what models to use and what data are important. Rittel and Webber suggest that wicked problems, because they are perceived differently by different interest groups with different values and goals, have no determinate solution because there is no agreement on the problem formulation.[22] They can be "resolved" by finding a temporary balance among competing interests and social goals, but as the situation changes, the problem changes and becomes more open-ended. Rittel and Webber explicitly mention that wicked problems have a way of coming back in new forms; as society addresses one symptom or set of symptoms, new symptoms appear, sometimes as unintended effects of treatments of the original problem.

Most environmental problems are wicked problems; they affect multiple values, and they impact different elements of the community differently, encouraging the development of multiple models of understanding and remedy. Resistance to unified problem formulation is endemic to wicked problems; they require iterative negotiations to find even temporary resolutions and agreements on actions. Another aspect of wicked problems—the temporal open-endedness which often attends wicked problems and brings them back in more virulent form as larger and larger systems are affected—may be susceptible to clarification through modeling. Ecologists have introduced "hierarchy theory" (HT) as a set of conventions to clarify space–time relations in complex systems.[23] HT can be characterized by two axioms (which happen to coincide with the second and third key characteristics of Adaptive Management listed in the Introduction). HT encompasses a set of models of ecological systems that are characterized by two constraints on observer and system behavior: (i) The system is conceived as composed of nested subsystems, such that any subsystem is smaller (by at least one order of magnitude) than the system of which it is a component, and (ii) all observations of the system are taken from a particular perspective within the physical hierarchy. A major addition, encouraged by environmental pragmatism, is to expand (ii) to (ii'): all observations and evaluations orient from a particular perspective within the physical hierarchy. An effect of this innovation is to make environmental values, evaluation, and social learning about values endogenous to the broader, adaptive management process.

This conceptual apparatus allows us to see human decision makers as located within layered subsystems and super-systems, with the smallest subsystems being the fastest-changing, and the larger systems changing more slowly, providing environments for the subsystems. Each individual person represents a small system that makes choices against the backdrop of a larger environment. These larger, slower-changing systems provide the environment for adaptation by subsystems (including organisms and places—composed of individuals and cultures). This convention allows us to associate temporal "horizons" with changing features of landscapes, as is illustrated in the famous metaphor used by Aldo Leopold, the forester and wildlife manager. Leopold set out to remove predators from the Forest Service ranges he managed in the southwestern United States. When the deer starved for lack of browse, he regretted his decision to extirpate wolves, chiding himself for not yet having learned to "think like a mountain."[24] He had not yet understood the role of the targeted species in the broader system. When he came to understand that role, he accepted responsibilities for the long-term consequences of his decisions and advocated wolf protection in wilderness areas.

Leopold intended to improve the lot of human consumers of nature's bounty—but his activity threatened larger-scale dynamics. Thinking like a mountain—or a watershed—requires accepting responsibility for the impacts one's decisions will have on subsequent generations. Accepting this responsibility is inseparable from adopting a larger ecophysical model of the system under management. At this point in time, armed with some knowledge of changing systems and how to model them, we begin to accept moral responsibility for actions that were once thought to be morally neutral. In both cases, accepting moral responsibility—and a sense of caring—were inseparable from adopting a changing causal model of what has happened to deer populations on Leopold's metaphoric mountain.

Using this framework of actions embedded within nested, hierarchical systems, it is possible to articulate a new approach to evaluating changes in human-dominated systems. Human management of the environment takes place within environmental systems as they are embedded in larger and larger—and progressively slower changing—super-systems. Each generation is concerned for its short-term well-being (personal survival economics), but also must be concerned to leave a viable range of choices for subsequent generations. Given our expanding knowledge of our impacts on the larger and normally slower-changing systems that form our environment, it seems reasonable also to accept responsibility for activities that can change the range of choices that will be open to posterity.

A concept of sustainability nicely "falls out" from this conception of adaptive management, in that a "schematic definition" of sustainability can be constructed on the axioms of adaptive management, provided only that prior generations accept responsibility for their impacts on the choice sets of subsequent generations. Given this rather sparse set of assumptions and hypothetical premises, it is possible to provide a simple and elegant definition of sustainability, or rather what might better be called a schema for sustainability definitions.[25] Because of the place-based

emphasis of adaptive management and the recognition of pervasive uncertainty, there is only so much that one can say about what is sustainable
at the very general level of a universal definition. Speaking at this level of
general theory, sustainability is best thought of as a cluster of variables; local communities can fill in the blanks, so to speak, to form a set of criteria
and goals that reflect their needs and values. While local determination
must play a key role in the details, adaptive management, and its associated definitional schema, makes evident the structure and internal relationships that are essential to more specific, locally applicable definitions
of sustainable policies. . . .

From this simple framework, a schematic definition of sustainability
emerges: individuals in earlier generations alter their environment, using
up some resources, leaving others. If all individuals in the earlier generations over-consume, and if they do not create new opportunities, then
they will have changed the environment that subsequent generations encounter, making survival more difficult. A set of behaviors is thus understood as sustainable if and only if its practice in generation m will not reduce the ratio of opportunities to constraints that will be encountered by
individuals in subsequent generations n, o, p.

Although the model has a "flat," schematic character, it could also be
given a richer, normative-moral interpretation, as is hinted at by use of
the terms *opportunities* and *constraints*. If we stipulate that the actors are
human individuals, then the simple model provides a representation of
intergenerational impacts of decisions regarding resources; our little
model can thus be enriched to allow a normative interpretation or analogue. If we accept that having a range of choices is good for free human
individuals, we can see the structure, in skeletal form, of the normative
theory of sustainability. An action or a policy is not sustainable if it will
reduce the ratio of opportunities to constraints in the choice sets of future people.

Each generation stands in this asymmetric relationship to subsequent
ones: choices made today could, in principle, reduce the range of free
choices available to subsequent generations. Thus, it makes sense to recognize impacts that play out on multiple, distinct scales. If it is agreed that
maintaining a constant or expanding set of choices for the future is good,
and that imposing crushing constraints on future people is bad, our little

model has the potential to represent, and relate to each other, the short- and long-term impacts of choice *and* to allow either a physical, descriptive interpretation or a normative one. . . .

V. Multiscalar Evaluation: An Adaptive Approach

Armed with this schematic definition and an associated conception of sustainability goal-setting as communities defining the variables—the indicators—that really matter to them as residents of a place, we can move boldly to introduce a new approach to evaluating environmental change. Rather than "chunking" nature and aggregating it into entities that are "commodities" and other entities that have intrinsic value and are "consumers," I suggest we set out to evaluate *development pathways*—which are possible paths that development and change can follow in a place. These pathways can then be evaluated *according to multiple indicators*—which are variables judged important enough to monitor in the process of adaptive management. Adaptive management, and public participation in its discourse, can thus provide a forum for discussion and revision of management goals. Accordingly, its discourse and deliberations must be normative as well as descriptive in nature. Public values will be embedded in the discussion, as arguments are made, compromise policies are forged, and participants try to influence policies by placing emphasis on one indicator or another. Once important variables are identified for monitoring, public discourse can address questions of priorities: which of the indicators is highest priority? Monitored variables would then represent social values indirectly, as easily measurable indicators are chosen and priorities are set.

In this way, values can be integrated into a rational decision process without being measured as increments in consumption or welfare associated with a particular chunk of nature, human or otherwise. Evaluation will be by multiple measurable indicators,[26] possibly including economic indicators, but applied holistically to paths of system change rather than as increments to an aggregated sum of utilities of individuals. Since these indicators measure trends in processes believed important by the community that inhabits a place, they allow the comparison of various possible futures according to a variety of value-laden yardsticks. Public debate about values would then shift away from its currently ideological formulation, which causes discourse to get stuck on the question of whose well-being counts, and toward real public policy choices about which variables to monitor as indicators, which goals to set with respect to management performance with respect to those indicators, and how to weight and prioritize the various indicators that emerge from public discussion and stakeholder negotiations. These questions will ultimately come down to questions about how communities, acting through an adaptive management process, expend their resources on management projects. Every management initiative thus becomes an experiment to learn how to do something better—as measured against the list of indicators endorsed as expressing community goals—and goals as well as accumulated scientific wisdom can be reconsidered in the light of new experience. . . .

This discussion, I fear, has been rather abstract, even though the changes I envision would be very concrete and practical, transforming ideologically strained and fractured dialogue about local and regional problems into an active search for indicators that express the true aspirations of the communities that are integrated into their places. Perhaps I can give a little specificity, if not concreteness, to my proposal by sharing briefly with you a fantasy I have regarding the paths of growth that take place in the Atlanta region I inhabit. I call it a fantasy because, I fear, it could only happen if there were almost unimaginable changes in the way participants in public discourse approach disputes about environmental goals, actions, and regulations. Suppose, however, that there were to emerge in the Atlanta area a public process of deliberation and discourse aimed at setting rational goals for environmental management, and that that process might even take on some of the characteristics of Habermas's "ideal speech community": a process open to all, in which ideas and values are evaluated according to reasons given and challenges to those reasons are backed up with countervailing reasons.[27] If that were to happen, I hope there might emerge an open and public discussion about what really matters, and that that discussion would eventually shift into a discussion of how to measure what really matters—to the question, that is, of what indicators to track, and what goals to set with respect to the various, accepted indicators.

One of the problems with pluralism is that when one sets no constraints on what endpoints are valued, members of a community will express so many valued endpoints that careful measurement—or even adequate discussion of the various values—becomes impossible. Consequently, the adaptive management process must encourage a careful search for "integrative" measures that apply at various scales on the ecological system that encompasses Atlanta and its rapid Northward growth. By an integrative measure, I mean an indicator that focuses on a process that can be expected to track multiple variables that have been identified by the community as important values, that define a place, and make it "home" to the people who live there. So, if my imaginative "ideal speech community" were to emerge in the Atlanta area, I would inject into that process the following synoptic indicator: the percentage of land in the extended metropolitan area that remains permeable to water. I would justify the choice of this indicator because success in reducing pavement and other impermeable surfaces in the process of development can be easily tracked by Landsat satellite imagery, and it can be expected to be a stand-in as a proxy for a number of widely shared values held by residents. Atlanta is sometimes called "the city of trees," and one of the shared values is to maintain the sense of a "city in a forest." But this is just the beginning of connections between our proposed proxy and social values in the region: such a synoptic indicator would draw support from wildlife lovers, from those who are concerned about water quality and water quantity, as success in maintaining permeable surfaces reduces run-off and allows water to be cleaned as it percolates into the aquifer. In other words, uniting behind this indicator would allow the community, driven by diverse values, to express goals—and criticize various development plans as negatively impacting the synoptic indicator, and as threatening the values residents associate with their place.

To illustrate the multi-scalar possibilities of the adaptive management approach to evaluating environmental change, it is also possible to consider what might be chosen as a broader-scale indicator of landscape health, extending beyond the boundaries of the Atlanta metropolitan region to encompass the ecosystem of the Southern Appalachians and the Piedmont, which forms the broader context of the city's expansion. Here, I would suggest adopting an indicator that would measure the percentage of landcover in the area that remains in mixed hardwood forest, the dominant ecosystem type before development and before the creation of pine plantation tree farms. Again, this variable is easily tracked through satellite

imagery, and I submit that it can act as a proxy for the healthy and bal-
anced development of the area, standing in for a variety of deeply held
values that express the love many residents have for their place. This
larger-scaled variable complements the permeable surfaces criterion that
is applied locally, embedding that smaller-scale criterion in a broad commitment to protecting native forests wherever possible.

VI. Conclusion

I have argued that, following the death of ideology—which is what is really being proclaimed by critics of environmentalism—there might
emerge a New Age of Adaptive Management, an age in which the bat-
tles over environmental goals will be argued out within a management
structure that addresses real world problems through an experimental and
experience-based model of social learning through deliberation and
compromise. After the Age of Ideology is truly dead—I fear it is only in a
permanent vegetative state, and I hope we now have the courage to pull
the plug on the rhetoric of old—it is time to advance into an adaptive
age where we explore diverse values, and seek to protect as many of our
true values as possible. If we cultivate a common language of indicators
and measurable goals, our deliberations will turn to questions of how to
achieve as many management goals as available resources allow. All of
these questions, unlike the questions provoked by the ideologues, can be
explored and learned about, and there are more-or-less answers that can
lead to compromise and win–win situations.

The Age of Ideology in environmentalism, while historically understandable as the sprawling United States of America chose a development
path across the West in the 18th Century, must now come to an end. The
rich rhetoric of those halcyon days has dealt nothing but frustration to
the advocates of environmentalism in the Century since, and especially in
the last decade with the ascendancy of the Right and the enshrining of
the ideology of Free Markets, as every possible solution to a problem gets
entangled in arguments about its ideological purity. Badly formulated
questions are answered badly; hence the current mess in environmental
policy, as federal commitments whiplash back and forth between the reg-
ulators (Democrats and Liberals) and the free marketeers (Republicans
and Conservatives), who remove or refuse to enforce them. If the passing

of the Age of Ideology is necessary to make way for the Age of Adaptive Management, and the shifting of arguments from polarized and all-or-nothing to negotiable differences about goals, priorities, and how to expand resources—then I say, let it die. But let us replace ideological environmentalism with adaptive management, a search for communication and cooperation, and a thirst for social learning.

Notes

1. Originally published as: Bryan G. Norton, "The rebirth of environmentalism as pragmatic, adaptive management," *Virginia Environmental Law Journal*, 24(3) (2005) 353–376. Reprinted with permission. References to Norton cite his book, *Sustainability: A Philosophy of Adaptive Ecosystem Management* (University of Chicago Press 2005).

2. Aldo Leopold, *A Sand County Almanac and Sketches Here and There* 132 (Oxford Univ. Press 1987) (1949).

3. Aldo Leopold, *The Essential Aldo Leopold: Quotations and Commentaries* 210–11 (Curt Meine & Richard L. Knight eds., 1999).

4. Michael Shellenberger & Ted Nordhaus, The Death of Environmentalism, *Grist Magazine*, Jan. 13, 2005, available at http://www.grist.org/news/maindish/2005/01/13/doe-reprint/ (last visited Apr. 24, 2006).

5. Bryan Norton & Ben Minteer, From Environmental Ethics to Environmental Public Philosophy: Ethicists and Economists, 1973–Future, in *The International Yearbook of Environmental and Resource Economics 2002/2003: A Survey of Current Issues* 373, 373–407 (T. Tietenberg & Henk Folmer eds., 2002).

6. See generally Gifford Pinchot, *Breaking New Ground* (Island Press 1998) (1947).

7. See generally John Muir, *A Thousand-Mile Walk to the Gulf* (William F. Bade ed., 1916).

8. Christopher D. Stone, Do Morals Matter? The Influence of Ethics on Courts and Congress in Shaping U.S. Environmental Policies, 37 *U.C. Davis L. Rev.* 13, 16 (2003).

9. Norton, supra note 4, at 149–90.

10. Lynn White, Jr., *The Historical Roots of Our Ecologic Crisis*, 155 Sci. 1203, 1203–07 (1967).

11. Id. See Norton, supra note 4, at 162–66, for a detailed account of the impact of White's paper on the history of environmental ethics.

12. For examples of the trend of focusing on these dualisms, see Richard Routley, Is There a Need for a New, an Environmental, Ethic?, in *Proceedings of the XVth World Congress of Philosophy* 205, 205–10 (Bulgarian Organizing Committee ed., 1973), and Holmes Rolston, III, Is there an Ecological Ethic?, 85 *Ethics* 93, 93–109 (1975). See generally Tom Regan, *The Case for Animal Rights* (1983).

13. See generally Norton, supra note 4; Norton & Minteer, supra note 9.

14. For a discussion of monism versus pluralism, see Christopher D. Stone, *Earth*

and *Other Ethics* 115–83 (Rick Hermann ed., Perennial Library 1988) (1987), especially Part IV. See also J. Baird Callicott, *Beyond the Land Ethic: More Essays in Environmental Philosophy* 141–83 (1999) (providing two essays written in response by J. Baird Callicott). On the empirical question of whether most Americans are pluralists or monists, Ben Minteer and Robert Manning have provided strong evidence that pluralism is in fact the dominant mode of value expression in the United States. Ben A. Minteer & Robert E. Manning, Pragmatism in Environmental Ethics: Democracy, Pluralism, and the Management of Nature, 21 *Envtl. Ethics* 191, 193, 199 (1999).

15. Andrew Light & Eric Katz, Introduction: Environmental Pragmatism and Environmental Ethics as Contested Terrain, in *Environmental Pragmatism* 1, 2 (Andrew Light & Eric Katz eds., 1996); Norton, supra note 4, at 86.

16. See generally Kai N. Lee, *Compass and Gyroscope: Integrating Science and Politics for the Environment* (1993); Norton, supra note 4.

17. See generally *Barriers and Bridges to the Renewal of Ecosystems and Institutions* (Lance H. Gunderson et al. eds., 1995); C. S. Holling et al., *Adaptive Environmental Assessment and Management* (C.S. Holling ed., 1978); Lee, supra note 20; Norton, supra note 4; *Panarchy: Understanding Transformations in Human and Natural Systems* (Lance H. Gunderson & C.S. Holling eds., 2002). Perhaps the closest analogue to adaptive management in Europe is "Ecological Modernization," which shares some tenets with adaptive management, but also differs in emphasis. See Maarten Hajer, *The Politics of Environmental Discourse: Ecological Modernization and the Policy Process* 24–30 (1995), for further examination.

18. Bernard Williams, *Ethics and the Limits of Philosophy* 132–54 (1985).

19. John Dewey, The Public and Its Problems, in 2 *The Later Works, 1925–1953: 1926–1927* 238 (Jo Ann Boydston & Bridget A. Walsh eds., 1984); Lee, supra note 20, at 130 32.

20. Horst W.J. Rittel & Melvin M. Webber, Dilemmas in a General Theory of Planning, *Pol'y Sci.*, June 1973, at 155, 155–69.

21. Id.

22. Id.

23. See generally T.F.H. Allen & Thomas B. Starr, *Hierarchy: Perspectives for Ecological Complexity* (1982); Norton, supra note 4, at 220–31.

24. Leopold, supra note 1, at 129–33.

25. Norton, supra note 4, at 356–65.

26. See Judith E. Innes & David E. Booher, Indicators of Sustainable Communities: A Strategy Building on Complexity Theory and Distributed Intelligence, *Plan. Theory and Prac.*, Dec. 1, 2000, at 173, 173–86 (discussing the promise and the requirements for success of processes designed to settle upon indicators of management success).

27. See generally Jurgen Habermas, *The Theory of Communicative Action* (Thomas McCarthy trans., 1984).

Part Five

Water: Life's Common Wealth

Chapter 18

Editors' Introduction

> A thing is right when it tends to preserve the integrity, stability, and
> beauty of the biotic community. It is wrong when it tends
> otherwise.
>
> —Aldo Leopold[1]

UNDERSTANDING AND EVALUATING our moral obligations requires making judgments regarding which aspects of a particular situation are ethically relevant. In this sense, the ideas of the previous section on water as a community resource are primarily concerned with the interests of humans. Alternately, and as this section considers, one may begin with a broader determination of what interests count as part of the moral equation, or who and what belongs in the moral community.

Arguments regarding moral consideration and the environment typically take three forms. The first is to extend the boundaries of the moral community by appealing to a common characteristic between humans and nonhumans. For example, Albert Schweitzer argued that we must respect the "will-to-live" wherever we find it, including in the lives of individual nonhuman animals and plants.[2] Schweitzer's arguments, and ones like them, typically depend on finding a common characteristic between human and other life, and then arguing that if we respect humans because they have this characteristic then we have to respect other creatures that share it.

A second way to extend indirect ethical consideration to nonhumans or the environment is to argue that in order to protect our own interests and to meet obligations to fellow humans we have a duty to protect the natural world, such as healthy ecosystems. This strategy has the effect of removing the need for argumentation regarding what (if anything) it is about the environment that warrants ethical consideration. This is the case because we assume that the obligations of humans establish a claim regarding the protection and use of those resources necessary for human flourishing, and hence must be protected.

In the literature on environmental ethics, and more recently on water ethics, debates regarding anthropocentric versus nonanthropocentric values have been commonplace. Especially virulent have been debates about what to make of the important work of Aldo Leopold, who extended moral consideration to natural communities in his essay, "The Land Ethic."[3] These debates have centered on whether Leopold's extension was based on the intrinsic value of communities or upon the value of communities to humans. Critically, and without entering into how these debates have polarized ethical discourse (see Norton's essay in this volume for a discussion), what is clear is that Leopold not only extends moral consideration to communities, he also derives ethical obligations from our position within them.

Deriving ethical obligations from our position as part of a community represents a third way in conceptualizing our relationship with life and the world. It goes beyond both the strategy of finding a common characteristic between humans and other beings, and the instrumental argument that we should respect and care for the environment to meet obligations for human purposes. One interpretation of this position is that it removes humans from the center of moral value. This "decentering" process, according to Thomas Berry, opens the possibility to see the world as a communion of subjects rather than as a collection of objects.[4] As a communion of subjects, each part of the natural world (humans included) occupies a unique position in relationship to all the others. As such, respecting these mutual relationships offers the basis for ethical deliberation.

The essays in this section fall broadly within this third perspective. This is the case because each of them, in their own way, conceives of humanity as one part of a unified whole. From this third perspective, any adequate ethic for water, the environment or natural resource policy, must begin by situating moral claims within the relationships upon which humans depend for life. For many early environmental ethicists, conceiving of our participation in relationship with the natural world involved Romantic and/or spiritual beliefs about the meaning and role of the natural world in human existence. For example, Henry David Thoreau believed that unmediated nature offers the route for individual transcendence beyond the learned and limited rules of social convention.[5]

Not all ethical positions that derive obligations from within a community require a spiritual or transcendent point of view.[6] However, as regards our perspective on the moral community, they do all influence claims regarding which actions are acceptable, and which are not. These claims have direct implications for developing a water ethic because water is necessary for both human and nonhuman lives. Further, once these ethical positions are applied, they have consequences for what are taken to be sound management principles. For instance, if we accept an argument that states all nonhumans have a right to water then we will need management principles that curtail human water use before we infringe on the rights of nonhumans.

Contents

This section considers the common wealth that water provides for communities. As such, it is particularly concerned with the value of water in communities of both humans and nonhumans. The first essay, by Peter G. Brown, argues that the received tradition of property has taken for granted that the world is composed of "resources" that are fully available for human uses. Brown contends that if we reject the assumption that water and other resources are here *for us* then we see that the water, forests, and land are already fully in use in the commonwealth of life. The second essay, by Sandra Postel, argues against purely supply-side prescriptions for meeting our obligations regarding water. Postel shows how such solutions invariably, and unethically, prioritize the rights of humans over those of nonhuman communities and the ecosystems upon which both depend. The third essay, by Carolyn Merchant, identifies the moral premises under different approaches to ecosystem management, especially as they have affected fishing policies. She argues for an ethic of partnership based on the mutual interdependence of human and nonhuman communities.

Notes

1. A. Leopold, *A Sand County almanac: with essays on conservation from Round River*. (New York: Oxford University Press, 1966), 262.

2. A. Schweitzer, *The philosophy of civilization*. (New York: Prometheus Books, 1987).

3. Leopold, 1966.

4. T. Berry, *The great work: our way into the future*. (New York: Bell Tower, 1999).

5. H. Thoreau, *Walden*. (Hungary: Könemann, 1999).

6. For instance, Norton's work (this volume) rests on a communal understanding of values that draws on the work of Jürgen Habermas, who considers our position within a "community of truth seekers" the basic condition for participation in the moral community. See, J. Habermas, *Moral consciousness and communicative action*. (Cambridge: MIT Press, 1990).

Chapter 19

Are There Any Natural Resources?[1]

Peter G. Brown

IS THE NATURAL WORLD a reservoir of resources for human gratification? The philosophers' answer, assuming one answer could be tallied reliably from many traditions over millennia of scholarship, would surely be yes, and by a wide margin.

Should we accept this answer as inevitable? Or has it been the rarely questioned premise making casually respectable an ever-more-audacious "power grab" by nature's one philosophizing species? to the detriment of many, most, or all other species? If the latter, and I assert that the latter more fairly suggests the truth, then how can we understand and resolve the problem into which we have led ourselves? This paper proposes a way.

Property in Three Traditions

What establishes legitimate property rights to things in the world not made by humans? What is "property" in natural resources? Are there any "natural resources" at all?

"Property" implies three clusters of rights. First, rights of exclusion, as in the right to keep others off, or away from, property. Second, rights of use, as in the right to do what one wishes to do with property. And, third, rights of disposition, as in rights to sell, give, or otherwise transfer property. In current institutional arrangements, property can be owned by one or more individuals, by groups such as tribes or clans, by legal entities such as corporations, or by nations, such as Egypt or the United States.

How these concepts are understood in practice differs across societies. Importantly, property can be owned portions of the earth itself; lands, riverbeds, waters, and even airspace can be owned. Alternatively, and in contrast, property can be the benefit stream arising from these portions of owned earth, as in a "usufruct" right, whereby the "fruits" of land or water—such as deer or fish or volumes of a river's flow—are possessed.

Anthropocentric thinking about natural resources is natural enough; we could hardly expect ourselves spontaneously to develop a fungal, arboreal, avian, or equine view. Justifying self-centeredness is another matter, however. In the philosophical West, three interrelated traditions have offered partially overlapping justifications for thinking that the world belongs to persons. These are the Judeo-Christian–liberal, the Aristotelian–Cartesian–rationalist, and the utilitarian or neoclassical economic.

The Judeo-Christian–Liberal Tradition

Particularly influential has been a British philosopher, John Locke, who accepted the Bible as authoritative, the world as a gift from God to humanity, and human beings as created in the image of God. On the matter of the gift he wrote: "The earth, and all that is therein, is given to men for the support and comfort of their being."[2] And on being created in the divine image: "God makes him in his own image after his own Likeness, makes him an intellectual Creature, and so capable of Dominion."[3] To these assumptions he added what he took to be a self-evident truth, that each person had ownership of his or her own body, though all ultimately were owned by God. We had a natural right to our bodies and to what we did with our bodies, provided we did not harm others and did not contradict God's laws as to the use of that "property" of the body, such as eating unholy foods, or engaging in sexual practices considered abominations. We established property rights over things in the world by mixing what we already owned—the labor of our own bodies—with what we did not own. For example, if we shot it, skinned it, and cooked it, then a deer belonged to us because we had mixed our labor with it. Similarly, if we enclosed a forest and converted it into farmland, thereby presumably increasing its usefulness to humanity, we could own the land itself. These ideas constituted "the labor theory of value," which in turn made plausible the establishment, distribution, redistribution, and defense of property without appeal to royal charter—without royalty at all, for that matter. Indeed, Locke's attitude toward monarchy was paralleled by his attitude toward aristocracy in general and toward wealth; contrary to the conservatives who would claim him as a proto-libertarian, Locke unquestionably saw property rights as subordinate to natural-law obligations. For instance, "[T]would always be a sin for any man of estate to let his brother perish for want of affording him relief out of his plenty."[4]

Locke argued that we can take from the commons—"as God . . . hath given the world to men in common"—only if there is "enough and as good" left for others.[5] This condition has often been called "the Lockean proviso." Taking land from the commons increased the resource base because cultivated land was so much more productive of what humans needed than was land in its natural state. Indeed, Locke saw an obligation to convert nature to human use so as to fulfill the natural-law obligation to "preserve all mankind." Converting a swamp to farmland helped avoid malnutrition, and, intuitively enough even in seventeenth-century medical thought, disease. The privatization of property satisfied Locke's proviso as long as the commons, the source of all surplus, remained undepleted. Moreover, the proviso could be satisfied even when all land had been appropriated, as long as gainful employment was created and surplus food generated.

The acceptance of money as a medium of exchange facilitated the conversion of waste into assets, as it created incentives to produce for distant markets. Farms in North America could produce grain for Europe, since barter was unnecessary, bringing additional assets "on line" in discharging our natural-law obligations. Yet, though he thought it necessary for complex civilizations such as his own, Locke saw money as a curse as much as a blessing. Previously, acquiring more than could be consumed before spoilage was hardly possible, but money made this quite possible, and great inequalities developed; our natural law obligations thus came to include redistribution. Money helped eliminate the waste of nature by increasing incentives for nature's conversion, but money also increased the waste of humanity by permitting over- and under-consumption and increasing opportunities for the indulgence of fancy.

Liberal moral philosophers in this tradition had trouble enough scaling the heights of monarchy. They were struggling to plant the flag of human rights above the reach of privilege and manipulation; other-than-human rights remained below, as in the writings of Immanuel Kant, who famously accorded nature no moral standing whatsoever. A core liberal concern became the distribution of *humans'* rights to nature's other-than-human bounty. Only in the nineteenth century would the inter-relatedness of these rights start to be asserted.

The Aristotelian–Cartesian–Rationalist Tradition

Another source of the doctrine that "humanity owns the earth" was Aristotle, though he did not offer an explicit theory of property. While he characteristically emphasized the continuity of mankind and nature, Aristotle also emphasized differences. As he observed in the Metaphysics, "the animals other than man live by appearances and memories, and have but little connected experience; but the human race lives also by art and reasoning."[6] The humanity-owns-the-earth tradition reached its zenith, or nadir, with René Descartes, who, among others, considered the ability to think the essential character of being human. He saw the rest of the world as "extension," as the taking up of space. Something could be either a thing or a mind. Descartes regarded other animals as things, "devoid of reason,"[7] or automata, acting out a mechanical destiny without cognition. This was a view, though put in different vocabularies, that has been carried forward by many others who consider the behavior of non-human animals to be determined exclusively, or at least very largely, by instincts or genetic programs. For these Aristotelian–Cartesian rationalists, all the world is an object to be used by humans—the only "subjects"—however humans wish.

The Utilitarian or Neoclassical Economic Tradition

Philosophical utilitarianism, which has come to be equated with the view that human preferences are the main unit of value, arose in response to the problems flowing out of the Protestant Reformation. Nearly continuous disputes, including religious wars, were fueled by an unfamiliar variety of beliefs about right and wrong, a variety attributable to a great divergence in moral premises. Utilitarianism was put forward as a common denominator for moral judgment.

Jeremy Bentham, in his 1789 book, *An Introduction to the Principles of Morals and Legislation*, had insisted that not only human beings but also any other form of life capable of suffering had to be included in moral calculations. John Stuart Mill joined Bentham in considering nonhuman animals: "Granted that any practice causes more pain to animals than it gives pleasure to man; is that practice moral or immoral? And if, exactly in proportion as human beings raise their heads out of the slough of self-ishness, they do not with one voice answer 'immoral,' let the morality of the principle of utility be forever condemned."[8] But despite such forceful declarations, J. S. Mill focused on the well-being of humans almost exclusively. The fundamental goal, he wrote, was the "greatest happiness of the greatest number." Every person's happiness counted equally, and actions had to be planned with this equality in mind. "The equal claim of every-body to happiness . . . involves an equal claim to all the means of happiness."[9] Property was to be allocated and governed so as to produce the greatest possible grand total amount of human happiness.

Utilitarianism's legacy discipline, microeconomics, preserves this all-human perspective. Indeed, when microeconomic techniques, including cost–benefit analysis, came to be applied in "animal science," they led, ironically, to the consideration of nonhuman animals only insofar as human owners and consumers were concerned. J. S. Mill's sentiment aside, nonhuman animals—a group including coral but excluding trees—have secured no moral standing through any calculation of "happiness."

Difficulties

These traditions each assumed that the world was made for humanity. Thus, they neatly explained—teleological explanations are nothing if not neat—the fit between human needs and earthly offerings, with the "fall of man" explaining any mismatch. This assumption was most explicit in Locke, who quoted scripture in support of his views. It was carried forward, less explicitly, in rationalism and utilitarianism. While not wholly irreconcilable with religious belief, modern science is sharply at variance with this particular account of humanity's relationship to the world.

Rather than being explained as the work of God, the fit of needs and offerings is credited to adaptive co-evolution. There is no empirical evidence that the world was made for humanity, and no hypothesis that it was can be falsified. Nor do we account for our intellect by citing its similarity to God's but as one among many complex products of our evolution. Locke, by way of his larger argument against absolutism, recognized some duties to what he called the "inferior creatures." He stressed that our dominion over them was like that of a shepherd over his flock, and that, while given to mankind in common, they were ultimately God's property, just like the rest of the world.[10] Hence, we had duties to refrain from wasting inferior creatures and to treat them with respect; this latter duty Locke did not explain further.

These traditions—with Bentham excepted and Mill suggestive—have taught that humanity, owing to distinctions of mind, differs in kind from the rest of nature. From a theological point of view, humanity had been created in the image of God. From an empirical point of view, nonhuman species had been programmed genetically, their actions those of automata. Today, we know better. Similarities between us and other species are fundamental and numerous. Most tellingly, the reasoning mind is not limited to primates or even chordata. Bees, for example, act intelligently as well as automatically.[11] We can no longer easily accept Descartes' view that the world of "subjects" is limited to persons and the world of matter defined by "extension." Nonhuman animals must be credited with intelligence, emotion, and sensation.

Anthropocentricity, the sine qua non of humanism, has become less and less satisfying in philosophy, even in utilitarianism. Anthropocentricity still dominates casual moralizing, clinical ethics, legal reasoning, and—most fatefully of all—microeconomics, but elsewhere its distorting effects have become sufficiently apparent to force it out of fashion. In environmental philosophy, anthropocentricity is mainly a dead letter; utilitarianism lives on, however, despite its failure to offer a satisfactory account of the foundations of moral obligation. This failure can be traced to embedded paradoxes.

The principle of utility appears to be one principle, but it contains two variables—happiness and its wide distribution—each of which we are supposed to maximize. It is impossible to maximize both at the same time, so we need a third rule about the management of conflict. But no third rule is supplied.

To add to these difficulties, in offering no place for the language of rights—Bentham referred to rights as "nonsense, nonsense on stilts"[12]—utilitarianism authorizes the ruthless exploitation of the minority, or even a relatively powerless majority, if we can show a net gain of total utility. Numerous attempts to rescue utilitarianism from this defect, by arguing that we can reconstruct the language of rights out of summary rules, have failed to persuade.[13] We still must decide whether any particular action will maximize utility if it overrides the rule.[14] *Rule* utilitarianism always collapses to *act* utilitarianism, and the rescue attempt fails. Much of modern "resource" economics tries to distance itself from the failures of utilitarianism by dropping the language of utility in favor of the language of preferences or tastes. Yet, if preferences and tastes are not connected to utility, then left completely mysterious is why one should care about them or why one should care about them on behalf of strangers.

Finally, a utilitarian should consider the well-being of at least some nonhuman animals, since some of these surely think, feel pleasure, and feel pain. A retreat to tastes and preferences worsens this anthropocentric problem considerably and leads to many absurd judgments. For example, in the logic of such a theory, earthworms would reveal a post-precipitation preference for sidewalks as contrasted with soil by crawling out of the latter and onto the former.

Once we recognize the revelation of this preference, should we not endeavor to satisfy it? Within the utilitarianism of Bentham, yes indeed; within the utilitarianism of neoclassical economists, certainly not—unless that answer would affect a human utility function, which it might, given the biomass of earthworms and their importance to agriculture, gardening, and lawn care.

If one does adopt utilitarianism, one may as well side with Bentham. In *An Introduction to the Principles of Morals and Legislation*, 1781, he wrote:

> The day may come, when the rest of the animal creation may acquire those rights which never could have been withholden from them but by the hand of tyranny. The French have already discovered that the blackness of the skin is no reason why a human being should be abandoned without redress to the caprice of a tormentor. [See Lewis XIV's Code Noir.] It may come one day to be recognized, that the number of the legs, the villosity of the skin, or the termination of the os sacrum, are reasons equally insufficient for abandoning a sensitive being to the same fate. What else is it that

should trace the insuperable line? Is it the faculty of reason, or, perhaps, the faculty of discourse? But a full-grown horse or dog is beyond comparison a more rational, as well as a more conversable animal, than an infant of a day, or a week, or even a month, old. But
suppose the case were otherwise, what would it avail? [T]he question is not, Can they reason? nor, Can they talk? but, Can they
suffer?[15]

The anthropocentric assumptions of the resource economics literature
are entirely *ad hoc*. The attempt to include nature in the calculus by
coming up with monetary values for "ecosystem services" fails to find an
exit from the metaphysical myopia of the mainstream view.[16] An argument offered in favor of this approach is that when the monetary value of
"nature" is set high, then attention is called to the high cost of ignoring
nature. While it appeals rhetorically, this argument perpetuates a false
view of humanity's place in the world and legitimates and extends a practice already much too common: trying to reduce every thing and every
one to market terms. Of the millions of nonhuman species in the world,
why all should be in service to man is not explained.

The ecosystem-services idea may in part be a holdover from the belief
that humans were created in the image of God and thus were entitled to
unique—or at least special—moral consideration. That this exceptionalist
belief is now under widespread reconsideration, both in theological cir-
cles and from the perspective of evolutionary biology, has not been taken
into account in utilitarianism or neoclassical economics, wherein the
well-being of nonhumans remains a concern only indirectly, as a function of human utility. That nonhuman animals or ecosystems could be of
noninstrumental value, having value in their own rights, is not considered. What we seek, and what I anticipate in the framework sketched below, is a broad "constitution of the world" in which considerations of
utility play a subordinate, yet still robust, role.

"Natural Resources" Re-evaluated

Is ours the only species fairly able to claim air, water, territory, and other
necessities of life? This question, which in few cultures would ever have
been taken seriously in the past, is no longer wholly unaskable, even in

law. The Endangered Species Act and the Species at Risk Act in the United States and Canada, respectively, were steps away from old presumptions, yet these bills might have been seen as mere elaborations on an old humanity-as-proprietor theme had they not departed from mainstream conceptions of privacy, property, and rights. Property-rights groups, whose reactions were and remain strongly negative, certainly recognized the departure as real.

Materially more ambitious have been attempts to repair ecological damage already done: attempts to restore salmon, condors, wolves, and so forth, to their former habitats. Significant, but radically insufficient, amounts of marine and terrestrial habitat have been set aside for particular species—or, in practice, for any species other than *Homo economicus*. Though the reasons for these set-asides have often included human well-being, including supposedly "sustainable" benign forms of commerce, such as eco-tourism, they have also included the well-being of other species in their own right.

Progress is grudgingly deliberate and far from slowing even the acceleration of anthropogenic extinctions, but clearly now progress is possible. Once we began walking the road of evolutionary, classical-genetic, and molecular-genetic understanding, the moral boundary between others and us began to blur. The world of human "subjects" and natural "objects" cannot be seen from or reached through science, whose modern lessons point in parallel more surely to "primitive" teachings, wherein peoples assumed themselves to be subjects among subjects. We have had to readjust our self-image, as Aldo Leopold wrote, "from conqueror of the land-community to plain member and citizen of it."[17] That said, our analytical capacity and our moral imagination make for us a responsibility that no other species shares or, as far as we can tell, even recognizes. This responsibility is hard to summarize, hard to square with our evolution as omnivorous, grasping materialists. Albert Schweitzer described this responsibility by its requirement, "reverence for life,"[18] a compellingly beautiful idea, both hopeful and poignant, immediate and remote, with myriad implications, many quite clear, yet some not clear at all.

Schweitzer sought the origin of his own demonstrably extraordinary conscientiousness, even the origin of moral motivation generally. When he felt—*felt*—he had found it, he set about to persuade civilization, then collapsing in vanity and war, and civilization's philosophers, deeply implicated in worldwide catastrophe, that he had found a principle well worth their consideration. He was steaming upstream, literally, in 1915:

> Lost in thought I sat on the deck of the barge, struggling to find the elementary and universal conception of the ethical which I had not discovered in any philosophy. Sheet after sheet I covered with disconnected sentences, merely to keep myself concentrated on the problem. Late on the third day, at the very moment when, at sunset, we were making our way through a herd of hippopotamuses, there flashed upon my mind, unforeseen and unsought, the phrase "Reverence for Life." The iron door had yielded: the path in the thicket had become visible.[19]

Reverence-for-life was not sentimentalism but a disposition, not a refusal to use the living world but a respectful affirmation of humanity's place within it, responsibility for it, and responsibility to it.

Schweitzer's approach was risky, susceptible as it was to dismissal as ethical intuitionism. You can safely claim the primacy of your intuitions, and I can safely claim the primacy of mine, as our two primacies cannot reliably be ordered or reconciled. Schweitzer realized this and sought corroboration in every source he knew.

First, reverence-for-life seemed a natural extension of the teachings of Jesus, particularly the two great commandments, as it helped align humanity with the spirit of divine love and broadened "neighbor" beyond persons to all living things.

Second, reverence-for-life was a "philosophy of the will," similar in kind to nineteenth- and early twentieth-century works of Nietzsche, Schopenhauer, Bergson, and Goethe, and also to prominent precepts of Hinduism. Similar in kind, yes, because most fundamentally around us we find the will to live, but reverence-for-life was hardly similar in content—or, most obviously in the case of Nietzsche, intent. All these antecedents Schweitzer faulted: they were self-centered, incomplete, or escapist.

Third, reverence-for-life shared with moral-philosophical contributions of Adam Smith and David Hume an emphasis on the role of sympathy, the ability to look at the world from another's point of view. But Schweitzer argued that sympathy went beyond point-of-view to the sharing of feelings and experience; sympathy was an extension of the self in the direction of the creative will of the universe.

Fourth, reverence-for-life was a source, not a product, of rational argument. It was, in this sense, then, mystical, and respectably so, as had been the activist evangelism of Paul the Apostle, whose career Schweitzer would analyze formally between the wars.[20] Reverence-for-life was a mysticism through which the self was not lost but enriched, the individual not suppressed but situated within an ultimately deathless whole.

Fifth, reverence-for-life was consistent with Darwin's argument, in *The Descent of Man*, that all differences between persons and other life forms were matters of degree, not of kind. Any attempt to draw a boundary of morality between humans and other species would fail. Darwin's picture hung above Schweitzer's desk. I accept this idea—reverence-for-life—as foundational but unfinished, and I propose to build upon it a capstone concept: the commonwealth of life.

Resource Use in "the Commonwealth of Life"

From the commonwealth-of-life perspective, most "natural resources" are already being used, either by persons or by members of nonhuman species. Canada is often said to have a fresh-water surplus, but this statement can make sense only from an anthropocentric point of view. All the fresh water in Canada—and everywhere else, too—is in reality already used, if not in every respect expended, in support of natural communities. Minerals within the earth's crust might be thought an exception, unless they supported subterranean organisms, as my colleague Frédéric Fabry has pointed out. Leaving unexplored any potential sympathies for "the deep subterranean biosphere," we are tempted to accept the use of minerals as untroubling for a commonwealth-of-life morality. But extraction raises more than the material, and commonwealth-of-life considerations come quickly into play. Deeply buried coal, though a product of Carboniferous life, may not now be hosting life, but its extraction, whether by shaft mining, strip mining, open-cast mining, or mountain-top removal, does affect life, drastically, through the leaching of associated substances, especially sulfur, through interactions with air and water, through the dispersal of particulates, through aerosolization of combustion products, and so on.

Then does a commonwealth-of-life morality oppose all human activity, all industry, all improvement? No, nor does it oppose digging by ants, chewing by beavers, gathering by bees, recycling by fungi, or flowering by dandelions. The difference between the commonwealth-of-life view and the standard anthropocentric view is a disagreement about resource scarcity. From the former perspective, all resources are already used; from the latter, resources increase only as anthropocentricity increases. Debates about scarcity are as much about metaphysical premises as about factual conditions.

So, how do we decide which human uses legitimately trump which nonhuman uses in which circumstances?

First, we should notice that legitimacy's burden of proof has been rebalanced. Human use must be supported by reasons, and the reasons offered cannot be concerned solely with human well-being. In the commonwealth of life we find obligations—human-to-nonhuman, if not consciously or enforceably the other way around as well—just as in political liberalism we find obligations that are human-to-human exclusively: noninterference and redistribution, for example.

Of course, what counts as a "reason," or as reasonable, is hard to establish. The dominance of the anthropocentric view guarantees that the well-being of nonhuman species will seem irrelevant, or at best instrumental to policy, except insofar as human industries are affected or human sentiments aroused. Arguments based on two of the three moral foundations of property considered above, the exception being Bentham's own original utilitarianism, explicitly assume this view, made all the more convincing by portrayal of nonhumans as automata—an early-modern characterization readily updated over the centuries to suit scientific advancement.

Second, the pre-analytical vision of the Western rational tradition screens out much of what we need to learn and consider; cultural anthropology and study of the world's religions can help restore it.[21] The taking of life and the use of resources on which life depends must occur reverently, which is to say thoughtfully and appreciatively. Many of the world's traditions, quaintly anachronistic though they may seem, have much to teach on environmental stewardship, attitudinally at least: nature and life as gifts, hunted animals as objects of respect, land and water as common homes.

While they have helped create much of our present problem, Western religious traditions do offer compensatory concepts: humanity's obligation to care for God's creation, which the Book of Genesis tells us God found to be "very good";[22] an Old Testament notion of right relationship with land;[23] and transcendental unity of self and universe—antithesis of the dualism that fated us to impasse.

Third, we must recognize that life takes life, whether directly or indirectly. Killing, resource use, and environmental alteration are inevitable, though not inevitably brazen. So, how should we think about killing and killing's variants? Here is how Harvey Feit summarized the traditional attitude toward hunted animals in the Cree culture of the James Bay region of Quebec. The animal killed in the hunt was considered a gift:

> The balance is reciprocal, and in return for the gifts, the hunter has obligations to the animals and *chuetenshu* (the north wind) to act responsibly. He is expected to completely use what he is given, to act respectfully toward the bodies and souls of the animals by observing the highly structured procedures for retrieving the animal, butchering it, consuming its flesh, and disposing of its remains. It is expected that men will kill animals swiftly, and avoid causing them undue suffering. It is also understood that men have the skill and technology to kill many animals, too many, and it is part of the responsibilities of the hunter not to kill more than he is given, and not to "play" with animals by killing them for fun or self-aggrandizement.[24]

This is a usufruct view of property. The hunters here were taking only what the land produced reliably in the long run. But the land's spontaneous productivity, and the sea's, cannot sustain a densely peopled world, even one whose citizens hope to improve their own behavior, nor can spontaneous productivity sustain the surplus needed to make, *inter alia*, science. Reverence-for-life—for lives lived in a commonwealth of life—must be a reservoir of practical ideas. Or it will fairly be dismissible as all aspiration and no implication.

What to do? Schweitzer is often criticized for failing to provide much guidance on how actually to implement his ethic. His own decisions seemed *ad hoc*. He fed dozens of fish to his pet pelican. He gave detailed instructions on how to get a snake that "stole" eggs to strangle itself on wire. Being Alsatian, he ate sausage.

Consider an analogy with pacifism. The pacifist is often confronted by the critic with a dilemma: kill the men who are threatening your citizens or let the citizens be killed. To this the pacifist replies, "I am not primarily concerned with what to do about these dilemmas when they arise, but I am concerned with preventing them from arising to begin with. So my emphasis is on disarmament, institutions such as a world court, and opting out of the war system."

Reverence-for-life was an admonition to live life so as to minimize such dilemmas, in number, in seriousness, and in consequence.

> Standing, as he does, with the whole body of living creatures under the law of this dilemma . . . in the will-to-live, man comes again and again into the position of being able to preserve his own life and life generally only at the cost of other life. If he has been touched by the ethic of Reverence for Life, he injures and destroys life only under a necessity, which he cannot avoid, and never from thoughtlessness. So far as he is a free man he uses every opportunity of tasting the blessedness of being able to assist life and avert it from suffering and destruction.[25]

We were being urged, first, to reconceptualize our behavior; second, to reform our institutions; and, third, to build a civilization deserving respect. Nothing less. The first task was hard enough, but also clear. Its accomplishment universally could never have been expected, and the safest bet was always that no progress along the prescribed line would ever occur. But progress has occurred, nowhere enough to satisfy, but far too much to support a total-futility claim. Schweitzer's second task has also been undertaken; indeed, many thousands worldwide now find careers in reformed institutions or in new institutions based on reformed ideas. Yet, progress along this second task's main front has slowed, right where the full-human-use argument meets the all-species-use argument.

To understand why, we might round up the usual suspects: economic interests opposing progressive change, monochromatic perspectives of mainstream journalists, difficulties organizing large numbers of people to further a diffuse cause. But the reasons are deeper, reaching to the sources of our traditions. Traditions which, as Schweitzer pointed out, assume the good is the human good and leave the rest of the biosphere in shadow. So, his argument comes full circle.

If we are to care for the commonwealth of life, we must care about the source of life's capacity for self-organization and maintenance. We find that source dutifully obeying all physical laws; one of these, the second law of thermodynamics or "entropy law," has special meaning for ethics. It suggests new ways to think about old responsibilities, setting us on a path toward Schweitzer's goal: a civilization worthy of respect.

Complex life is an exception in the universe; whether it be a frequent exception or an absolute rarity or a unique terrestrial endowment none yet can say confidently.[26] The universe as a whole is entropic—conforming to the second law's insistence about the degradation of energy and the tendency toward uniform simplicity. On Earth, for billions of years now, life has been swimming against the tide, an eddy of complexity in a gathering sea of simplicity, all made possible, but never certain, by core heating and continuous exogenous inputs of solar energy captured by plants and converted into what we call nature. Energy degrades in the process, but a surplus arrives daily. Menacing the commonwealth of life now is anthropogenic multifocal ecological simplification, a dismantling of natural complexity at the system level, if not the organismal, demonstrably faster than sunlight, photosynthesis, and DNA can compensate. *Preservation of the capacity for self-organization and maintenance—formally, preservation of the global anti-entropic capacity—must underlay our ethics.*

How much of the endowment making self-organization possible belongs to mankind? A widely noted estimate has put human consumption of the products of terrestrial photosynthesis at around forty percent.[27] With *Homo sapiens* just one of thirteen- to fifteen-million species, this seems a bit much. Over half the grain grown in North America is fed to livestock and only then as meat, milk, and eggs to humans, a practice requiring vast acreages of simplified plantings. Imagine the flourishing of life foregone. *We should leave substantial self-organizational scope for the other living things with whom we "share the light," or, as Locke might have applied his proviso in an environmentally aware era, we should leave them "enough and as good."*

The hallmark of our membership in the commonwealth of life should be the health of the ecosphere: what Aldo Leopold called "land." Since he knew health was hard to define, Leopold began with its opposite. He said the symptoms of land sickness were "abnormal erosion, abnormal intensity of floods, decline of yields in crops and forests, decline in carrying capacity . . . , a general tendency toward the shortening of species lists and of food chains, and a world wide dominance of plant and animal weeds."[28] Seen from this perspective, the highest and best use of land is not what will bring the greatest economic return but what will bring resilient flourishing of life and the maintenance of capacity for self-renewal. Human uses of land dominated by economic considerations must be seen in the context of the well-being of the landscape as a whole. *For the earth as a whole, preservation of self-organizational capacity must trump traditional economic arguments.*

The commonwealth-of-life idea invites us to notice, as Schweitzer did in text and life alike, that we reside in two spheres: the transcendent and the temporal. We identify as a matter of course with ourselves and with the whole of which we are a part, a fact well appreciated by J. S. Mill—though forgotten by his intellectual progeny. We are participants in what James Carse has called "an infinite game," as contrasted with a finite game, like baseball, with set boundaries in space and time, unchangeable rules during the game, and definite winners and losers.[29] "In the infinite game, to play is to win."[30] Those who are better at playing help those not so adept, both directly and through institutional adaptation conscientiously considerate of a long and fruitful future.[31] We would look, like Schweitzer, "right through death"[32] toward life, flowering and abundant.

Notes

1. Originally published as: Peter G. Brown, "Are there any natural resources?" *Politics and the Life Sciences* 23 (2004): 12–21. Reprinted with permission.

2. John Locke, *Two treatises of government*, Peter Lasiert, ed. (Cambridge: Cambridge University Press, 1960), Second Treatise, § 26.

3. Ibid., First Treatise, § 30.

4. Ibid., First Treatise, § 42.

5. Ibid., Second Treatise, § 33.

6. Aristotle, Metaphysics, Book A (1), Lines 25–7.

7. René Descartes, *Automatism of brutes in selections*. (New York: Charles Scribner's Sons, 1927), 360.

8. John Stuart Mill, "Whewell on moral philosophy," in *John Stuart Mill and Jeremy Bentham: utilitarianism and other essays*. (Middlesex: Penguin, 1987), 253.

9. John Stuart Mill, "Utilitarianism," in *Essential works of John Stuart Mill*. (New York: Bantam Matrix, 1965), 247.

10. Locke, First Treatise, § 39.

11. D. R. Griffin, *Animal minds*. (Chicago: University of Chicago Press, 1992).

12. Jeremy Bentham, "Anarchial fallacies; being an examination of the declaration of rights issued during the French Revolution," in *Works of Jeremy Bentham*, ed. John Bowring, Volume II (New York: Russell & Russell, 1962), Article II, p. 501.

13. Henry Sidgwick, *The methods of ethics* [1874], 7th ed., reissue (Chicago: University of Chicago Press, 1962).

14. J. J. C. Smart and B. Williams, *Utilitarianism? for and against*. (Cambridge: Cambridge University Press, 1973), 100–107.

15. Jeremy Bentham, An introduction to the principles of morals and legislation (1781), Chapter XVII: Of the Limits of the Penal Branch of Jurisprudence; § 2. Jurisprudence, its branches; XXIX, 2.

16. Robert Costanza et al., *Nature*, 387, 15 May 1997, 253–260.

17. Aldo Leopold, *A Sand County almanac*. (New York: Oxford University Press, 1989), p. 204.

18. Albert Schweitzer, *Out of my life and thought*. (New York: Henry Holt and Company, 1933), 186.

19. Ibid., 185.

20. Albert Schweitzer, *The mysticism of Paul the Apostle* [1931] (Baltimore: Johns Hopkins University Press, 1998).

21. Colin Scott, "Science for the West, myth for the rest? The case of James Bay Cree knowledge construction," in *Naked science: anthropological inquiry into boundaries, power, and knowledge*, ed. Laura Nader. (New York: Routledge, 1996), 69–86.

22. Matthew Scully, *Dominion: the power of man, the suffering of animals and the call to mercy*. (New York: St. Martin's Press, 2002).

23. Herman E. Daly and John B. Cobb, Jr., *For the common good*. (Boston: Beacon Press, 1989), 102–5.

24. Harvey A. Feit, "Waswanipi Cree management of land and wildlife: Cree ethno-ecology revisited," in *Native people, native lands: Canadian Indians, Inuit and Metis*, ed. B. Cox (Ottawa: Carlton University Press, 1992), 75–91.

25. Schweitzer, 1933, p. 272.

26. Peter D. Ward and Donald Brownlee, *Rare earth: why complex life is uncommon in the universe*. (New York: Copernicus, 2000).

27. P. M. Vitousek, et al., "Human appropriation of the products of photosynthesis," *BioScience* 36(6) (June 1986): 368–373.

28. Aldo Leopold, "The land-health concept and conservation" in *For the health of the land: previously unpublished essays and other writings*, ed. Baird Callicott and Eric T. Freyfogle (Washington, DC: Island Press, 1999), 219.

29. James Carse, *Finite and infinite games*. (New York: The Free Press, 1986).

30. Stewart Brand, *The clock of the long now*. (New York: Basic Books, 1999), 187.

31. Ibid., 161.

32. Ibid., 147.

Chapter 20

The Missing Piece: A Water Ethic[1]

Sandra Postel

NOW FOR THE MILLION-DOLLAR QUESTIONS: Why has so much of modern water management gone awry? Why is it that ever greater amounts of money and ever more sophisticated engineering have not solved the world's water problems? Why, in so many places on this planet, are rivers drying up, lakes shrinking, and water tables falling?

The answer, in part, is simple: we have been trying to meet insatiable demands by continuously expanding a finite water supply. In the long run, of course, that is a losing proposition: It is impossible to expand a finite supply indefinitely, and in many parts of the world the "long run" has arrived.

For sure, measures to conserve, recycle, and more efficiently use water have enabled many places to contain their water demands and to avoid or at least delay an ecological reckoning. Such tried-and-true measures as thrifty irrigation techniques, water-saving plumbing fixtures, native landscaping, and wastewater recycling can cost-effectively reduce the amount of water required to grow food, produce material goods, and meet household needs. The conservation potential of these measures has barely been tapped.

Yet something is missing from this prescription, something less tangible than drip irrigation lines and low-flow showerheads, but, in the final analysis, more important. It has to do with modern society's disconnection from nature's web of life and from water's most fundamental role as the basis of that life. In our technologically sophisticated world, we no longer grasp the need for the wild river, the blackwater swamp, or even the diversity of species collectively performing nature's work. By and large, society views water in a utilitarian fashion—as a "resource" valued only when it is extracted from nature and put to use on a farm, in a factory, or in a home.

Overall, we have been quick to assume rights to use water but slow to recognize obligations to preserve and protect it. Better pricing and more open markets will assign water a higher value in its economic functions, and breed healthy competition that weeds out wasteful and unproductive uses. But this will not solve the deeper problem. What is needed is a set of guidelines and principles that stops us from chipping away at natural systems until nothing is left of their life-sustaining functions, which the marketplace fails to value adequately, if at all. In short, we need a water ethic—a guide to right conduct in the face of complex decisions about natural systems that we do not and cannot fully understand.

The essence of such an ethic is to make the protection of freshwater ecosystems a central goal in all that we do. This may sound idealistic, yet it is no more radical a notion than suggesting that a building be given a solid foundation before adding thirty stories to it. Water is the foundation of every human enterprise, and if that foundation is insecure, everything built upon it will be insecure, too. As such, our stewardship of water will determine not only the quality but the staying power of human societies.

The adoption of such a water ethic would represent a historic shift away from the strictly utilitarian approach to water management and toward an integrated, holistic approach that views people and water as interconnected parts of a greater whole. Instead of asking how we can further control and manipulate rivers, lakes, and streams to meet our ever-growing demands, we would ask instead how we can best satisfy human needs while accommodating the ecological requirements of freshwater ecosystems. It would lead us, as well, to deeper questions of human values, in particular how to narrow the wide gap between the haves and have-nots within a healthy ecosystem.

Embedded within this water ethic is a fundamental question: Do rivers and the life within them have a right to water? In his famous essay, "Should Trees Have Standing? Toward Legal Rights for Natural Objects," legal scholar Christopher D. Stone argued more than 35 years ago that yes, rivers and trees and other objects of nature do have rights, and these should be protected by granting legal standing to guardians of the voiceless entities of nature, much as the rights of children are protected by legal guardians.[2] Stone's arguments struck a chord with U.S. Supreme Court Justice William O. Douglas, who wrote in a famous dissent in the 1972 case *Sierra Club v. Morton* that "contemporary public concern for protecting nature's ecological equilibrium should lead to the conferral of standing upon environmental objects to sue for their own preservation. . . . The river, for example, is the living symbol of all the life it sustains or nourishes—the fish, aquatic insects, water ouzels, otter, fisher, deer, elk, bear, and all other animals, including man, who are dependent on it or who enjoy it for its sight, its sound, or its life. The river as plaintiff speaks for the ecological unit of life that is part of it."

During the next three decades, U.S. courts heard cases brought by environmental groups and other legal entities on behalf of nature and its constituents. In water allocation, concepts such as "instream flow rights" began to take hold, although these rights often received too low a priority to offer meaningful protection of river health. With freshwater life being extinguished at record rates, a more fundamental change is needed. An ethical society can no longer ignore the fact that water-management decisions have life-or-death consequences for other species. An ethically grounded water policy must begin with the premise that all people and all living things should be given access to enough water to secure their survival before some get more than enough.

On paper, at least one government has grounded its water policy in precisely such an ethic. South Africa's 1998 water law establishes a water reserve consisting of two parts. The first is a non-negotiable water allocation to meet the basic drinking, cooking, and sanitary needs of all South Africans. (When the African National Congress came to power, some 14 million poor South Africans lacked water for these basic needs.) The second part of the reserve is an allocation of water to support the long-term sustainability of the nation's aquatic and associated ecosystems. The water determined to constitute this two-part reserve has priority over licensed uses, such as irrigation, and only this water is guaranteed as a right.

At the core of South Africa's policy is an affirmation of the "public trust," a legal principle that traces back to the Roman Empire, that says governments hold certain rights and entitlements in trust for the people and are obliged to protect them for the common good. In addition to the public trust, another rule fast becoming essential for freshwater ecosystem protection is the "precautionary principle," which essentially says that given the rapid pace of ecosystem decline, the irreversible nature of many of the resulting losses, and the high value of freshwater ecosystems to human societies, it is wise to err on the side of protecting too much rather than too little of the remaining freshwater habitat.

The utilitarian code that continues to guide most water management may fit with prevailing market-based socioeconomic paradigms, but it is neither universal nor unchanging. The American conservationist Aldo Leopold viewed the extension of ethics to the natural environment as "an evolutionary possibility and an ecological necessity." More recently, Harvard biologist Edward O. Wilson noted in his book, *Consilience*, that ethical codes historically have arisen through the interplay of biology and culture.[3] "Ethics, in the empiricist view," Wilson observes, "is conduct favored consistently enough throughout a society to be expressed as a code of principles."

In other words, ethics are not static; they evolve with social consciousness. But that evolution is not automatic. The extension of freedom to slaves and voting rights to women required leaders, movements, advocates, and activists that collectively pulled society onto higher moral ground. So it will be with the extension of rights to rivers, plants, fish, birds, and the ecosystems of which they are a part. As societies wrap their collective minds around the consequences of global environmental change—rising temperatures, prolonged droughts, chronic water shortages, disappearing species—it may well be that a new ethic will emerge, one that says it is not only right and good but necessary that all living things get enough water before some get more than enough. Because in the end, we're all in this together.

Notes

1. Reprinted with permission from Sandra Postel, "The missing piece: a water ethic," *The American Prospect*, Volume 19, Number 6: May 27, 2008. www.prospect

.org. The American Prospect, 1710 Rhode Island Avenue, NW, 12th Floor, Washington, DC 20036. All rights reserved. Postel's original essay, "A water ethic" appeared in her book, *Last oasis: facing water scarcity*. (New York: W.W. Norton, 1992).

2. C. Stone, *Should trees have standing? Towards legal rights for natural objects*. (New York: Avon Books, 1974). Original in 1972.

3. E. O. Wilson, *Consilience: the unity of knowledge*. (New York: Alfred A Knopf, Inc., 1998).

Chapter 21

Fish First! The Changing Ethics of Ecosystem Management[1]

Carolyn Merchant

FISH FIRST! If we think about the theme of "fish first!," we see many nuances. Is it the most important thing for the individual fisher, for example, to take fish first above every other consideration? Or, should fish be caught first for the good of society and only secondarily for the good of the individual? Or, should the fish themselves come first before all human considerations? Do humans or fish or both have rights? Under what circumstances do fish win by being at the table rather than on the table? Each approach to policy entails a particular approach to management, and each form of management entails an underlying environmental ethic. We can see these approaches illustrated in the history of changing policies, ethics, and ways of managing the fisheries in the Pacific Northwest from the 19th century to the present. By identifying the ethical approaches underlying earlier policies, we can formulate the grounds for new ethics to guide future policy and management choices.

The first fisheries in the Pacific Northwest, started in 1823, occurred for the purpose of trading and marketing the chinook salmon. The period from the 1820s to the 1880s was marked by the progress of the *laissez-faire* market economy.[2] *Laissez-faire* capitalism was rooted in what we might call the "egocentric ethic," the ethic that pertains to individual fishers, or fishing companies, taking fish from the rivers and sea (Figure 21-1). Individual humans had rights of ownership over individual stocks of fish. The basic ethical, economic, and policy assumption behind the egocentric ethic is: what is good for the individual is good for society as

```
┌─────────────────────────────────────────────┐
│            Egocentric Ethics: Self            │
│                                               │
│       Maximization of Individual Self-Interest:│
│          What Is Good for the Individual      │
│            Is Good for Society as a Whole     │
│                                               │
│       Mutual Coercion Mutually Agreed Upon    │
│                                               │
├───────────────────────┬───────────────────────┤
│  Self-Interest        │  Religious            │
│  Thomas Hobbes        │  Judeo-Christian Ethic│
│  John Locke           │  Arminian "Heresy"    │
│  Adam Smith           │                       │
│  Garrett Hardin       │                       │
└───────────────────────┴───────────────────────┘
```

Figure 21-1 Egocentric ethics.

a whole.[3] An unregulated fishing economy, managed by individual and corporate fishers, and based on the freedom of the seas, developed as the West Coast was settled in the 19th century.

The second assumption behind the industries' development and management was that the fisheries were basically inexhaustible. If one particular fishery lost its productivity and profits declined, then the fishers could move onward to another fishing ground, leaving the first one alone to recover.[4]

A third assumption of the *laissez-faire* economic approach and its underlying egocentric ethic was that fish were basically passive objects. They were not living fish possessing individual spirits within them, which were equal to or even more powerful than a human being, but were entities of lesser value. They were passive resource objects that could be taken out of the environment. As commodities to be extracted from the state of nature, they could be turned into profit. Like the gold that had been discovered in California, fish were treated as gold nuggets, serving as the coin of trade.[5] The policy of taking fish from the commons, that is, from the state of nature treated as a commons for everybody, as a free-for-all, has been characterized by environmental historian Arthur McEvoy as the "fisherman's problem."[6] Based on the idea of the "tragedy of the commons," popularized by ecologist Garrett Hardin in 1968, fishing by individuals for profit degrades the environment.[7] When done

competitively, it means there are powerful incentives to overfish, especially under common property regimes. When resources are owned in
common, but used competitively, the advantage to each individual fisher
is plus one, but the overall problem of the degradation of the commons is
shared equally by all. So the loss is much, much less than minus one.
Hardin's characterization of the "tragedy of the commons" led him to
propose extremely tight coercive regulation as a solution, or "mutual coercion, mutually agreed upon." His solution, based on the assumption
that human beings are an economically maximizing species, ignored the
cooperative actions of subsistence-oriented peoples both in medieval
Europe and in native and colonial America.[8]

A fourth assumption of the *laissez-faire* approach to fisheries management was that the fish themselves, once extracted from the commons, are
forms of private property. Private property is a bundle of human rights
and privileges obtained when an individual withdraws a resource from
the commons. These ideas go back to the 17th century political philosophers Thomas Hobbes and John Locke who wrote about rights to ownership of private property—mixing one's labor with the soil, as Locke
put it.[9] The idea of mixing your labor as a fisher with the seas to extract a
fish is that, in that very act, you create ownership of the fish or the entire
catch. Humans' property rights take precedence over the rights of fish to
continue to exist. Barbara Leibhardt-Wester has proposed a very interesting comparison between Western culture's notion of private property as
a bundle of human rights and privileges, with that of the Yakima Indian
tribe of the Columbia River basin as a sacred bundle of relationships and
obligations between humans and other organisms, such as fish.[10]

The Western idea of property stems from the Roman notion of bundles of sticks or fasces; symbols of authority and justice carried by Roman lictors as symbols of power, exemplified most blatantly in modern
times by the fascist symbol of a bundle of sticks, emblem of the Italian regime of Mussolini. By contrast, the Yakima believed there were sacred
bundles of magical objects given to an individual by a guardian spirit, defined, not as rights and privileges as in the Western system, but as relationships and obligations to other human beings, to the tribe, to nature,
and to the spirit world. Thus under *laissez faire* capitalism, a very different

ethic replaced the native American belief system for managing the commons in the Pacific Northwest.

These nineteenth century efforts to extract fish from the oceans and rivers and export them as marketable commodities under the *laissez faire* system led to a collapse of the fisheries on the West Coast. In the 1850s, the first gill-nets were used on the Columbia River below Portland. They were combined with purse seines, traps, and squaw nets during the decade of the 1850s and 1860s. In 1879, fish wheels were introduced on the Columbia River; these were like ferris-wheels with movable buckets, attached either to a scow or to rock outcrops along the edge of the river. They operated day and night scooping fish out of the river and dumping them down shoots into large bins on the shore to be packed and salted. By 1899, there were 76 fish wheels on both sides of the river. In 1866, the canning industry began operating on the banks of the Columbia near Eagle Cliff, Washington, and by 1883, there were 39 canneries shipping to New York, St. Louis, Chicago, and New Orleans.[11]

What were the consequences of unregulated fishing? In 1894, the Oregon Game and Fish protector observed, "It does not require a study of statistics to convince one that the salmon industry has suffered a great decline during the past decades, and that it is only a matter of a few years under present conditions when the chinook of the Columbia will be as scarce as the beaver that was once so plentiful on our streams."[12] In 1917, John H. Cobb of the U.S. Bureau of Fisheries pronounced, "Man is undoubtedly the greatest present menace to the perpetuation of the great salmon fisheries of the Pacific Coast. When the enormous number of fishermen engaged, and the immense quantity of gear employed is considered, one sometimes wonders how any of the fish, in certain streams at least, escape."[13]

The solution of "mutual coercion, mutually agreed upon" (Garrett Hardin's approach) would have required extreme policing and strict laws leveled on the fisheries. The idea of a police state was certainly not compatible with the then current notion of *laissez-faire* and certainly not with the idea of the freedom of the seas. How then was the problem of the egocentric ethical approach to the decline of the fisheries resolved? It was approached by the passage of laws and regulations that would help to manage the fisheries and the fluctuating fish populations.

The new approach exemplified a second environmental ethic, the utilitarian or homocentric ethic that arose in the United States and in the Pacific Northwest as a result of more general problems of resource management. Forests, along with fish, wild animals, and bird—all organisms that were renewable, but in decline during the 19th century—were affected. The homocentric approach, or human society first and fish second, stems from the utilitarian ethic of 19th century philosophers Jeremy Bentham and John Stuart Mill.[14] It is concerned with the questions: What is the social good, rather than the individual good? What is the public interest, rather than the private interest of the individual or corporation? (Figure 21-2). The utilitarian approach to conservation ethics, as modified by Gifford Pinchot and W. J. McGee in the early 20th century, is based on the concept of "the greatest good for the greatest number for the longest time" and on the idea of duty to the whole human community.[15] But like the egocentric ethic, it gives precedence to the rights of the human species over those of nonhuman species. As applied to fisheries, homocentric ethics underlie the policies and practices of regulating and controlling the *laissez-faire* market.

In the United States, the concept of legal limitation was set out by the Supreme Court, which decreed in 1855 that those businesses "affected

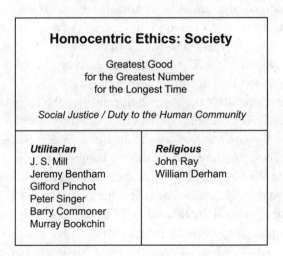

Figure 21-2 Homocentric ethics.

with a public interest" could be regulated.[16] Regulation entailed the utilitarian idea of cost–benefit analysis—that is, one must weigh both the benefits and the costs resulting from competing interests. In California, an important precedent was that of mining interests versus farming interests, two groups that each had a stake in the quantity and quality of the water flowing out of the Sierra. The rights and privileges of the two different interest groups were assessed in terms of costs and benefits, while natural resources such as fish were considered externalities. In the 1870s, California made fish and game state property to be regulated for the public good.[17] The State Board of Fish Commissioners was created "to provide for the restoration and preservation of fish in the waters of this state."[18]

The U.S. government participated in helping to manage and regulate fisheries through the creation of the U.S. Fish Commission. The first director, Spencer Fullerton Baird, promoted research and development along the Pacific coast to determine the varieties of fish distributed in coastal waters and to map the places where they occurred in greatest abundance.[19] If one knew the numbers associated with particular species in a fishery, that fishery could be managed according to the idea of maximum sustainable yield. The logistic curve, defined by Pierre François Verhulst in 1849, revealed the carrying capacity, or the maximum number of individuals that could be sustained without damage to the environment, while the fluctuation point represented the level of maximum sustainable yield, basically one-half of the number of individuals at the carrying capacity.[20] Fishers were to take only as many fish as the fish themselves reproduced in a given season.[21]

During the late 19th and early 20th centuries, the fisheries employed a homocentric ethic, exemplified by the idea of maximum sustainable yield, as the best approach to regulation and management. Yet there was still an enormous decline in the fisheries. Regulations were instituted in Oregon and Washington to control the technologies used. Fish wheels were outlawed and access to times of fishing curtailed. In 1877, for example, Washington closed the fisheries in March and April and again in August and September to give the fish a chance to reproduce. Oregon followed suit in 1878. The states also regulated the kind of gear that could be used. The mesh sizes of the nets were specified, and their use was limited to only a third of the width of the river. In 1917, purse seines were prohibited, and in 1948 size regulations were instituted limiting catchable fish to those above 26 inches in length.[22]

A bigger threat to the fisheries, however, occurred in the 1930s. This was the construction of large dams along the Columbia River and its tributaries. Dams for hydropower and flood control are examples *par excellence* of the homocentric ethic dedicated to the public good. Yet the public good did not coincide with the good of fish. Fish ladders and elevators had only limited effect in sustaining fish migrations, particularly those downstream.[23] The Chief Engineer of Bonneville Dam initially proclaimed, "We do not intend to play nursemaid to the fish."[24] In 1937, George Red Hawk of the Cayuse Indians observed, "White man's dams mean no more salmon."[25] By 1940, the catch of Coho salmon amounted to only one tenth of that taken in 1890. In 1938, the Director of Research for the Oregon Fish Commission, Willis Rich, said, "The decline is well below the level that would provide the maximum sustained yield. Such regulations and restrictions as have been imposed on the Columbia River salmon fisheries apparently have had very little effect in so far as they may act to reduce the intensity of fishing."[26] In 1948, the Army Corps of Engineers reported that over 300 dams had been built in the Columbia Basin: "Yet only in a few instances has any thought been paid to the effect these developments might have had on the fish and wildlife."[27]

It seemed clear that even this second approach to environmental ethics and management, the utilitarian or homocentric ethic, was ineffective. The concept of "the greatest good for the greatest number for the longest time" still meant human society first and fish second. By the 1950s, it began to give way to a third approach—the ecocentric approach, first formulated as the "land ethic" in 1949 by Aldo Leopold.[28] The ecocentric ethic is based on the idea that fish are equal to other organisms, including human beings, and therefore have moral consideration (Figure 21-3). As Leopold put it, "A thing is right when it tends to preserve the integrity, beauty, and stability of the biotic community. It is wrong when it tends otherwise."[29] We could expand his idea of the land ethic and call it a "land and water ethic." As such, "it enlarges the boundaries of the community to include soils, waters, plants, and animals

```
┌─────────────────────────────────────────────────────┐
│              Ecocentric Ethics: Cosmos                │
│                                                       │
│           Rational, Scientific Belief-System          │
│               Based on Laws of Ecology                │
│                                                       │
│                Unity, Stability, Diversity,           │
│           Harmony of Ecosystem, Balance of Nature     │
│                                                       │
├───────────────────────────┬───────────────────────────┤
│  Eco-Scientific           │  Eco-Religious            │
│  Aldo Leopold             │  American Indian          │
│  Rachel Carson            │  Buddhism                 │
│  Deep Ecologists          │  Spiritual Feminists      │
│  Restoration Ecologists   │  Spiritual Greens         │
│  Biological Control       │  Process Philosophers     │
│  Sustainable Agriculture  │                           │
└───────────────────────────┴───────────────────────────┘
```

Figure 21-3 Ecocentric ethics.

[including fish] or collectively: the land."[30] It changes the role of *homo sapiens*, Leopold said, "from conqueror of the land community to plain member and citizen of it."[31] There is an intrinsic value to all living and nonliving things, and all have a right to survive. Fish, as well as humans, have rights and can even have standing in a court of law.

The idea that began to emerge in the 1950s and 1960s was that the fish themselves had a right to survive and that one should cooperate with each stock's own strategy for survival. The interaction between harvesting and environmental change and cooperation with the species' own strategy for survival reflected the new ecocentric approach to management. The conclusion that arose from these ecological considerations was that "the benefit to the nation occurs by leaving the fish in the ocean."[32] This was a policy of fish first and people second, or fish for the sake of the fish.

Developed in conjunction with this ecocentric approach to management was the idea of the optimum sustainable yield, a modification of maximum sustainable yield. The optimum level of harvest is the level that can be obtained indefinitely without affecting the capacity of the population or the ecosystem to sustain that yield. In practice, it meant that the population should be maintained at something like 10% above that of the maximum sustainable population. The optimum yield was the maximum sustainable yield as modified by any relevant economic, social, or ecological factor.[33] It meant that endangered species must be taken into consideration and that there would be limited entry to the fisheries. The idea of freedom of seas was challenged. Both the Fisheries Conservation and Management Act of 1976 and the Marine Mammal Protection Act of 1972 were based on the idea of maintaining the health and stability of marine ecosystems with the goal of obtaining an optimum sustainable population.[34]

What problems arise from this ecocentric approach? One problem is that even the idea of optimum sustainable yield retains certain kinds of assumptions. It is based on the idea, current in the 1960s and 1970s, that ecology reflects the balance of nature.[35] It retains the assumptions that the fish population will follow the classical logistic curve, that there is a fixed carrying capacity, that there is an absolute maximum sustainable level, and that nature left undisturbed is constant and stable. These are the classical assumptions of the concept of the balance of nature which was the motivating inspiration behind the ecocentric ethic and the environmental movement of the 1970s.[36] But the notion of the balance of nature has recently been challenged by ecologists, particularly population ecologists, and by ideas of chaos theory and complexity theory.[37] Chaos theory questions the idea of the constancy and stability of nature, the idea that every organism has a place in the harmonious workings of nature, that nature itself is fixed in time and space like the environment in a petri dish in a modern scientific laboratory—and the idea that the logistic curve is a permanent and final explanation.

Ecologist Daniel Botkin has proposed the idea of discordant harmonies as an alternative to the concept of the balance of nature. Botkin says, we must move to a deeper level of thought and

confront the very assumptions that have dominated perceptions of nature for a very long time. This will allow us to find the true idea of a harmony of nature, which as Plotinus wrote so long ago, is by its very essence discordant, created from the simultaneous movements of many tones, the combination of many processes flowing at the same time along various scales, leading not to a simple melody, but to a symphony sometimes harsh and sometimes pleasing.[38]

The idea of discordant harmonies, theories of the chaotic and complex behavior of nature, raise the consideration that natural disturbances can in some cases be more rapid and drastic (as in fires, tornadoes, and hurricanes) than disturbances by human beings (forest harvesting, real estate development, and dam construction, for example). Moreover, natural and anthropogenic disturbances in conjunction with each other can amplify negative effects on the environment. Such observations have led to a questioning of earlier approaches—not only the egocentric and homocentric, but even the ecocentric approach—to environmental ethics and ecosystem management.[39]

As we go into the twenty-first century, I propose that we consider a new kind of ethic, which I call a partnership ethic—a synthesis between the ecocentric approach and the social justice aspects of the homocentric approach.[40] It is based on the idea that people and nature are equally important (Figure 21-4). Both people and fish have rights. We have the possibility of a win–win situation. For most of human history, up to the 17th century, nature had the upper hand over human beings, and humans fatalistically accepted the hand that nature dealt. Harvests, famines, and droughts were considered God's way of punishing human beings for acting in an unethical way. Since the 17th century, however, the pendulum has swung the other way and Western culture has developed the idea that

Partnership Ethics: People and Nature

—Equity between the human and nonhuman communities
—Moral consideration for both humans and other species
—Respect for cultural diversity and biodiversity
—Ecologically sound management is consistent with the continued health of both the human and nonhuman communities

The Greatest Good for the Human and Nonhuman Communities Is in Their Mutual Living Interdependence

Figure 21-4 Partnership ethics.

humans are more powerful than nature and that we, as European Americans, can dominate, control, and manage it.[41] Because humans are above nature, we can control the fisheries, for example, through such ideas as logistic curves and maximum or optimum sustained yields. We need to bring the pendulum back into balance so that there is greater equality between human and nonhuman communities.

The partnership ethic I propose for consideration is a synthesis of the ecocentric approach based on moral consideration for all living and non-living things, and the homocentric approach, based on the social good and the fulfillment of basic human needs. All humans have needs for food, clothing, shelter, and energy, but nature also has an equal need to survive. The new ethic questions the notion of the unregulated market, eliminating the idea of the egocentric ethic, and instead proposes a partnership between nonhuman nature and the human community.

A partnership ethic holds that the greatest good for human and nonhuman communities is in their mutual living interdependence. A human community in a sustainable relationship with a nonhuman community is based on the following precepts: first, equity between the human and nonhuman communities; second, moral consideration for both humans and other species; third, respect for both cultural diversity and biodiversity; fourth, inclusion of women, minorities, and nonhuman nature in the code of ethical accountability; and fifth, that ecologically sound management is consistent with the continued health of both the human and the nonhuman communities.[42] We might come back to the notion that Barbara Leibhardt-Wester proposed in her comparison of native and European Americans—the idea of the "sacred bundle." Like the Native American sacred bundle of relationships and obligations, a partnership ethic is grounded in the notions of relation and mutual obligation.[43]

What would a partnership ethic mean for ecosystem management? How would it be implemented in the fisheries professions? Each stock of fish has a home spawning stream and an ocean habitat connected over many miles of river. Each stock has a season for returning to its primal ecological community to reproduce. Seasonal changes, as well as chaotic disturbances in ocean currents, temperature changes, and predation, affect recruitment. So do human disturbances, such as timber removal, erosion, watershed pollution, dams, and fishing quotas and regulations. In each linked human and nonhuman biotic community, all the parties and their representatives must sit as partners at the same table. This includes knowledgeable fishers (individuals, corporate, and tribal representatives), foresters, dam builders, conservationists, soil and fishery scientists, community representatives, and spokespersons for each stock of fish affected. The needs of fish and the needs of humans should both be discussed. Examples of such efforts at partnerships include resource advisory committees, watershed councils, self-governing democratic councils, collaborative processes, and cooperative management plans.

Consensus and negotiation should be attempted as partners speak together about the short- and long-term interests of the interlinked human and nonhuman communities. The meetings will be lengthy and might continue over many weeks or months. As in any partnership relationship, there will be give-and-take as the needs of each party are expressed, heard, and acknowledged. If the partners identify their own egocentric, homocentric, and ecocentric ethical assumptions and agree to start anew from a partnership ethic of mutual obligation and respect, there is hope for consensus. A partnership ethic does not mean that all dams must be blasted down, electricity production forfeited, and irrigation curtailed for the sake of salmon. It means that the vital needs of humans and the vital needs of fish and their mutually linked aquatic and terrestrial habitats must both be given equal consideration. Indeed there is no other choice, for failure means a regression from consensus, to contention, and thence into litigation.

Many difficulties exist in implementing a partnership ethic. The free market economy's growth-oriented ethic, which uses both natural and human resources inequitably to create profits, presents the greatest challenge. The power of the global capitalist system to remove resources, especially those in Third World countries, without regard to restoration, reuse, or recycling is a major roadblock to reorganizing relations between production and ecology. Even as capitalism continues to undercut the grounds of its own perpetuation by using renewable resources, such as fish, faster than the species or stock's own recruitment, so green capitalism attempts to Band-Aid the decline by submitting to some types of regulation and recycling. Ultimately new economic forms need to be found that are compatible with sustainability, intergenerational equity, and a partnership ethic.

A second source of resistance to a partnership ethic is the property rights movement, which in many ways is a backlash against both environmentalism and ecocentrism. The protection of private property is integral to the growth and profit-maximization approaches of capitalism and egocentrism and to their preservation by government institutions and laws. While individual, community, or common ownership of "appropriate" amounts of property is not inconsistent with a partnership ethic, determining what is sustainable and hence appropriate to the continuation of human and nonhuman nature is both challenging and important.

As a start, we might propose an ethic for the American Fisheries Society, inspired by that proposed for the Society of American Foresters: partnership with the land and the aquatic habitat is the cornerstone of the fisheries profession; compliance with its canons demonstrates respect for the land and waters and for our commitment to the wise management of ecosystems.

So, as we move into the twenty-first century, the idea of a partnership between human beings and the nonhuman community in which both are equal and share in mutual relationships is the ethic that I would propose. A partnership ethic will not always work, but it is a beginning, and with it there is hope.

Notes

1. Originally published as: C. Merchant, "Fish first! The changing ethics of ecosystem management," *Human Ecology Review* 4(1) (1997): 25–30.
2. A. Netboy, *Salmon of the Northwest: fish versus dams.* (Portland, OR: Binfords and Mort, 1958).
3. C. Merchant, "Environmental ethics and political conflict: a view from California," *Environmental Ethics* 12(1) (1990): 45–68.
4. A. McEvoy, *The fisherman's problem: ecology and law in the California fisheries, 1850–1980.* (New York: Cambridge University Press, 1986).
5. Ibid.
6. Ibid.
7. G. Hardin, "The tragedy of the commons," *Science* 162 (1968): 1243–1248.
8. McEvoy, 1986; S. Cox, "No tragedy on the commons," *Environmental Ethics* 7(1) (1985): 49–69; R. White, *The Organic Machine* (New York: Hill and Wang, 1995).
9. J. Locke, *Second treatise of government,* ed. R. H. Cox (Arlington Heights, IL: Harlan Davidson, 1982); C. MacPherson, *The Political Theory of Possessive Individualism: Hobbes to Locke* (New York: Oxford University Press, 1962).

10. B. Leibhardt-Wester, "Law, environment, and social change in the Columbia River basin: the Yakima Indian Nation as a case study, 1840–1933" (Ph.D. diss., University of California, Berkeley, 1990).

11. Netboy, 1958; C. Smith, *Salmon fishers of the Columbia*. (Corvallis: Oregon State University Press, 1979).

12. Netboy, 1958.

13. Netboy, 1958, 39.

14. Merchant, 1990.

15. G. Pinchot, *Breaking new ground*. (Washington, DC: Island Press, 1947), 326.

16. McEvoy, 1986, 117.

17. Ibid., 118.

18. Ibid., 101.

19. Ibid.

20. D. Botkin, *Discordant harmonies: a new ecology for the twenty-first century*. (New York: Oxford University Press, 1990).

21. McEvoy, 1986.

22. Netboy, 1958, 28–30; J. Crutchfield and G. Pontecorvo, *The Pacific salmon: a study of irrational conservation*. (Baltimore, MD: Johns Hopkins University Press, 1969).

23. Netboy, 1958.

24. A. Netboy, *The salmon: their fight for survival*. (Boston: Houghton Mifflin, 1974), 287; D. Iltis, "Salmon in the Pacific Northwest." (Unpublished paper, 1995). In possession of author.

25. Netboy, 1958: 48; Iltis, 1995.

26. Netboy, 1958: 39.

27. Ibid., 34.

28. A. Leopold, *A Sand County almanac*. (New York: Oxford University Press, 1968), original in 1949.

29. Leopold, 1968, 225.

30. Ibid., 204.

31. Ibid.

32. McEvoy, 1986, 227.

33. Botkin, 1990.

34. McEvoy, 1986; Botkin, 1990.

35. Botkin, 1990.

36. Ibid.

37. Botkin, 1990; J. Gleick, *Chaos: the making of a new science*. (New York: Viking, 1987); R. Lackey, "Pacific salmon, ecological health, and public policy," *Ecosystem Health* 2(1) (1996): 1–8; M. Waldrop, *Complexity: the emerging science at the edge of order and chaos*. (New York: Simon and Schuster, 1992).

38. Botkin, 1990, 25.

39. R. Lackey, "Ecological risk assessment," *Fisheries* (1994) September: 14–18.

40. C. Merchant, *Earthcare: women and the environment* (New York: Routledge, 1996).

41. Ibid.

42. Ibid.

43. Ibid.

Part Six

Ethics in Complex Systems

Chapter 22

Editors' Introduction

[M]an must not revel either in the inventory of his "qualities" nor in his achievements; his freedom is unfathomable; he can be the author of the best and the worst; he has to reposition his being in relation to what caused him to emerge in the world and in relation to the life that supports him and whose sense he bears.

—Dominique Janicaud[1]

SO FAR THIS BOOK HAS CONSIDERED some of the main ethical traditions influencing water use decisions, especially within the context of modern management concerns. This final section looks to the future of our relationship with water and our growing appreciation of the complexity of social and ecological systems. To do so it considers two ways forward:[2] On the one hand, governing a complex system may be understood in terms of the need for more extensive and more effective management. On the other, complexity may lead us to a position of humility as we realize how little we understand of Earth's systems or the effects of our actions on them. It is not necessary to see these two avenues as mutually exclusive. In a certain sense, they both point toward the same goal of making decisions regarding water under conditions of uncertainty. Here we introduce some of the basic elements necessary for understanding Earth as a complex system and outline how the essays in this section offer new perspectives for the future of water management.

James Lovelock postulated that the entire Earth, understood as a single organism, could be characterized as one large, self-organized system.[3] Lovelock's theory, referred to as the Gaia hypothesis, built upon findings by Erwin Schrödinger and other natural scientists, which suggested that organisms, in fact life itself, emerged in a manner consistent with the laws of thermodynamics.[4] Early ecologists, such as Eugene Odum, argued that these self-organizing systems operate at numerous different scales—from individual cells, to organs of the body, and through to populations, ecosystems, and the entire biosphere.[5] In the decades that followed, complex systems' theory developed. It emphasized the inherent instability of self-organizing entities and their propensity for non-linear and difficult-to-predict behavior.

These findings called into question a basic assumption of management: that ecosystems were inherently stable and that the goal of environmental policies was to establish a desired baseline of ecosystem functioning and to use this baseline as a goal toward which to manage. The results of this approach have been disappointing, even disastrous. For example, the assumption that forests naturally stabilize as mature stands of tall, uniform species of trees was used by the U.S. Forest Service to try to produce the maximum sustainable yield of forests. Yet these attempts failed because they did not appreciate the complex conditions under which forests develop or the natural changes that characterize them.[6]

An alternative approach based on a better understanding of the behavior of complex systems and the types of management best suited for their governance was developed. In the 1970s, C. S. Holling and others pioneered the field of adaptive management to give effect to these insights.[7] This perspective rejects the assumption of stability and replaces it with that of change in recognition that ecological systems often exhibit non-linear responses to disturbances; likewise, our attitudes toward management must therefore countenance the inherent uncertainty of trying to manage complex systems.[8] As Norton's essay in this volume emphasizes, key features to this approach are (1) its emphasis on social learning as the result of management experiments;[9] (2) the development of pragmatic, objective-oriented partnerships with affected stakeholders;[10] and (3) a closer consideration of the different, and interacting scales at which management affects social and ecological systems, from the relatively fast biological scales such as those of human lives to the long, geologic scales such as those of carbon sequestration by oceans.[11]

Contents

This final section presents two essays on ethics and the complex systems of which the hydrological cycle is a part. The first, by Malin Falkenmark and Carl Folke, argues that earlier traditions of water management and their *ex post* attempts to deal with the impacts of social activities have failed to reflect the fact that the world is made up of complex, interlocking systems. Rather, management must be based on a whole systems perspective. In response, they present an alternative system of water management that recognizes visible, "blue water" and invisible, "green water" (such as that used in evapotranspiration) in a manner that balances human well-being and ecosystem needs. This position is called ecohydrosolidarity, which emphasizes the ethical right to a just sharing of the rainfall used in human development and the freshwater needed for sustaining the ecosystem services that provide for human well-being. They critique, and then provocatively expand upon, the idea of integrated water resource management and the need to promote an adaptive attitude toward complexity that includes surface, subsurface, and atmospheric water. The overall goal is to secure a sustainable use of dynamic landscapes by recognizing the interplay of terrestrial and aquatic ecosystems and their continued production of vital ecosystem services.

The second essay, by Peter G. Brown and Jeremy J. Schmidt, agrees with the idea that future efforts in water management must be premised on an ethic that treats humans and nature as a dynamic, mutually interdependent system. However, rather than explore how our existing water management paradigms can be improved upon, they focus their attention on how humans—and their management actions—are conceived of as part of larger narratives that legitimate attitudes toward water. From their perspective, Earth's complexity requires an upfront acknowledgment not only of uncertainty but also of our ignorance. As such, they critique some of the underlying ideas of modern water management and argue for an ethic they call compassionate retreat. From this perspective, what is also needed in future water management efforts is a recovery of those ethical attitudes of respect and reciprocity for nature that have been lost in modern management that prioritize scientific rationality as the basis for water management.

Notes

1. D. Janicaud, *On the human condition*, E. Brennan (trans.). (New York: Routledge, 2005), 11.

2. See, E. Lövbrand, J. Stripple, and B. Wiman, "Earth system governmentality: reflections on science in the Anthropocene," *Global Environmental Change* 19 (2009): 7–13.

3. J. Lovelock, *Gaia: a new look at life on Earth.* (New York: Oxford University Press, 1979).

4. E. Schrodinger, *What is life?* (New York: Cambridge University Press, 2006).

5. E. Odum, *Fundamentals of ecology.* (Philadelphia: Saunders, 1953).

6. N. Langston, *Forest dreams, forest nightmares: the paradox of old growth in the inland West.* (Seattle: University of Washington Press, 1995).

7. C. S. Holling (ed.), *Adaptive environmental assessment and management.* (New York: John Wiley & Sons, 1978).

8. L. Gunderson, C. S. Holling, and S. Light (edss), *Barriers and bridges to the renewal of ecosystems and institutions.* (New York: Columbia University Press, 1995).

9. C. Walters, *Adaptive management of renewable resources.* (New York: MacMillan, 1986).

10. L. Gunderson, "Adaptive dancing: interactions between social resilience and ecological crises," in *Navigating social–ecological systems*, ed. F. Berkes, J. Colding, and C. Folke (Cambridge, UK: Cambridge University Press, 2003), 33–52.

11. L. Gunderson and C. S. Holling (eds.), *Panarchy: understanding transformations in human and natural systems.* (Washington, DC: Island Press, 2002).

Chapter 23

Ecohydrosolidarity: A New Ethics for Stewardship of Value-Adding Rainfall

Malin Falkenmark[1] and Carl Folke[2]

Introduction

Humanity continues to undermine the life support system of the planet, reflected in the continuous decline of ecosystem services.[3] Many rivers are running dry, many water systems are severely polluted, and many land systems have passed ecological thresholds. In the past, environmental consequences of interventions with land and water have been addressed in the *ex post* perspective,[4] as illustrated by the recent GEO 4 report with its detailed cause/effect analyses of a whole gamut of environmental challenges.[5] In the past, focus has been on environmental impact assessment and on analysis of experienced symptoms of ecological change rather than on finding ways to minimize environmental damage. While ecosystems have continued to degrade, strong driving forces have continued to work and will be further exacerbating this massive undermining of the life support system.[6] In this situation, constructive and implementable proposals are urgent of *what can be done to mitigate such impacts* and the resulting biodiversity decline.

What has not been properly understood is the fundamental involvement of water phenomena in the ecological degradation processes. The base for the past approach was laid during a period of widespread water blindness, culminating in the Brundtland Commission's report on environment and development in 1987.[7] Awareness of water's function on land remained focused on erosion, while the infiltrated rain in the root zone, that is, the life-giving green water, was seen as "soil."[8] Land was seen as two-dimensional, with limited attention paid to the water in the root zone without which the land remains infertile. What was neglected was freshwater's fundamental role as the blood of the life-support system of the biosphere as a whole.[9] Also neglected was the role of water flows in linking the land and water systems as well as freshwater's role as ecosystem determinant: green water in relation to terrestrial ecosystems, blue water to aquatic ecosystems.[10]

This chapter will illustrate the opportunity to benefit from water's many different roles in a catchment, thereby linking humans and ecosystems and allowing a move toward conscious *ex ante* balancing between different societal uses on the one hand and ecological functions in nature on the other, striving toward what we here call ecohydrosolidarity—the ethical right to a just sharing of the rainfall over catchments and in landscapes that provides freshwater for human development and simultaneously accounts for the critical role of freshwater in generating ecosystem services for human well-being. To remedy the past shortcomings, adequate attention has now to be paid to water's flow through the landscape, benefiting from its integrating function for human well-being directly through freshwater use by people and indirectly in sustaining ecosystem dynamics and resilience, generating critical ecosystem services. This broader view of water properly acknowledges fundamental land–water–ecosystem linkages and should be captured in a catchment-based, integrated approach to governance, like the recent calls for adaptive water management of river basins.[11]

We also need to identify fundamental thresholds in related ecosystems; introduce resilience-building toward human-induced change; identify water's roles in resilience building; introduce an "L" for "land" use in the integrated water resources management tool (IWRM), changing it to ILWRM; and develop a mode of adaptive management to human interventions in the landscape.[12] This would make it possible to move toward a governance system, characterized by navigating toward *catchment-based compatibility* between the main interests and phenomena of land use, water use, and sustained ecosystem functions.[13]

This chapter stresses the need for such a broader adaptive landscape management approach as a basis toward *ecohydrosolidarity* in interdependent social–ecological systems. Social–ecological systems research recognizes that systems of people and nature are coupled systems, and not just occasionally linked, but strongly interdependent.[14] Freshwater plays a fundamental role in providing basic life support in such systems. Eco-hydrosolidarity expands the challenge from sharing blue water resources to developing flexible governance structures that account for the role of water in all its dynamic functions in catchments. The ecohydrosolidarity lies in an explicit accounting of value-adding of rainfall for the productive capacity and resilience of the life-support systems that sustain human well-being and societal development.

We propose active stewardship of water partitioning in dynamic landscapes as a management strategy toward ecohydrosolidarity. Here we summarize main characteristics related to water's essential functions in the life-support system and its inherent ability to link terrestrial and aquatic systems. We highlight the importance of rainwater partitioning at the ground level and its relation to land use and ecosystem services, including food production, and call attention to the opportunity that it opens for active management of landscape activities toward ecohydrosolidarity; we then address the dynamics originating from precipitation variability and anthropogenous system changes; and finally highlight water and ecosystem resilience and resilience building with examples of thresholds involved and how they could be approached from a water perspective.

Opportunity to Benefit from Water-Based Catchment Linkages

Water—a Key Element in the Life-Support System

Water is a key element of the biosphere in both the micro and the macro scales.[15] On the one hand it is a major component of living tissues and cells; on the other it has fundamental energy distribution functions in the global system through three mutually balancing sets of water-related twin processes: physically (evaporation/condensation), chemically (crystallization/solution), and biologically (water molecule splitting/reassemblage through respiration).[16] For these reasons, water plays a central role in the self-organization of complex adaptive ecosystems[17] and thereby for the provisioning of many ecosystem services.[18]

Humanity shapes the processes of the biosphere and is simultaneously fundamentally dependent on its proper functioning. The hydrological cycle is critical in this context. Due to a multiple set of functions of primary importance in land/water/ecosystem management, management must incorporate a whole set of different water-related perspectives: in particular body functions/health perspective; socioeconomic functions/income raising and energy production perspectives; biomass production function/food, fuelwood, timber, forest, carbon sequestration perspectives; carrier functions/erosion and pollution mobility perspectives; and habitat functions/aquatic ecosystem perspectives.

Multiple Roles Also in Environmental Impact Generation

A fundamental challenge in the social–ecological system is the fact that development involves a number of landscape-based manipulations: both of the *water components* to meet social water needs (municipal, industrial, irrigation, energy production, cooling and heating, etc.); and of the *land and vegetation components* to meet land-based needs and biomass production (agricultural production, forestry, urbanization). Water's roles in the landscape also result in cause–effect linkages, so that all these manipulations tend to generate water-related environmental impacts; the water manipulations related to water flows and seasonality, the land manipulations related to rainwater partitioning between vapor flow and liquid flow, altering river flow and seasonality, water table, etc. By these changes ecosystem determinants are being influenced, leading to various forms of ecological impacts, many of which are difficult to avoid. The side effects tend to develop in steps, involving impacts first of the water itself, next on organisms that depend on water, and finally within ecosystems of which they are part. This ecological cascade may continue in a multiscale fashion, with diverse links producing even distant effects, through, for example, atmospheric transport or degradation of resources and ecosystem services across nations, causing social and economic consequences.

Water's Role for Land Productivity

Water's flow in the landscape defines the spatial unit for addressing upstream/downstream conflicts of interests. When ecosystem thresholds are being approached, future options for societal development are constrained. To some extent the effects are avoidable, but unavoidable manipulations indicate the need for *trade-off striking* and the existence of *ethical considerations*.

Evidently, the past, *ex post* approach to environmental problems has to be replaced by one of active, *ex ante* perspective on societal linkages with the life-support system. Both a sustainable land productivity and a sustainable water flow system must be secured. To this aim, the ongoing shift in thinking on water's functions in the landscape will be supportive.[19] The past approach, inherited from the water resources engineering era, has its focus on liquid water flow solely—*blue water*. This means incorporating only one third of the true water resource, constituted by the precipitation over the continents, and addressing water in agriculture only in terms of irrigation. The current approach is now shifting toward seeing continental precipitation as the basic water resource, and directing adequate interest to the naturally infiltrated soil moisture—*green water*. This is the water that supports most plant production. The green water evaporates during use, and this consumptive water use incorporates two thirds of all precipitation over the continents.

The blue-green approach puts a finger on the importance of *partitioning changes* of the incoming precipitation in its contact with the ground level—changes that are essential for the generation of ecosystem services in dynamic landscapes (Figure 23-1). Such changes are especially evident in the tropics where the potential evapotranspiration is high. The green water conceptualization makes it possible to address, for instance, linkages between forests and water, and to bury many past myths in that regard.[20]

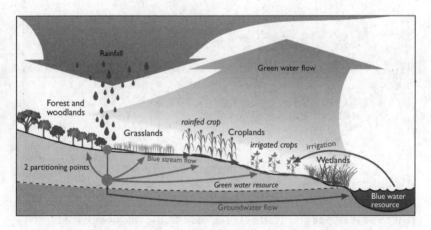

Figure 23-1 Water partitioning at the land surface between green water flow through vegetation and blue water flow used by human society.

Compromise-Building and Ecohydrosolidarity

As already indicated, water's movement through the catchment generates water-related causal chains between human activities related to food, water and energy supply, and income-generation activities, in the disturbance end, and ecosystem goods, such as biomass harvest, and services such as the role of biodiversity in pollination, in the target end. *The long-term goal will be to find criteria for the protection of the capacity for sustainable production of the life support system in the catchment.*

In view of water's flow, the catchment is a useful spatial unit for overview and compatibility analyses (Figure 23-2). It makes it possible to integrate the whole series of considerations required: water needs, land use needs, terrestrial ecosystems and their goods and services, as well as aquatic ecosystems and the goods and services that they provide. By reconciliation of conflicts of interest, such compatibility analyses of human livelihood interests, on the one hand, and unavoidable environmental consequences, on the other, should strive toward ecohydrosolidarity.

Securing resilience to ecological disturbances

Intergenerational equity involves the need to secure sustainable land productivity and long-term resilience to sustain and enhance crucial ecosys-

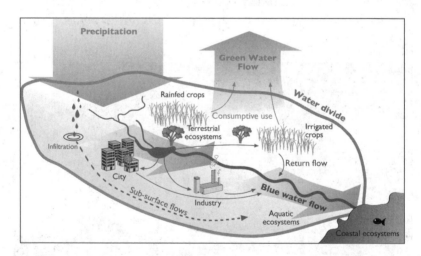

Figure 23-2 Blue and green features to be addressed in catchment-based trade-offs.

tem services for human well-being. Humanity increasingly alters the conditions, entering a spectrum of disturbances, to which organisms have evolved, which can lead to increased variability and uncertainty about the capacity of the environment to sustain society with essential goods and services.[21]

What has to be secured is resilience to disturbances in terms of capacity to absorb continuous change, persist, and continue to develop. This means addressing the resilience of the system as a buffer to disturbance, and biological diversity as insurance from a functional perspective.[22] Resilience is a measure of the amount of disturbance that can be absorbed before the ecosystem passes a threshold between one stable state such as tropical forest to another such as tropical grassland (i.e., undergoes a *regime shift*).[23] Human redirections of freshwater from its natural pathways may undermine the capacity of an ecosystem to redevelop following a disturbance, losing the services it used to generate.[24] The challenge is, in other words, to find compromises between obligations to environmental conventions and fundamental livelihood needs of the inhabitants to secure safe water, land productivity, aquatic goods and services of downstream ecosystems, on the one hand, and on the other resilience of terrestrial ecosystems to natural and human-made disturbances in order to secure ecosystem services and fundamental human well-being.

Ecohydrological catchment management involves coupling of green and blue freshwater issues to issues of ecosystem management in the landscape.[25] Although still largely an unexplored area, it is quite obvious that freshwater plays fundamental roles to maintain ecosystems' resilience to change. *Basic principles are now needed for the balancing of incompatible interests in a catchment.*

But such principles must be developed with due attention to *precipitation variability* and the uncertainties linked to that variability. Adding value through stewardship of rainfall is not a static process but highly dynamic. In a situation with degraded lands in the catchments, rainfall may rapidly be transformed to runoff and lost to coastal waters or in dry regions to the atmosphere through evaporation. The challenge is to make use of freshwater's role in the self-organized processes of living systems,[26] to make productive use of precipitation, and to catch rain and rainfall pulses before they are lost from the landscape.[27] It implies expanding the perspective of management from blue water uses only to also include green water in an active water-partitioning management of terrestrial and aquatic ecosystem services.

Land-Based Water Management

Effects of land cover conversions on water fluxes, local freshwater circulation through moisture feedback, and potential links to global climate processes is attracting increasing interest.[28] Here we develop the perspective of water partitioning management in catchments/landscapes. Starting with rainfall as the freshwater input, we identify eight significant partitioning features that redirect water flows. These are not new but have seldom been discussed together in a systems picture of the aforementioned integrated land and water resource management (ILWRM). We believe this approach has the potential to improve freshwater management for human well-being and help prepare for and even possibly avoid unpleasant surprises of, for example, water scarcity and droughts on the one hand and, for example, floods on the other.

The approach will be especially important in dry climate tropics where evapotranspiration plays a much larger role in the water partitioning between green and blue water resources than in the temperate zone. Thus, for a country like Kenya, the green water resource amounts to over 90% of the total water resource (Figure 23-3), as compared to 65% for the planet as a whole. All water is involved in generating both social services and ecological functions and services, the latter determining the ecological resilience of a catchment/basin. For many poor semiarid countries, where blue water will not be sufficient to produce the food needed to meet a growing demand, a mixture of green and blue water management strategies will be required.

The basic aim of the land-based water-partitioning management that we propose is to make productive use of rainwater while passing through the catchment from the upstream land areas, dominated by green water use and blue water generation, to the downstream areas dominated by blue water use and environmental flow. The management involves a balancing of *water for direct human uses* in terms of both blue water–based uses and green water–based uses, on the one hand, and on the other *water required to sustain the capacity of ecosystems* to generate essential ecosystem

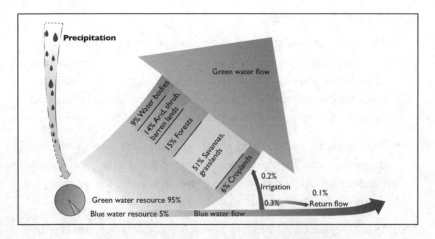

Figure 23-3 Partitioning of the rainfall over Kenya between green water in areas with different land cover, forming evapotranspiration, and blue water in rivers and aquifers. Also shown are blue water withdrawals and their partitioning between consumptive water use and return flow back to the river system. The darker arrow indicates the amount that has to be reserved as environmental flow to support aquatic ecosystems.

services for human well-being, in terms of both blue water–dependent aquatic ecosystems and green water–dependent terrestrial ecosystems. It also means to secure convective precipitation through moisture feedback, to secure environmental flow for aquatic ecosystems, and to secure measures against drought phenomena and protection against flood-based phenomena.

Upstream and Downstream Water Partitioning Components

Water partitioning management for freshwater use, ecosystem services, and human well-being involves a large number of components—in *recharge areas upstream* as well as in *discharge areas downstream* in the landscape. One aim is to make productive use of precipitation and to catch rain and rainfall pulses before they are lost from the landscape. The endeavors basically involve knowledge-based balancing upstream between terrestrial ecosystems of various kinds and runoff generation for rivers and aquifers, and downstream between wetlands, cities, and aquatic ecosystems, involving the following components.

Recharge Area Activities

- Managing of *vegetation* to secure crop production (currently 50 to 60% of global crop production is rain-fed), timber production, greenhouse gas sequestration through forestry, productive grasslands for livestock, local moisture-feedback cycles, and numerous other terrestrial ecosystem services

- Managing of *infiltration* to secure green water availability, improve soils and the numerous terrestrial ecosystem services dependent on the water holding capacity of soils, secure drought protection and good crop yields

- Manage *rainwater harvesting* to secure local water during dry spells for supplementary irrigation, household water needs, etc., by capturing runoff in tanks to make water available for critical phases of crop production and other ecosystem services.

- Manage *groundwater recharge* to secure protection against flash floods and base flow generation, and thereby reduce effects of undesired floods

Discharge Area Activities

- Manage *flood flow* by storing water surplus in reservoirs to secure flood protection, minimize inundations and flood damage, and maximize downstream water security for human needs

- Manage *groundwater seepage* in water-fed wetlands to secure wetland ecosystems and their role as stepping stones for migrating mobile links species[29] of significance in ecosystem dynamics and development, and in regulating ecosystem services.

- Manage *reservoir outflow* to secure flood pulses for inundation-dependent flood plains used for pastures and for aquatic ecosystems and support pasture-oriented food production and related ecosystem services, and for flushing of pollutants and silt

- Manage *trade-offs* between human withdrawals for cities and industry and aquatic ecosystems to secure adequate environmental flow

The time is mature to start to address such water interactions in catchments and landscapes. It has previously been done for parts of the systems, for example, the trade-off between vegetation management and freshwater for direct human use, which led to the Working for Water Program of South Africa.[30]

Hydro-Unit-Based Approach

In this sense, we envision the possibility to develop schemes of "hydro-unit"-based land management under different land uses and with different partitioning characteristics as a central feature of the ecohydrosolidarity perspective. Such an approach would put the finger on critical trade-offs of water use in catchments/landscapes but also on how to make improved use of the bloodstream of the biosphere by creating water partitioning synergies between different uses and enhance overall catchment productivity. The landscape could be tentatively divided into such hydro-units, which would require an explicit attention to upstream/downstream freshwater interactions and to blue/green water tradeoffs, with a focus on green water management upstream and blue water availability downstream.

Ecohydrosolidarity Perspective

Needless to say, the water partitioning management approach outlined here would entail a major shift in thinking of current freshwater management and governance. The shift entails a holistic view of catchments and their interdependent social–ecological systems with institutions and multigovernance systems that develop an adaptive management approach for navigating ecohydrological solidarity within and between regions and nations. However, our plea for starting with rainfall and explicitly accounting for both green and blue water flows, identifying their synergies, trade-offs, and redirections with rainfall dynamics through active management and stewardship, may not be too far away. Part of the approach is captured in I(L)WRM and might be incorporated into attempts to develop catchment-based management of direct water uses by humans and water uses for bundles of ecosystem services. Efforts such as the European Union's Freshwater Directive and the legislation approach taken in South Africa, integrating forest and water management, may lead the way.

Tipping Points, Thresholds, and Ecosystem Resilience

However, there is an additional and profoundly important feature that needs to be incorporated in a water partitioning management approach for ecohydrosolidarity—the *freshwater–ecosystem resilience connection.*

Ecologists have shown that ecosystems may tip over from one dynamic state (stability basin) to another and that such regime shift increasingly is the result of human actions causing loss of resilience.[31] Among those are lakes shifting from clear water to muddy water systems; savannas shifting from productive grasslands to unproductive bush lands, with mismanagement of fire, grazing, and rainfall involved in such shifts; reefs that shift from coral to algal dominance; and many others.[32] Resilience—the capacity of a system to persist and continue to develop in the face of changes, often rapid and unpredictable, like storms, floods, fire, pest outbreaks—is a central feature that needs to be actively managed to sustain the generation of terrestrial and aquatic ecosystem services. Folke contrasted conventional freshwater and resource management as still often practiced, on the one hand, with more dynamic and adaptive management, and governance systems required for building resilience to deal with change, including climatic change, on the other.[33] Insights are increasing on the social challenges in developing adaptive water management in catchments and river basins.[34]

Hydrological Modifications and Major Ecosystem Shifts

Gordon and others recently investigated the link between modifications of hydrological flows for agricultural production and catastrophic ecosystem regime shifts.[35] They identified evidence for three categories of water/agriculture-related regime shifts in the hydrological cycle with strong implications for water partitioning management:

- *Agriculture and aquatic systems,* including changes in runoff quality and quantity that lead to regime shifts in downstream aquatic systems; examples include regime shifts in lakes in relation to fertilizers transported through runoff or through sediment loading into rivers

- *Agriculture and soil,* in which changes in infiltration and soil moisture result in terrestrial regime shifts (e.g., grazing by livestock reducing vegetation cover), setting in motion a feedback that decreases nutrient and water accumulation or destabilizes water in the root zone. Other such examples include rise in the water table due to reductions in evapotranspiration, caused by replacement of deep-rooted trees with annual crops, causing salinization; or rapid yield decline in semiarid croplands caused by shortened fallow period.

- *Agriculture and the atmosphere*, in which changes in evapotranspiration result in regime shifts in the climatic system itself, or in terrestrial ecosystems as a consequence of such shifts. Examples include the shifts between wet savanna systems and dry savanna systems in the Sahara and the Sahel, transitions of forests to savannas in the Amazon region, and possible changes in the monsoon behavior as a consequence of land cover change.[36]

Figure 23-4 illustrates the differences between gradual ecosystem change (1) and three different ecosystem shifts (2–4) using precipitation–vegetation interactions as an example. In (1) the relation between rainfall is linear (i.e., the more it rains the more vegetation), in (2) precipitation above a certain level may cause a threshold effect with rapid increase of vegetation into a new stability landscape, in (3) precipitation interacts with two different stability landscapes through a hysteresis effect, and in (4) such change may be irreversible.[37]

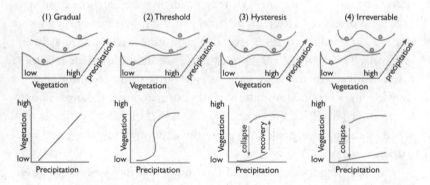

Figure 23-4 Differences between gradual ecosystem change (1) and three different ecosystem shifts (2–4) using precipitation–vegetation interactions as an example.[38]

Deforestation on Borneo for timber and soybean production to global markets is an example of a human-induced water-related ecosystem regime shift. Bornean rain forest dynamics are driven by El Niño–induced droughts that trigger mast reproduction among trees and fauna, thereby serving as a trigger for rain forest regeneration. Curran and others have shown that in Indonesian Borneo (Kalimantan), concession-based timber extraction, oil palm plantation establishment, and weak institutions have produced highly fragmented and vulnerable forests with low resilience.[39] As a consequence, El Niño currently triggers droughts and wildfires and erodes the basis for rural livelihoods.[40] Page and others estimated that the widespread El Niño–related wildfires of Borneo in 1997 released between 0.81 and 2.57 Gt of carbon to the atmosphere, equivalent to 13 to 40% of the mean annual global carbon emissions from fossil fuels.[41]

Indirect Role of Freshwater in Ecological Disturbances

The role of water as a direct disturbance is well studied (e.g., floods and drought debates). However, the indirect role of freshwater in ecological disturbance, like fire, insect outbreaks, and pulses of grazing, is an unexplored area. It is well known that human actions alter the magnitude, frequency, and duration of such disturbances or compounded perturbations,[42] but the role of freshwater dynamics in compounded perturbations has scarcely been investigated.

Sudden ecosystem regime shifts, involving water redirections and impacts through land use changes, may result in huge surprises and irreversible changes with losses of essential ecosystem services causing severe impacts on livelihoods and social and economic well-being locally and regionally. For example, rural poor people are significant beneficiaries of forest biodiversity and ecosystem services. In a study commissioned by the G8+5 environment ministers, it was estimated that the gross domestic product (GDP) of the poor in India would increase by almost 60% when attempts were made to capture the economic value of these non-marketed services.[43]

The 2008 report of the World Resources Institute stresses the livelihood significance of managing for social–ecological resilience to secure essential ecosystem services including food production.[44] Needless to say, the water–resilience–ecosystem services nexus is critical in this context. Water resources management urgently needs to broaden its scope and become engaged in active stewardship of this dynamic. Water-partitioning management of catchments and landscapes, which we have started to explore here, may be a fruitful avenue in this context, with potential to form a sound basis for ecohydrosolidarity among people.

Conclusions

This chapter has addressed some fundamental shortcomings when it comes to conventional perspectives of "environmental protection" and their focus on ecosystem health. The *ex post* approach has focused mainly on environmental impacts of various societal activities, identified symptoms of environmental degradation, and tried to conserve and protect nature from human actions. This has generated a feeling in the general debate that humans and nature are two separate systems and that environmental protection is equivalent to "no touch"—a goal difficult to implement in an era with triple squeeze acting on the life-support system as subject to the effects of population growth, socioeconomic expansion, and climate change. In the meantime, environmental degradation has continued to increase, expand, and intensify, and ecological systems have been observed to pass thresholds moving them to degraded states.

In this chapter, we have explored the possibilities to switch this approach into an *ex ante* approach by recognizing the essential role of freshwater in generating both terrestrial and aquatic ecosystem services. In this sense, freshwater management significantly expands from the narrow blue water focus that hitherto has dominated management to a focus on rainfall over catchments and the role of what we call water partitioning management in this context. The overarching goal is to secure sustainable use of landscapes by recognizing the freshwater interplay and requirements of terrestrial and aquatic ecosystems and their continued production of vital ecosystems services.

Eight pathways for value-adding stewardship of rainfall through water partitioning management have been identified, explicitly connecting in a holistic manner freshwater, ecosystem services, and human well-being. They have been clustered under *recharge areas upstream* and *discharge areas downstream* and account for rainfall pulses. The purpose is to direct freshwater into productive activities in landscapes.

Hence, we propose an active stewardship of the landscape as management strategy, based on compromise-building and ecohydrosolidarity.

262 ETHICS IN COMPLEX SYSTEMS

This is basically a broad-based adaptive management with rainwater partitioning processes at the land surface in focus, especially since these processes are influenced by and respond to land-use alterations. As a management tool, we propose structuring the landscape into what we call *hydro-units under different land use*. This would make it possible to carry out a dynamic catchment-based planning and analysis of alternative land-use patterns and their compatibility, improving productive use of not only rainfall as such, but also rain variability in order to create synergies and value added in the generation of bundles of ecosystem services.

A new framework for analyzing the critical role of freshwater in landscape processes has been explored and developed in this chapter. We hope that the perspective will stimulate the development of new governance structures for integrated and adaptive landscape management. We believe that the rainwater–ecosystems perspective in the catchment context presented here could provide a foundation for institutional developments toward ecohydrosolidarity among people.

Notes

1. Stockholm International Water Institute; Stockholm Resilience Center, Stockholm University, SE-10691 Stockholm, Sweden.

2. Stockholm Resilience Center, Stockholm University, SE-10691 Stockholm, Sweden; Beijer Institute of Ecological Economics, Royal Swedish Academy of Sciences, PO Box 50005, SE-10405 Stockholm, Sweden.

3. Millennium Ecosystem Assessment, *Ecosystems and human well-being: synthesis.* (Washington, DC: Island Press, 2005).

4. M. Falkenmark and C. Folke, "The ethics of socio-ecohydrological catchment management: towards hydrosolidarity," *Hydrology and Earth System Sciences* 6 (2002): 1–9.

5. GEO-4, Global Environment Outlook. Environment for Development (United Nations Environment Program, 2008).

6. Millennium Ecosystem Assessment, 2005.

7. M. Falkenmark, "Water and sustainability: a reappraisal," *Environment: Science and Policy for Sustainable Development* 50 (2008): 4–16.

8. M. Falkenmark and J. Lundquist, "World freshwater problems—call for a new realism," *Background report 1, comprehensive assessment of the freshwater resources of the world.* (Stockholm Environment Institute, 1997).

9. M. Falkenmark and C. Folke, "Freshwater and welfare fragility—introduction," *Philosophical Transactions of the Royal Society London, Biological Sciences* 358 (2003): 1917–1920.

10. J. Rockström, L. Gordon, C. Folke, M. Falkenmark, and M. Engvall, "Link-

ages between water vapor flows, food production and terrestrial ecosystem services," *Conservation Ecology* 3 (1999): 5; M. Falkenmark and J. Rockström, "Assessing the water challenge of a new green revolution in developing countries," *Proceedings National Academy of Sciences* 104 (2007): 6253–6260.

11. C. Pahl-Wostl, J. Sendzimir, P. Jeffrey, J. Aerts, G. Berkamp, and K. Cross, "Managing change toward adaptive water management through social learning," *Ecology and Society* 12 (2007): 30.

12. See for examples: C. Folke, "Freshwater for resilience: a shift in thinking," *Philosophical Transactions of the Royal Society London, Biological Sciences* 358 (2003): 2027–2036; J. Sendzimir, P. Magnuszewski, Z. Flachner, P. Balogh, G. Molnar, A. Sarvari, and Z. Nagy, "Assessing the resilience of a river management regime: informal learning in a shadow network in the Tisza River Basin," *Ecology and Society* 13 (2007): 11.

13. E. Enfors, L. Gordon, G. Peterson, and D. Bossio, "Making investments in dryland development work: participatory scenario planning in the Makanya Catchment, Tanzania," *Ecology and Society* 13 (2008): 42.

14. V. Galaz, T. Hahn, P. Olsson, C. Folke, and U. Svedin, "The problem of fit among biophysical systems, environmental regimes and broader governance systems: insights and emerging challenges," in *Institutions and Environmental Change: Principal Findings, Applications, and Research Frontiers*, ed. O. Young, L. A. King, and H. Schroeder (Cambridge, MA: MIT Press, 2008), 147–186.

15. Falkenmark and Folke, 2002; 2003.

16. W. Ripl, "Water: the bloodstream of the biosphere," *Philosophical Transactions of the Royal Society London, Biological Sciences* 358 (2003): 1921-1934.

17. S. Levin, *Fragile dominion: complexity and the commons*. (Reading, MA: Perseus Books, 1999).

18. Rockström et al., 1999.

19. M. Falkenmark and J. Rockström, "Towards more resilient land and water resources management," Draft editorial, *Journal of Water Resource Planning and Management* (2009).

20. I. Calder, *The Blue Revolution: land use and integrated water resources management.* (London: Earthscan, 1999).

21. C. Folke, S. Carpenter, B. Walker, M. Scheffer, T. Elmqvist, L. Gunderson, and C.S. Holling, "Regime shifts, resilience and biodiversity in ecosystem management," *Annual Review of Ecology, Evolution and Systematics* 35 (2004): 557–581.

22. Ibid.

23. M. Scheffer, S. Carpenter, J. Foley, C. Folke, and B. Walker, "Catastrophic shifts in ecosystems," *Nature* 413 (2001): 591–596.

24. L. Gordon, G. Peterson, and E. Bennett, "Agricultural modifications of hydrological flows create ecological surprises," *Trends in Ecology and Evolution* 23 (2008): 211–219.

25. L. Gordon, W. Steffen, B. Jönsson, C. Folke, M. Falkenmark, and Å. Johannessen, "Human modification of global water vapor flows from the land surface," *Proceedings National Academy of Sciences* 102 (2005): 7612–7617.

26. Ripl, 2003.

27. R. Sivanappan, "State of the art on soil and water conservation, water harvesting and eco-restoration in Western Ghats," SIDA Workshop on Water Harvesting (Tamil Nadu, India, 1989).

28. Gordon et al., 2005; S. Rost, D. Gerten, A. Bondeau, W. Lucht, J. Rohwer, and S. Schaphoff, "Agricultural green and blue water consumption and its influence on the global water system," *Water Resources Research* 44 (2008): W09405; S. Rost, D. Gerten, A. Bondeau, W. Lucht, J. Rohwer, and S. Schaphoff, "Agricultural green and blue water consumption and its influence on the global water system," *Water Resources Research* 44 (2008): W09405; M. Kravcik, J. Pokorny, M. Kovac, and E. Toth, "Water for the recovery of the climate," *A new water paradigm.* Available: www.water paradigm.org (accessed, 2007).

29. J. Lundberg and F. Moberg, "Mobile link organisms and ecosystem functioning: implications for ecosystem resilience and management," *Ecosystems* 6 (2003): 87–98).

30. B. Van Wilgen, R. Cowling, and C. Burgers, "Valuation of ecosystem services: a case study from South African fynbos ecosystems," *Bioscience* 46 (1996): 184–189.

31. Scheffer et al. 2001; Folke et al. 2004.

32. B. Walker and J. Meyers, "Thresholds in ecological and social–ecological systems: a developing database," *Ecology and Society* 9 (2004): 3.

33. Folke, 2003.

34. See Pahl-Wostl et al., 2007.

35. Gordon et al., 2008.

36. Ibid.

37. For further explanation see Scheffer et al., 2001.

38. Modified from Gordon et al., 2008.

39. L. Curran, S. Trigg, A. McDonald, D. Astiani, Y. Hardiono, P. Siregar, I. Caniago, and E. Kasischke, "Lowland forest loss in protected areas of Borneo," *Science* 303 (2004): 1000–1003.

40. Ibid.

41. S. Page, F. Siegert, J. Rieley, H. Boehm, A. Jayak, and S. Limink. "The amount of carbon released from peat and forest fires in Indonesia during 1997," *Nature* 420 (2002): 61–65.

42. R. Paine, M. Tegner, and E. Johnson, "Compounded perturbations yield ecological surprises," *Ecosystems* 1 (1998): 535–545; Folke et al., 2004.

43. TEEB, "The economics of ecosystems and biodiversity," Available at: http://ec.europa.eu/environment/nature/biodiversity/economics/index_en.htm (accessed, 2008).

44. World Resources Institute, "Roots of resilience: growing the wealth of the poor," World Resources Institute in collaboration with UNDP, UNEP and the World Bank. (Washington, DC: World Resources Institute, 2008).

Chapter 24

An Ethic of Compassionate Retreat

Peter G. Brown and Jeremy J. Schmidt

The more the island of knowledge expands in the sea of ignorance, the larger its boundary to the unknown.

—L. S. Rodberg and V. F. Weisskopf[1]

What makes . . . the Gaia Hypothesis so inspiring? . . . the awareness of our being anchored in the earth and the universe, the awareness that we are not here alone nor for ourselves alone, but that we are an integral part of higher, mysterious entities against whom it is not advisable to blaspheme. This forgotten awareness is encoded in all religions.

—Vaclav Havel[2]

WE NEED A FUNDAMENTAL SHIFT in perspective within water management. To attain such a goal, we must reconsider how efforts in modern water management have, in general, focused on scientific and technological advances and assigned a declining importance to cosmology, religion and ethics, areas formerly used to provide a context for the ends of human knowledge and action. A good place to start is to critically evaluate ideas in the broader Western narrative that have tended to privilege human welfare, scientific knowledge, and technological know-how. The alternate view we suggest, that of *compassionate retreat*, positions water use decisions in a different, although not wholly new narrative. In this narrative, the rightful role of humans is more modest and is mindful of two factors. The first addresses scientific uncertainties about water's role in earth systems and the potentially detrimental effects of acting on inherently limited knowledge.[3] The second enumerates humanity's duties of respect and reciprocity as an increasingly influential and potentially responsible member of Earth's living communities.

A central problem with the ethical narrative underlying much of modern water management is that policy decisions are conceived of primarily as epistemological (i.e. scientific or technological) questions, whose primary focus is on how to achieve a certain view of human welfare. This underlying narrative fails to consider how beliefs about human welfare legitimate actions that impact the hydrological cycle. It also fails to consider the non-epistemological aspects of moral experience that influence our acceptance of different water use practices; some of these include issues of aesthetics, compassion, fairness, temperance, habit and custom. As such, the criteria for right and wrong and their applications are not adequately situated in relation to either the empirical realities of the hydrological cycle or facts about moral experience and human obligations.

In questioning the basic tenets of the narrative of modern water management, we should not seek to consolidate water use decisions under a single model of decision making, such as those management paradigms that emphasize epistemic claims over moral concerns. Rather, we should recognize that all knowledge is partial and limited; and all management actions affecting water have moral dimensions. And, as the epigraphs to this essay imply, we would suggest that effective, ethical water management systems must take into account three things. (1) The uncertainties still rife in modern management, which reflect a very incomplete understanding of complex social and ecological systems. In fact, given our limited understanding in some cases it might be prudent to confess ignorance. (2) A revised—though by no means new—view of the relationship between humans and the rest of life and the world. In framing this part of the argument, we are drawing on Aristotle's distinctions between scientific knowledge (*epistêmê*), technological know-how (*technê*), and practical wisdom (*phronêsis*). (3) How a revised perspective may help water managers to begin thinking about ethical behavior in times of crisis, and ultimately how to turn from a management perspective focused primarily on scientific and technological knowledge towards what we call "compassionate retreat." From the perspective of compassionate retreat, water management would begin by recognizing that modern societies, as the dominant ecological force in the Anthropocene, must operate in view of their potential to degrade, whether temporarily or permanently, the productive capacity of different ecosystems.[4] Within this framework, human managers would seek a relationship wherein knowledge and actions are situated within the systems they seek to manage, and operate in a manner that will increase their practical wisdom as they encounter uncertainties and complexity. This approach would also require a deep respect, growing out of the recognition that human beings are part of the universe and its expression in the exuberance of life on Earth.

Some Ethical Assumptions of the Modern Management Narrative

The past century has witnessed fierce debates over the role of philosophical and ethical values in science. In particular, there has been a fundamental questioning of the so-called deductive-nomological method, wherein particular truths are rationally inferred (often experimentally) from universal laws about the way the world works. More recently, similar debates have arisen in ethics, particularly in the model of applied ethics, wherein correct action in a particular case is, in theory, rationally deduced from general moral principles.[5] Without entering in on the details of these arguments, one development evolving from this discussion has been the reinterpretation of modern science and ethics in narrative terms. Such narratives reflect particular points of view; they are often stories of peoples that provide a way of understanding where they have come from and where they may be going, rather than objective theories regarding what they ought to do. These narratives share traits with myths and stories, such as having a beginning, a middle and an end, the latter sometimes being foretold, such as in the apocalypse in the biblical Book of Revelation or the predictions of the Book of the Hopi. Although we seldom recognize it, from a narrative perspective, modern water management is conditioned by its own cultural story. This story grounds and defines the values that it derives for making water use decisions and provides the context for the ends toward which its policies aim.

Modern water management arose within the context of the mainstream Western narrative, which begins with humanity as the main focus of moral concern, separate from and generally understood to be superior to the rest of the world. From this beginning, nature has been viewed (in the main) as something to be transformed in the service of humanity, in recent centuries by using scientific knowledge and industrial technology.[6] What is especially noteworthy about these initial normative premises is that they are prescientific—they took on many of their main features centuries before the scientific revolutions of the last several centuries, and have undergone little substantial revision in light of these monumental discoveries, such as those that have shaped our understandings of evolutionary biology. Within this old Western narrative, water's value is often tied to the type and quality of human life promoted within a culture. For instance, the essays commenting on Christianity in this volume emphasize that attitudes toward water are important due to the role of water in meeting obligations to fellow humans and their commitments of belief.[7] The essays that comment on Islamic and Hindu beliefs regarding water situate these beliefs within the larger cultural narratives of which these religions are a part and which influence the legitimacy of different legal or social claims to water.[8]

The scientific and technological developments of the last three centuries have used these underlying Western beliefs about the primacy of human needs and our inherent superiority over other creatures on Earth. They have advocated what have been presented as universal truths regarding the nature of our knowledge about the world and how to govern its systems. Although firmly based within a cultural narrative, a main feature of the modern approach to natural systems management has been this assumption of its universal claim to truth. For example, in the case of scientific positivism, a belief system that emerged in the late 19th and early 20th centuries, narratives of any kind were proclaimed to be nonscientific, metaphysical beliefs that should be eradicated from serious management thinking. Yet, the attempt to categorize them as such is itself based on the Western cultural narrative current at the time. It is important to note as well that the conceptual roots that explain the hydrological cycle in supposedly scientific terms are embedded within the 18th and early 19th century quest of "natural theology" to give a rational account of the amount and behavior of water on Earth—a window into the "mind of God."[9]

In this context, the term *natural theology* refers to an era of inquiry that sought to reconcile the emerging fields of scientific knowledge (after the Renaissance) with the Christian belief that the world was created by God. From this perspective, advances in such things as Newtonian mathematics, and their ability to give a rational account of natural phenomenon, were thought to confirm the general belief that the world functioned according to the dictates of a provident creator who had established the natural laws that govern the earth. Hence, to understand natural law was to understand the "mind of God." And, to explain natural processes through the techniques of modern science and philosophy provided a firm foundation for knowledge and justification to have faith in reason.

From the perspective of natural theology, the main epistemological problem regarding water was the seeming excess amount of it on Earth, a point we will return to later. In fact, up until the 19th century the central question puzzling natural theologians was why a perfect God would have put so much water on the earth.[10] The vastness of the seas and oceans, whose saltiness rendered them less useful, combined with the fact that freshwater in rivers appeared to flow wastefully into the ocean were problematical. How were they reconcilable with the wisdom of a God for whom all things had a purpose in the divine economy of the world in the service of humanity?[11] Answering this question drove the investigations that led to the scientific account of water's behavior now referred to as the hydrological cycle. However, as the concept of the hydrological cycle matured into an accepted account of water's behavior, its origins in this specific theological and cultural narrative slowly faded from view in favor of a rational point of view grounded in empirical observation.

Despite this shift to empirical science, the values inherent in the larger theological narrative were uncritically carried over in the project of making water a "resource" that could serve the Western ideal of human welfare. For instance, a common sentiment in late 19th century North America was the pressing need to capture surface waters from rivers and lakes into human systems before they flowed "wastefully" out to the sea.

In 1888, Major John Wesley Powell, an influential figure in North American water policy and former head of the U.S. Geological Survey, proclaimed that human diversions of water were key to the progress of Western civilization. Powell's arguments are emblematic of how water management shifted from its beginnings in natural theology to an Enlightenment ideal of human superiority. This view assumed that human reason, judgment, and science could make wonderful and endlessly productive improvements upon water's natural dispensation.[12]

Simple models of hydrological cycles are inadequate for understanding the actual behavior of water in complex ecosystems. For example, they almost universally failed to predict the often catastrophic changes to biophysical systems that are caused by human interference in natural cycles via large dams, intensive irrigation or changes in land cover. In 1909, with incomplete knowledge of the complex interrelationships between water and the environment, W. J. McGee declared water a natural resource that could (and should) be controlled by humans through technology, quantified through better science, and put to use for the greatest good of society.[13] Once head of the American Association for the Advancement of Science and a Secretary for the Inland Commission on U.S. Waterways, McGee's arguments found favorable hearing within the Progressive Era movement in American environmental politics.

The Progressive Era movement of the early 20th century was, in terms of environmental issues, concerned with the degradation and exploitation of natural resources. In particular, there was concern that without strong government leadership and management, the proclivity of selfish entrepreneurs to maximize profits would leave few resources for the future. In response, progressives argued for a larger role for government in natural resource policy from both the conservationist and "wise use" of all resources, as in the philosophy of utilitarians such as McGee.[14] The impact of declaring water a resource meant that it could be used in concert with other natural resources, such as forests, in service of the Progressive Era ideal of human progress.[15] Progress, at least, as measured in the utilitarian ethic of the day. As such, water became one factor in service to political liberalism's idea of human-centered values, in which the Earth's natural systems can be integrated and managed to achieve this goal for all.

David Feldman has described in careful detail how the political economy of U.S. water resource policy throughout the 20th century has been based on utilitarian claims.[16] Stephen Kraft has argued that these utilitarian notions are embedded in a larger narrative of utilitarian ethics received in western legal traditions.[17] Such an ethic fit its times perfectly, in its promotion of liberal ideas that legitimated living wherever one wants, having as many children as desired, and achieving an affluent life style. After World War II, these ideas were promoted on an even larger scale, under the guise of national and international "development." As part of a subsequent, broader narrative, the achievement of material wealth and increased industrial production then became part of an international, global project to alleviate poverty through increased living standards for all. The prophetic gospel of this management movement was "resource efficiency," and its goal was the harnessing of global resources entirely in the service of human production and consumption.[18] In the neoliberal version of this narrative, goods and services could be supplied at the lowest possible prices to consumers by using sufficiently liberalized or "free" markets. These markets could access free-flowing capital and operate without the tariffs and quotas that were previously seen as necessary for the protection of national interests. In partial support of this narrative, more than 45,000 large dams have been constructed to harness water for human development, changing the operation of the water cycle on a global scale.[19]

The unfettered promotion of water resource development was critically confronted at the Conference on Water in Mar Del Plata, Argentina, in 1977, a conference that marks the dawn of global water policy discourse. There, the momentum of the development project and its implicit assumptions were criticized for prioritizing normative views, those remnants of natural theology, that assumed water resources were abundant.[20] In place of abundance, it was put forward that water should be conceived of as universally scarce, due to its inequitable distribution in time and space. Subsequently, water scarcity provided the grounding proposition for a new global era of policy and planning.[21] Yet the axiom of scarcity was no more value-neutral than the narrative of abundance, for it assumed that water resources were inequitably distributed based on existing human populations and patterns of resource use.

Hence, even though the political contests that beset modern water policy discourse are well documented, there has been common consent that some combination of science, rational planning, and technology provide the necessary keys to remedy scarcity[22]—rather than to question the location, size, or social values of human communities or their attendant demands for water.

Since the 1970s, many authors have documented the failures of excessively rational, "command-and-control" approaches to water governance and their inability to adequately regulate or adapt to the complexity of human behavior. In this regard, the late 20th and early 21st century witnessed a major shift in the water narrative towards a kind of demand management based on "full-cost pricing," or generally increasing the economic cost of water to encourage conservation—making water into a tradable commodity that is a discrete, private, and marketable good.[23] Where increases in human happiness were formerly seen as a "good" on the supply-side of water, demand-side management through pricing was promoted by authors such as Anderson and Leal as a means for making sure that water went to those who placed a high value on it, largely as a way to reduce demand through increased water use efficiency.[24]

Pricing water is not a straightforward exercise in supply and demand. Rather, it is intrinsically tied to the regulations that govern such things as acceptable water uses and legitimate water rights. And these regulations cannot be divorced from the politics of their creation and enforcement.[25] A pricing system without constraints opens management efforts to the danger that water—a key to the functioning and basic existence of all life on Earth—will go only to those able to pay for it. For instance, in early 2009 the government of Madagascar announced a deal with private investors from South Korea, who sought to lease half of Madagascar's arable land (1.3 million acres) for an agreed-upon sum, to grow water-intensive crops that South Korea lacks the capacity to produce. This scheme clearly put too low a value on the country's land and water and brought about the fall of Madagascar's government. The deal was quashed, but it illustrates how poor systems of water pricing have the capacity to destabilize entire regions.[26] This little story also graphically illustrates that the idea of efficient prices ultimately rests on the empirically unsubstantiated conceit that the world was made for the use of humanity—even to the point of permitting certain individuals or groups to use it all. We feel it is necessary to deeply reconsider the basic assumption that, even in the distant future, scientific knowledge and technological know-how will be able to allow, or even *ought to allow*, complete human management of the hydrological cycle.

The Problem of Ethical Principles in Complex Systems

There is little doubt that, for better but more often for worse, the scale of human activity on Earth is affecting the entire hydrological cycle, from global land-cover changes to carbon emissions that alter ocean acidity, and changes in rainfall patterns. Such awareness presents us with a fundamental crisis of values; that is to say, it presents us with a stark choice in the human narrative, a choice that will to some extent govern the sequence of events determining life's future on this planet. Within the current narrative, water is seen as crucial in supporting human populations, which are typically growing in both size and wealth, regardless of the most pressing needs of the natural landscapes around them. The latter are viewed as valuable only in terms of the services they provide in support of the former.

In reality, complex natural systems present a direct challenge to an ethical viewpoint that rests on a single and/or inflexible principle. Devising and then acting on *any* single principle or standard (such as price) will inevitably alter the hydrological system of which the good is a part, as it legitimates some and constrains other water uses. Where such an ethic is based on deducing actions from overarching principles, such as the preeminent rights of humans or laws of supply and demand, it typically offers very little ability to respond to its own effects. This is the case because recognizing deleterious effects, and responding to them, would appear irrational in the context of the assumed and inflexible narrative. For example, if the good of achieving material wealth for humans requires increased water supplies, the problems that arise as a consequence of increased water use rarely cause managers to question the overarching goal of increasing human wealth.

From humanity's perspective, so long as the actions guided by ethical systems were small in relation to the vast and complex systems of the planet, the disconnect between natural complexity and what were taken to be the universal and necessary means of rationally discharging ethical obligations may not have made much difference, or at least we were blissfully unaware of such effects. But the distance has closed between the impacts of our normative actions and the world's complex biophysical systems. This closure has revealed a suspect inference in the assumptions of the basic narrative of modern water management: that material and moral progress are of a piece.[27]

Organizing water management around a single theory of value standards will constrain future avenues for social and biological evolution and adaptation, including avenues that the managers may not have considered or may yet not know about. This is an extremely unethical and unscientific basis for any action. According to evolutionary science, it is adaptation and flexibility that have provided biological survival for all lifeforms. Constraining adaptation and evolution of natural systems as radically as we are already doing today will close off future survival for many complex forms of life. If we are to avoid such a path by recognizing our limited knowledge of the ecosystems and cycles on which we depend, we should consider the role of multivariate decision systems that, other things being equal, are likely to work longer because they provide more options from which to respond to the feedback of complex systems. We would do this in the complete understanding, however, that no system of human principles can be as complex as the system(s) in which they operate. So, from a decision-making perspective, purely rational and technocratic management cannot go far enough in helping us through the current water crisis. What we also need is a new narrative that positions scientific knowledge and technological know-how as part of the broader systems people seek to manage, and which include the cultural, religious and ethical values by which the managers and users are informed.

The Age of Crises and a New Narrative

Our previous ethical systems have contributed to the current water crisis. Yet, if we are to offer a new direction for management, we must rethink the beginning, middle, and end of our water narrative. As we noted in the introduction to this essay, Aristotle offers sound advice. In his *Nichomachean Ethics*, he distinguishes three types of knowledge.[28] The first is pure knowledge, or *epistêmê*, which is the root word for "epistemology" and the types of knowledge claimed by modern science. For Aristotle, this knowledge proceeded from necessary and universal truths about un-changeable objects (i.e. mathematical axioms or water's chemical makeup as H_2O). The second is applied knowledge, or *technê*, which is the root for "technology" and the types of knowledge employed in our productive capacity, or know-how, in reasoning out how to produce such things as a house, a hydroelectric dam, or a modern sewage treatment system. The third is practical wisdom, or *phronêsis*, which has no modern equivalent[29] but may be interpreted as a prudential type of reasoning characterized by those who are able to reason not only about what is good for them, but are also able to deliberate about what is conducive to the good life in general.[30]

For the purpose of critically engaging the ethic and narrative of mod-ern water management, it is helpful to show how its emphasis on scien-tific epistemology (epistêmê) and technological reasoning (technê) has excluded the virtues of practical wisdom (phronêsis) that offer a route to an improved, ethically conscious form of water management.[31] First, where epistêmê emphasizes that scientific knowledge is often built from necessary and unchanging truths, such as the ocean's role in absorbing heat trapped by greenhouse gases and helping to moderate temperature differences on the earth, phronêsis offers the opportunity to deliberate on water's many changing relationships with other chemicals and biological organisms in complex, adaptive systems. Or again, where technê is con-cerned with productive knowledge, for example improved irrigation methods or conveyance infrastructure, phronêsis is concerned with prac-tices based on experiential wisdom. Excellent examples of this come from Paul Trawick's study in chapter fifteen of this volume on the evolu-tion of successful principles for communal water management that have evolved in many regions of the world.[32] Another caveat about our cur-rent system is that technê takes advantage of luck, as in Canada where rel-atively large stores of freshwater are dammed for large-scale electricity production based on a "myth of abundance."[33] By contrast, phronêsis does not depend on the serendipity of finding (or being rich enough to create) the right type of external environment conditions for achieving the good life. We can conclude that phronêsis is a type of knowledge dis-tinguished from both scientific theory and technological production by its emphasis on the necessary flexibility required to act virtuously that, in the case of water management, means recognizing the limits imposed by being part of a complex, adaptive system.

With these distinctions in mind, it can be argued that acting ethically is not just a matter of acquiring enough knowledge to adequately solve a problem. Instead, ethical experiences are qualitative and require that we fully recognize our limited knowledge. Managing water cycles and supplies must be based on practical wisdom, which could potentially include ideas of 'full-cost accounting' or increased water efficiency, but only if these efforts were deemed prudent through reasoned debate that included much more than just economic deliberations. The notion of *compassionate retreat* first suggests that our actions ought to be guided by, but can never be reduced to, scientific or technological knowledge. It then implies that our attitude toward water ought to appreciate humanity's position as just one part within a very complex and interwoven set of systems. It also includes a clear acknowledgment of our relative ignorance concerning how that system evolved, how its different component parts (i.e., different species) emerged, and the full effects and implications of our interactions with it.

A safer, more equitable and long-lasting version of water management would require using scientific knowledge to construct a different narrative regarding how the world came to be and what place humanity holds within it relative to other forms of life. Here are some of the elements of such a narrative, presented in reference to the old one it seeks to amend:[34] First, the universe should not be viewed as having been brought into being by a Creator. Rather, the universe is itself Creative, or self-organizing in the Gaia hypothesis sense, and, by a long series of emergent steps, has given rise to extremely complex processes, such as Earth's living ecosystems and the organisms that live within them.[35]

We now know that lifeforms are creative influences that help construct both natural ecosystems and the Earth's vast biophysical systems, such as the atmosphere and the water cycle. Human beings would therefore not be viewed as having a qualitatively distinct status due to their creation in God's image. Rather, humans would be seen as members of natural communities that are the result of long-term emergent processes.[36] Whereas water once held primarily a human-focused, instrumental value, the new narrative would value water as essential to the flourishing of all forms of life, not just our own. Such a perspective was and remains part of many religious beliefs, especially among indigenous and traditional peoples.[37] But even within the world's dominant modern religions, water is usually held as sacred; behaving in accordance with this theological belief has been lost from modern forms of management.[38]

Under compassionate retreat, natural systems would not be considered simple mechanisms, where the consequences of intervention would always be believed to be reversible or amenable to "remediation," as they are now. Instead, natural systems, such as wetlands, taiga, or coral reefs would be appreciated both for their complexity and their necessity. Science has made it abundantly clear that each system has innumerable feedback loops prone to change, in which small perturbations may result in significantly different states of affairs. As Madeleine Cantin Cumyn argues in this volume, ascertaining water's value to human communities might begin by understanding that there are no real surpluses of water.[39]

Although the narrative just outlined is tentative, there are numerous authors who have been working to fill out what types of values ought to inform management decisions and to excise from them these very old cultural assumptions about human superiority or the priority of liberal, individual values. Joseph Sax, for instance, emphasizes the roots of several legal traditions in a communal right to natural resources. Importantly, this right is not simply the aggregate of individual claims, because it is not possible to trade these claims without communal effects.[40] In place of the independent, controlling shares of water awarded to individual humans, corporations, or governments in the past, Sandra Postel, Greta Gaard, and Carolyn Merchant all highlight the interdependence of human and natural systems. They argue that respect for one is intrinsically tied to respect for the other.[41] Alternate views of property and the plurality of claims to water are provided in this book by Peter G. Brown, Rajendra Prahdhan, and Ruth Meinzen-Dick, who argue that both natural and human systems *already* have legitimate claims on water as parts of complex natural, cultural, and legal systems. And therefore, any changes to the governance and management of watersheds, however well-intentioned, is well-advised to consider that predictive techniques, such as economic forecasts, are not well suited for policy making in complex, nonlinear systems. Hence they risk jeopardizing the survival of local systems that, at least in some cases, are working well.

While we should be careful not to read the views expressed by the other authors of this book as automatically supporting our own, for in many cases significant differences remain, it is important to consider how a new and clearer water ethics discourse is emerging within the context of environmental ethics, environmental law, and natural resource policy. In all these disciplines, common criticisms have been made of the policies that have dominated the ethics of 20th and early 21st century development. Seeing these criticisms as part of an emerging literature is therefore not only an observation of familial resemblance, it is a statement that the water ethics literature is assembling rungs on a ladder that should help us all to think more ethically and responsibly in the current and clearly exacerbating water crisis. From the perspective of these frameworks, there is an ethical imperative to reduce the scale and intensity of human intervention in the hydrologic cycle, and to thoughtfully reverse many of the interventions that have already been made. These changes must be accompanied by fundamentally rethinking the ends toward which water management is aimed.

Collapse and the Ethics of Compassionate Retreat

According to the World Economic Forum, the world water crisis is closely interlinked with other crises facing humanity as the new millennium gets under way, including climate uncertainty, intermittent but often severe shortages of staple grains, rampant and increasing consumption of goods, political destabilization in developing countries, foreign oil dependence and energy security in Europe and North America, crises in urban water supply and sanitation, and global human health and population increases and shifts.[42] These are all examples of systems under increasing stress. We think it is important to see these interconnected phenomena as signals that fundamental rethinking of our circumstances is required—a fundamental shift in perspective and in the scale of our demands on Earth's life-support systems.

At this time in history our ethical systems face immediate and critical tests. As Falkenmark and Folke make clear, systems that are greatly disturbed may collapse or "flip" from one set of behaviors to another.[43] In the water sector, the potential for many such collapses is imminent due to the effects of climate perturbation on droughts, floods, sea level rise, aquifer depletion and contamination, ice melt, ocean acidification, and saltwater intrusion. A new ethic needs to help us prepare for the likelihood of ecological, economic, and social collapse. However, from the perspective of constructing a vitally needed new narrative, we must think critically about what such collapses portend, and about reconstruction thereafter.

Jared Diamond defines social and ecosystem collapse as a "drastic decrease in human population size and/or political/economic/social complexity over a considerable area, for an extended time."[44] The nascent literature on social responses to collapse postulates five pathways that normally occur after social or environmental collapse.[45] (1) One is where complex human and natural systems are not able to reemerge as they once were. Remnants of previous civilizations, such as those Mayan groups whose water use rituals contributed to ecological and social collapse, exemplify a road to be avoided if possible.[46] (2) Another may be referred to as template regeneration. When the crisis is past, there is a reassertion of old ideologies and worldviews, and little is learned from the experience of collapse. A contemporary example was produced in the film *Crapshoot: The Gamble with Our Wastes*, which links contemporary sanitation problems with a failure to rethink the basic Roman assumption of mixing water with waste: namely, that once mixed, nature's processes or our technological prowess will allow us to safely separate them later. The conclusion of this and legal work in the same vein is clear. We have repeated the Roman pattern of poor reasoning in modern sanitation, and now are faced with wastewater problems at a much more vast scale.[47] (3) The opposite of regeneration is a new system that contrasts strongly with the preexisting template or narrative—sometimes with a foreign source. An example of this is the replacement, in the United States, of the Iroquois self-understanding with the Judeo-Christian understanding of the European settlers. (4) In the fourth pathway, social or natural complexity does not reemerge at all. After collapse the capacity of the system is too weak to support human and natural diversity, such as when floods erode topsoil and permanently curtail productivity or fossil aquifers collapse from over-pumping and can no longer store groundwater. (5) A final option is called orthopraxy. In these cases, marginalized groups practice the orthodoxy of the dominant group but do not internalize it. For instance, Australian aboriginal groups have persisted using their own values but also argue for rights to both water and land within the system imposed by their colonizers.[48]

To the degree that we can influence the timing and nature of collapses and their aftermath, this typology provides some guidance on what to do—tempered by strong humility that our control over events is likely to be limited in many cases and nonexistent in others. For example, it is apparent that as climate changes are amplified by positive feedback loops, future generations will have no timely prospect of reversing the process. It is also obvious that they must avoid template regeneration if at all possible, since, as we have already argued, that narrative has been a major cause of our current, multiple crises. Avoiding past mistakes, however, will not be enough; a water ethic must be seen as constitutive of, and complementary to, much broader social and moral obligations. In this sense, it requires carefully readjusting our water use patterns in a manner that honors our obligations of respect and reciprocity toward how the rest of life flourishes.

On the one hand, modern water management has not fully appreciated its roots in the broader Western narrative and has not come to terms with the ways this narrative has proven to be problematical. On the other, simple models of the hydrological cycle and attendant assumptions of either universal abundance or scarcity fail in their ability to capture natural complexity. So as a first step, water management must expand to include an ethic of virtue—where the quest is not only for improved decision-making frameworks, but is also for persons who act out of recognition that scientific and technological knowledge must be situated in relation to deliberations on ethics, fairness, temperance, and justice and which include great humility regarding the types and ends of human knowledge. *In this sense, a water ethic must be seen as moderating, rather than managing, the human–environment relationship.*

We want to point out that we are arguing that any notion of including a virtue ethic for water must be situated within humanity's position as one part of many complex socio-ecological systems. With considerable foresight and drawing on one form of phronêtic wisdom, Aldo Leopold argued that as members of a complex ecological community, humans must acknowledge that ethics bear on those actions involving "deferred reactions" that have consequences not discernable to the average person.[49] This is because, within complex systems, it is not likely that we will always be able to connect or single out direct causal relationships. Like C. S. Holling and others who view the world as a complex adaptive system, we are arguing that people need to "manage" water by minimal intervention.[50] The virtue of a water ethic would therefore lie in the fact that managers and users needn't understand the complexities of water in all of its manifold processes in order to behave in a manner respectful of it. This would answer any objectives that what we are suggesting would complicate water management by adding more criteria to its goals. Indeed, trying to manage in such multitudinous ways would present intractable, probably impossible levels of calculation. We are rather arguing that humanity's primary relationship with life and the world should be one of respect and reciprocity, wherein we use our existing knowledge toward ends that are conducive to a good life for the entire community of life that is dependent on water. To start with, we should not assume that natural water is in any way inequitably distributed over time and space. Rather, the incongruence between supply and demand should cause us to reflect on the size and characteristics of human communities and patterns of resource use, not only on water supply.

The quadrupling of the human population and the economic expansion of several hundred percent in the 20th century have placed a crucial choice before us: live with a denuded, simplified, dangerous, and quite possibly dying world; or embrace what we're here calling *compassionate retreat*. At this turning point, humankind is facing some of the most difficult choices of our history. There are large and often rapidly growing human populations living in areas like sub-Saharan Africa, where chronic droughts are very likely to be increased in magnitude and intensity by climate change. The same holds true for the U.S. Southwest and large parts of Australia. It is growing increasingly unlikely that it will be feasible to continue to support these areas' current populations in situ. Nor is it possible to legitimately support the high-consumption societies of which the two latter places named are a part.

Compassionate *retreat* starts with the recognition that the size of the human population and the massive consumption already under way (and nearly universally aspired to) are not consistent with an ethic of respect and reciprocity, and especially do not accord with the human ability to understand or to manage complex systems. Rather than maintain the conceit that we can somehow get out of the problems we have created through management based only on science and technology, this new narrative proposes a form of strategic retreat, similar to those used in a battle that cannot be won. It offers the option of significant reductions in the scale and escalation of our problems, which will allow us more time to assess and respond. There is moreover a concomitant and urgent need to think through and move toward steady-state economies, such as advocated by Peter Brown, Herman Daly, and Peter Victor.[51] Ultimately, compassionate retreat aims for an overall impact that approximates what Daly calls "the biocentric optimum"—that level of activity consistent with abundant human and nonhuman life and needs. Technological advances can play a major role in reducing the overall scale of the human impact, but technical advance alone is not sufficient to deal with the excessive scale of the human enterprise at this stage in history.

There are several dimensions to the *compassionate* side of this strategic retreat. The first is to recognize that modern water management has failed to appreciate and understand the influence of its roots in Western values, worldviews, and religion.[52] It should start by sharply and systematically questioning that narrative and then should take an open stance toward alternate ideas and beliefs that will have positive effects on how decisions affecting water are made. Modern science's account of the evolution of the Universe offers one possible narrative, using its own version of human origins and of our collective relationship to Earth, one which is fundamentally different from the older, prescientific Western narrative in which current water management approaches are embedded. But we can enrich our understanding of compassionate retreat from existing cultural sources as well. For instance, Chinese philosophy has a strong history of using water's behavior as the natural model—displaying humility, leadership, and perseverance—for principles from which ethical and even political obligations are derived.[53]

A second approach is to recognize that our current water use patterns, though in many cases both unsustainable and ethically indefensible, have committed us to certain obligations to human and nonhuman communities that now depend upon them. Solutions to long-standing problems should seek low-technology alternatives, such as solar water disinfection (SODIS), which uses the sun's ultraviolet rays to purify water, already in use purifying water for over two million people. Such noninvasive technologies represent proven ways to increase community involvement in human health and sanitation in the latitudes most affected by water-related illnesses without large changes to complex systems and in the areas of the world where drinking-water needs are the most severe.[54] Under compassionate retreat, any new water developments must be premised on the fact that the hydrological cycle is already fully in use by the world's interdependent communities, both human and nonhuman. And finally, there is a need to redistribute material wealth away from the excessively rich to the desperately poor, at the same time that we redesign the economies of the wealthy countries away from high consumption, gradually, so as to cushion damaging jobs while evolving good ones. This change will require new global institutions respectful of community rights to water, which have the power to severely curb and redirect the current emphasis on individual and business liberalism.[55]

What we are able to offer here, as a conclusion to this book, is a preliminary vision of a future that is most urgently in need of construction. It is also clear from the contents of this book that in finding a new ethic for water, we can draw on elements of humanity's shared moral and scientific heritage and reposition them within a narrative that puts science and ethics together in living within complex systems. In this sense, although we have argued here that humanity's underlying water narrative needs reconstruction, the process of creating the new one may involve reusing stones from the building that is being torn down. We are all inheritors of rich moral teachings that can be deployed as elements in a narrative and ethic that envisions and helps to bring into being a flourishing Earth.

Notes

1. L. Rodberg and V. Weisskopf, "Fall of parity," *Science* 125 (1957): 627–633. At 632.

2. V. Havel, "The need for transcendence in the post-modern world," Speech delivered at Independence Hall, Philadelphia, July 4, 1994.

3. B. Vitek and W. Jackson (eds.), *The virtues of ignorance: complexity, sustainability and the limits of knowledge.* (Lexington: University of Kentucky Press, 2008).

4. P. M.Vitousek, H. A. Mooney, J. Lubchenco, J.M. Melillo, "Human domination of earth's ecosystems," *Science*, 277 (1997) no. 5325: 494–499.

5. B. Hoffmaster and C. Hooker, "How experience confronts ethics," *Bioethics* 23 (2009): 214–225.

6. C. Merchant, *Reinventing Eden: the fate of nature in Western culture.* (New York: Routledge, 2004).

7. Patriarch Bartholomew, "Byzantine Heritage" this volume.

8. Faraj Al-Awar, Mohammad Jamel Abdulrazzak, and Radwan Al-Weshah, "Water ethics perspectives in the Arab Region," this volume; R. Pradhan and R. Meinzen-Dick, "Which rights are right? Water rights, culture, and underlying values," this volume.

9. Yi-Fu Tuan, *The hydrological cycle and the wisdom of God: a theme in geoteleology.* (Toronto: University of Toronto Press, 1968).

10. Ibid.

11. Ibid.

12. J. W. Powell, "The course of human progress," *Science* 11 (1888): 220–222.

13. W. J. McGee, "Water as a resource," *American Academy of Political and Social Science* 33(3) (1909): 37–50. Also in this volume.

14. For an interesting overview and primary documents see, E. Stradling (ed), *Conservation in the progressive era: classic texts* (Seattle: University of Washington Press, 2004).

15. See for background, J. Westcoat, "Watersheds in regional planning," in *The American planning tradition: culture and policy*, ed. R. Fishman (Washington: Wilson Centre, Smithsonian Institutions, 2000), 147–172.

16. D. Feldman, *Water resources management: in search of an environmental ethic.* (Baltimore: John Hopkins University Press, 1995); D. Feldman, *Water policy for sustainable development.* (Baltimore: Johns Hopkins University Press, 2007).

17. S. Kraft, "Surface water and groundwater regulation and use: an ethical perspective," this volume.

18. Wolfgang Sachs, *Planet dialectics: explorations in environment and development.* (London: Zed Books, 1999).

19. Large dams are classified as those over 15 meters high or, if between 5–15 meters, impounding more than three million cubic meters of water. World Commission on Dams (2000). *Dams and development: a new framework for decision-making.* Retrieved March 9, 2009, from: http://www.dams.org//docs/overview/wcd_overview.pdf.

20. A. Biswas (ed.), *United Nations water conference.* (Oxford: Pergamon Press, 1978).

21. Ibid.

22. K. Conca, *Governing water: contentious transnational politics and global institution building.* (Boston: MIT Press, 2006).

23. E. Freyfogle, "Water rights and the common wealth," *Environmental Law* 26 (1996): 27–51.

24. T. Anderson and D. Leal, "Priming the invisible pump," this volume.

25. B. Haddad, *Rivers of gold, desiging markets to allocate water in California*. (Washington, DC: Island Press, 1999); M. Robertson, "Discovering price in all the wrong places: the work of commodity definition and price under neoliberal environmental policy," *Antipode* 39 (2007): 500–526.

26. National and international protests have slowed development. See, Sarah Haughn, "Outsourcing irrigation, farming discontent," *Circle of Blue/WaterNews*, 23 February 2009, http://www.circleofblue.org/waternews/world/africa/outsourcing-irrigation-farming-discontent/ (accessed April 21, 2009).

27. As Mohatma Gandhi remarked on such equations, "They say that before we can think or talk of their [those in India living on one meal per day] moral welfare, we must satisfy their daily wants. With these, they say, material progress spells moral progress. And then is taken a sudden jump: what is true of thirty millions is true of the universe. . . . I need hardly say how ludicrously absurd this deduction would be." Mohatma Gandhi, "Economic and moral progress," in *Mahatma Gandhi: the new economic agenda*, ed. P. C. Joshi (New Delhi: Har-Anand Publications), 236–237.

28. Aristotle, *The Nichomachean ethics*. (New York: Oxford University Press).

29. Bent Flyvberg, *Making social science matter: why social inquiry fails and how it can succeed again*. (Cambridge: Cambridge University Press, 2001).

30. Aristotle, *Nichomachean ethics*. (Indianapolis: Hacket Publishing, 1985), at VI; H. Gadamer, *Truth and method*, 2nd edition. Translated by J. Weinsheimer and D. Marshall. (New York: Continuum, 2000).

31. We gratefully acknowledge the input of May Sim in this paragraph.

32. P. Trawick, "Encounters with the moral economy of water: general principles for successfully managing the commons," this volume.

33. K. Bakker (editor), *Eau Canada: the future of Canada's water*. (Vancouver: UBC Press, 2007).

34. See also, T. Berry, *The great work: our way into the future*. (New York: Bell Tower, 1999).

35. E. Schneider and D. Sagan, *Into the cool: energy flow, thermodynamics and life*. (Chicago: University of Chicago Press, 2005).

36. Ibid.

37. G. Chamberlain, *Troubled waters: religion and the world's water crisis* (New York: Rowman & Littlefield Publishers, Inc., 2008).

38. Since we have critiqued the nonempirical basis of religion above, we do not advocate that religion offers grounds for the new narrative. Rather, religious systems are one part of it. For recent work on religion and water see, S. Shaw and A. Francis (eds), *Deep blue: critical reflections on nature, religion and water*. (London: Equinox, 2008).

39. Madeleine Cantin Cumin, "The legal status of water in Quebec," this volume.

40. Joseph Sax, "Understanding transfers: community rights and the privatization of water," this volume.

41. See this volume, Sandra Postel, "The missing piece: a water ethic;" Greta Gaard, "Women, water, energy: an ecofeminist approach;" Carolyn Merchant, "Fish first! The changing ethics of ecosystem management."

42. World Economic Forum, "The bubble is close to bursting: a forecast of the main economic and geopolitical water issues likely to arise in the world during the next two decades," *Draft for discussion at the World Economic Forum Annual Meeting 2009.* (World Economic Forum: January, 2009). Accessed April 21, 2009, at: http://www.weforum.org/pdf/water/WaterInitiativeFutureWaterNeeds.pdf.

43. M. Falkenmark and C. Folke, "Ecohydrosolidarity: a new ethics for steward-ship of value-adding rainfall," this volume.

44. J. Diamond, *Collapse: how societies choose to fail or succeed.* (London: Penguin Books, 2005), 6.

45. The last four categories draw on G. Schwartz, and J. Nichols, *After collapse: the regeneration of complex societies* (University of Arizona Press, 2006).

46. L. Lucero, *Water and ritual: the rise and fall of classic Maya rulers.* (Austin: University of Texas Press, 2006).

47. J. Benidickson, *The culture of flushing: a social and legal history of sewage.* (Vancouver: UBC Press, 2007).

48. V. Strang, "Blue, green and red: combining energies in defence of water," in *Deep blue: critical reflections on nature, religion and water,* ed. S. Shaw and A. Francis (London: Equinox, 2008), 253–274.

49. Aldo Leopold, *A Sand County almanac: with essays on conservation from Round River.* (New York: Oxford University Press, 1966), 239.

50. C. S. Holling and G. Meffe, "Command and control and the pathology of natural resource management," *Conservation Biology* 10 (1996): 328–337.

51. P. Victor, *Managing without growth: slower by design, not disaster.* (Northampton, MA: Edward Elgar Publishing, 2008), P. Brown and G. Garver, *Right relationship: building a whole earth economy.* (San Francisco: Barrett-Kohler Publishers, Inc., 2009).

52. G. Chamberlain, *Troubled waters: religion, ethics and the global water crisis.* (Lanham, Maryland: Rowman and Littlefield, 2008).

53. S. Allan, *The way of water and sprouts of virtue.* (Albany, NY: State University of New York Press, 1997).

54. R. Meierhofer, "Solar water disinfection helps reduce the global diarrhea burden," *IWRA Update: newsletter of the International Water Resources Association,* 22 (April, 2009): 5–9.

55. R. Petrella, *The water manifesto: arguments for a world water contract.* (New York: Palgrave, 2001).

Acknowledgments

WE WOULD LIKE TO THANK members of our advisory board for their input, direction, and helpful criticisms on earlier drafts of this volume: Madeleine Cantin Cumyn, Malin Falkenmark, H. Patrick Glenn, Chandra Madramootoo, Bryan G. Norton, Christiana Peppard, Sandra Postel, Henry Shue, Mary Evelyn Tucker, and Mike Young.

A special thanks for the support of Chandra Madramootoo, Dean of McGill University's Faculty of Agricultural and Environmental Sciences. In addition, we are grateful for comments on the final essay from Peter Adams, Worth Bateman, Sheldon Chow, Paul Heltne, Jessica Labreque, Bano Medhi, Philip Osano, May Sim, and William Vitek. Special thanks to Holly Dressel for helpful edits on the final essay. Jeremy Schmidt would like to thank Rachel Harvey for her ongoing support and advice, it is greatly appreciated.

Contributors

Mohammad J. Abdulrazzak, United Nations Educational, Scientific and Cultural Organization, Cairo, Egypt.

Faraj Al-Awar, Regional Consultant, Water Resources Planning and Management, Beirut, Lebanon.

Radwan Al-Weshah, United Nations Educational, Scientific and Cultural Organization, Cairo, Egypt.

Terry L. Anderson, Executive Director, Property & Environment Research Center (PERC), Montana. Coauthor of *Free Market Environmentalism* (1991; revised, 2001) and *The Not So Wild, Wild West* (2004), among others.

His All Holiness Ecumenical Patriarch Bartholomew, spiritual leader of Orthodox Christians and a leader of Religion, Science and the Environment, a movement with major international symposia on the state of the world's water.

Augustin Berque, Directeur d'études, L'Ecole des Hautes Etudes en Sciences Sociales, Paris.

Peter G. Brown, Professor, Departments of Natural Resource Sciences, Geography and School of the Environment, McGill University.

Madeleine Cantin Cumyn, former Wainwright Chair in Civil Law, Emeritus Professor of Law, McGill University.

Thomas Dietz, Director, Environmental Science and Policy Program, Assistant Vice President for Environmental Research, Michigan State University.

Malin Falkenmark, Professor, Senior Scientist at the Stockholm International Water Institute and Stockholm Resilience Center.

Carl Folke, Professor and Science Director of the Stockholm Resilience Centre and Director of the Beijer Institute of Ecological Economics of the Royal Swedish Academy of Sciences.

Greta Gaard, Associate Professor, Department of English, University of Wisconsin, River Falls. Author of *Ecological Politics* (1998) and *The Nature of Home* (2007), among others.

Steven E. Kraft, Professor and Chair, Department of Agribusiness Economics, Co-Director of the Environmental Resources and Policy PhD Program, Southern Illinois University, Carbondale.

Donald R. Leal, Director of Research, Property & Environment Research Center (PERC), Montana. Coauthor of *Free Market Environmentalism* (1991; revised, 2001) and *Enviro Capitalists* (1997).

William J. McGee (1853–1912). At the time of original publication W. J. McGee was Secretary of the U.S. Inland Waterways Commission.

Ruth Meinzen-Dick, Senior Research Fellow, Environment and Production Technology, International Food Policy Research Institute, Washington, DC.

Carolyn Merchant, Professor of Environmental History, Philosophy and Ethics. Department of Environmental Science, Policy and Management, University of California, Berkeley. Author of *The Death of Nature* (1980) and *Reinventing Eden* (2003), among others.

Bryan G. Norton, Distinguished Professor of Philosophy, Science and Technology, Georgia Institute of Technology. Author of *Sustainability: A Philosophy of Adaptive Ecosystem Management* (2005), among others.

Elinor Ostrom, Senior Research Director, Workshop in Political Theory and Policy Analysis, Indiana University. Founding Director, Center for the Study of Institutional Diversity, Arizona State University.

Sandra Postel, Director of the independent Global Water Policy Project and lecturer, writer, and consultant on international water issues. Author of *Last Oasis* (1992), *Pillar of Sand* (1999), and, with Brian Richter, *Rivers for Life* (2003), among others.

Rajendra Pradhan, a legal anthropologist, is the Chair, Social Science Baha, Kathmandu, Nepal. Author of *Law, History and Culture of Water in Nepal* (2003), among others.

Joseph L. Sax, James H. House and Hiram H. Hurd Professor of Environmental Regulation, Emeritus, Boalt Hall, Faculty of Law, University of California, Berkeley.

Jeremy J. Schmidt, PhD Candidate and Trudeau Scholar, Department of Geography, University of Western Ontario. Member of the UNESCO working group on Water Ethics and Water Resource Management.

Paul C. Stern, Director, Committee on the Human Dimensions of Global Change, The National Academies, National Research Council, Washington.

Paul Trawick, Senior Lecturer in Ecological Anthropology, Department of Natural Resources, School of Applied Sciences, Cranfield University. Author of *The Struggle for Water in Peru* (2003), among others.

Advisory Board

Cumyn, Madeleine Cantin, Former Wainwright Chair in Civil Law, Emeritus Professor of Law, McGill University.

Falkenmark, Malin, Professor, Senior Scientist at the Stockholm International Water Institute and Stockholm Resilience Center.

Glenn, H. Patrick, Peter M. Laing Professor of Law, McGill University.

Madramootoo, Chandra, Dean of the Faculty of Agricultural and Environmental Sciences, McGill University, Montreal, Canada.

Norton, Bryan G., Distinguished Professor of Philosophy, Science and Technology, Georgia Institute of Technology.

Peppard, Christiana, PhD Candidate, Department of Religious Studies, Yale University and Scholar in Residence, Cathedral of St. John the Divine, New York City.

Postel, Sandra, Director of the Global Water Policy Project, Los Lunas, New Mexico.

Shue, Henry, Senior Research Fellow Emeritus, Merton College and Professor Emeritus of International Relations, Oxford.

Tucker, Mary Evelyn, Senior Lecturer and Research Scholar, School of Forestry and Environmental Studies and the Divinity School, Yale University. Co-director, Yale Forum on Religion and Ecology.

Young, Mike, Director, The Environment Institute and Research Chair in Water Economics and Management, School of Earth and Environmental Sciences, University of Adelaide.

Index

Note: page numbers in italics refer to illustrations

Justice, Rawls' theory of, 110–12
Just savings principle, 111

Kant, Immanuel, 206
Kesterson National Wildlife Refuge, 94
Killing, 215
Knowledge, types of, 274–76
Kraft, Stephen, 271

Labor theory of value, 204–5, 229
LaGrande Complex (James Bay I), 69
Laissez-faire capitalism, 227–30
Land productivity, water's role in, 250–51, *251*
Law and legal issues: cultural values and, 40–41;
    ethical formalism and, 106, 112–13; interna-
    tional, 45–46; legal limitation, 231–32; legal
    pluralism, *41*, 41–42; Public Trust Doctrine,
    46–47, 224; Quebec's Beauchamp Report,
    168; regional differences in U.S., 89; *res com-
    munis* in Quebec, 167, 169–75; standing for
    natural objects, 222–23; statutory, 46–47;
    transfers and community rights, 118–21; util-
    itarian basis of, 105, 107
Legitimization of water rights, 43–44
Leibhardt-Wester, Barbara, 229, 237
Leopold, Aldo: land ethic, 200, 211, 218, 224,
    233–34; pragmatism and, 179, 180, 183; on
    right and wrong, 199, 233; virtue ethic and,
    280–81; wolves and, 188–89
Leroi-Gourhan, André, 137n32
Liberal moral philosophy, 204–6
Linear model of power production, 71
Locke, John, 204–5, 207–8, 218, 229
Lockean proviso, 205
Logistic curve, 232
Long-term benefits, 81
Lovelock, James, 244

Madagascar, 272
Marcelino Botin Foundation Water Workshop
    (2007), 5
Market-driven economics, 31–32
Market failure, 108–9
Markets. *See* Water markets and transfers
Master Model, the, 62
Mastery over nature. *See* Dominion model
Maximum sustainable yield, 232, 234–35, 244
McEvoy, Arthur, 228
McGee, W. J., 231, 270
McInerney, J., 110, 114n10
Metropolitan Water District (MWD), 95
Microeconomic approach, 81–82, 207
Mill, John Stuart, 11, 79, 207, 208, 218

Mineral extraction, 213
Modern disconnection from life basis of water,
    221–22
Modern ontological *topos*, 133–35, 137n32
Modern water management model: epistemo-
    logical vs. non-epistemological factors, 266;
    ethical assumptions of, 267–73; practical wis-
    dom excluded from, 275–76; problems with
    221–226; rethinking of, 265–66. *See also* An-
    thropocentrism; Utilitarianism
Monetary reductionism, 109–13
Moral community, 201
Moral consideration, 199–201, 236
Moral economy of water, 163
Muir, John, 181, 183, 270
Multi-scalar modeling, 184, 221–226

Narrative perspective, 267–68, 282
National Energy Systems Company
    (NESCO), 70
Native Americans, 65–68
Naturalism, methodological, 185–86
Natural theology, 269–70
Nature: aporia of humans and nature, 130–32;
    assumed as immutable, 107; balance of, 235–
    36; dualisms and oppression of, 60–61
Negotiation, 238
Neo-liberal, free-market economics, 31–32
Nepal, 52
Newlands Reclamation Act (1902), 93
Newton, Isaac, 133
Nez Perce nation, 66
Nonhuman community: Bentham on, 209–10;
    common characteristics approach, 199–200;
    decentered community approach, 200–201;
    duty-to-protect approach, 200; ecocentric
    ethic, 233–36; Locke on, 205–6; partnership
    ethic, 236–39; utilitarianism and, 206–7. *See
    also* Commonwealth-of-life perspective
Northwest Power Planning Council
    (NPPC), 65
Norton, Bryan, 10–11, 82–83

Objectification, 133
Odum, Eugene, 244
Ogallala Aquifer, 100
Open access systems, 141, 147–48. *See also*
    Community-based management and
    commons
Optimum sustainable yield, 234–35
Original sin, 63
Orthodox Church, 25–28
Ostrom, Elinor, 142–43, 156, 159